D0763018

EDMUND HUSSERL

(1859–1938)

Edmund Husserl
*Philosopher
of Infinite Tasks*

Northwestern University

STUDIES IN *Phenomenology &*

Existential Philosophy

Maurice Natanson

Edmund Husserl

*Philosopher
of Infinite Tasks*

NORTHWESTERN UNIVERSITY PRESS

EVANSTON   1973

Maurice Natanson is Professor of Philosophy and Fellow of Cowell College at the University of California at Santa Cruz.

IN MEMORY OF MY FATHER
CHARLES NATANSON
OF THE YIDDISH THEATER

Contents

Preface

"Origin is the goal."
—Karl Kraus

ABOUT FIFTEEN YEARS AGO, in a critical but friendly review, a colleague warned me against becoming Husserl's expositor. Apart from brief excursions into the vicinity of that danger, I have heeded his advice. Nor do I think that with this volume I have succumbed to the temptation. A genuine exposition of Husserl's thought would require a treatise which would dwarf what is attempted here. The seventeenth-, eighteenth-, and nineteenth-century background of his work would have to be examined; all of Husserl's books would have to be presented, summarized, and reviewed in turn; some schema would have to be constructed for ordering the transitions and developments in his philosophy; an account of the relevant archival material would have to be given; and a considerable apparatus of reference to the secondary literature would have to be organized. The alternative to such an undertaking is the writing of monographs on limited topics. What I have tried to do here is quite different. In place of an exposition I have sought to guide the reader through some fundamental aspects of phenomenology, to acquaint him with the essential problems which Husserl faced, and to bring him into relationship with the radical implications of phenomenological method. For this purpose, I have concerned myself with the entire corpus of Husserl's work, but I have focused the discussion on about a dozen books which I consider pivotal. What I offer, then, is a start rather than a finish.

If this book is not an exposition of Husserl, neither is it a critique of phenomenology. Such a venture would demand a vantage point I do not possess, for I am too closely associated with phenomenology to be able to serve as its critic. At the same time, I have not sought to develop a particular interpretation which might challenge other phenomenologists to defend this or that position within Husserl's thought. That kind of critical partisanship would have turned this effort into a work of interest only to a narrow circle. It is my belief that phenomenology has, in addition to the legitimate development of its own specialized literature, a broader function to serve at this point in history: to demonstrate to a larger audience the necessity for specialization. In concrete terms, that means the defense of philosophy in a form which is accessible to nonphilosophers but which does not compromise the force of philosophical thought. It may be that the audience I envisage is a phantom of an imagination formed by a desire to be faithful to Husserl and to sell as many copies of this book as possible. It is hard to make good sense of the usual conglomerate subsumed under the rubric of audience: experts in the field but also the serious layman, students of the discipline but also those in related fields, adepts but also interested novices. It all seems to translate into "anyone with the price of a copy." No doubt there is some bad faith involved in the notion of audience; yet there is a genuine element of hope that despite the paradoxes and even absurdities of defining a readership, there may exist a band of individuals willing to move beyond both patronization and provinciality. The word "comrade" once described the reader I have in mind.

Although I have attempted neither a full-fledged exegesis nor a large critique of Husserl, there is plenty of exposition and criticism included in this book. Both come by way of an interpretive approach to phenomenology. My idea is to establish an outline of phenomenological philosophy by displaying and analyzing its central themes. Although I have tried to give a trustworthy account of his views, I have not simply trailed after Husserl's doctrine but have endeavored to comprehend it in my own critical terms. In strong measure, then, the chapters which follow are a philosophical response to phenomenology; they represent my own inroad to Husserl's teaching. Necessarily, such a response requires a selective procedure. What I take to be the major themes in phenomenology are discussed at some length, but there are also problems which, significant as they may be, are not even mentioned. I offer no justification for the choices I have made. This book will have to justify itself. But the reader should know that if there are substantive difficulties in phenomenology which are ignored, it is not because I prefer to shield its originator from attack. I am not Husserl's bulldog. At the same time, the reader should recognize that I have not hesitated to move away from traditional Husserlian territory when I thought it appropriate. The discussion of existentialism might have raised Husserl's interest; it would certainly have raised his eyebrows. So, too, the section on the concept of "application" in philosophy is hardly to be construed as the work of a marcher doing the lockstep. Throughout, I try to honor Husserl by retaining my own independence. I offer the reader a way and perhaps a method of reading Husserl.

For the most part, I have equated "Husserl" with "phenomenology." Although my interest is not biographical, it might be helpful to give a very brief summary of his personal history. Edmund Husserl was born in Moravia, then within the Austrian Empire but now part of Czechoslovakia, on April 8, 1859, of middle class Jewish parents (he was later baptized as a Protestant). His father was a merchant. After a Gymnasium education in Vienna, Husserl entered the University of Leipzig to do work in mathematics and the physical sciences. In 1878 he moved to the University of Berlin to do further work in mathematics with the illustrious Professors Kronecker and Weierstrass. In 1881 he left Berlin for Vienna, where he took his doctorate with a dissertation on the calculus of variations. Following that, he held, for a brief time, an assistantship under Weierstrass. From 1884 to 1886 Husserl returned to further studies in Vienna, but this time he decided to go to hear the philosophical lectures of Franz Brentano. Brentano had a decisive effect on him: Husserl decided to devote himself to philosophy. His university career then followed, starting at the University of Halle, where he was a *Privatdocent* from 1887 to 1901, continuing at Göttingen (1901–16), and ending at Freiburg in Breisgau, where he was a full professor until his retirement in 1928. He died on April 27, 1938.

At this point it might be helpful to list the publications I have emphasized so that the reader can see what Husserl wrote at various stages in his career.[1]

Philosophie der Arithmetik, 1891

1. In some instances I have indicated the original date of publication or composition in brackets. My reliance on these works is not altogether reflected in the number of footnotes devoted to them, for I have tried to avoid extensive annotation as well as detailed cross references.

Logical Investigations, 1900–01 (2nd edition, 1913)
The Phenomenology of Internal Time-Consciousness [1904–10], 1928
The Idea of Phenomenology [1907], 1947
"Philosophy as Rigorous Science" (*Logos* article), 1911
Ideas, 1913
Ideen II [1912–28], 1952
Ideen III [1912], 1952
"Phenomenology" (*Encyclopaedia Britannica* article), 1927
Formal and Transcendental Logic, 1929
Experience and Judgment [1929 and after, but including some earlier material], 1973
Cartesian Meditations, 1931
The Crisis of European Sciences and Transcendental Phenomenology [1934–37], 1954 (a portion published in 1936).

An article originally published in *Kant-Studien* by Eugen Fink, one of Husserl's most knowledgeable assistants, deserves to be mentioned here, for its contents were fully endorsed by Husserl:

"The Phenomenological Philosophy of Edmund Husserl and Contemporary Criticism" [1933], 1970

Other writings by Husserl have been drawn upon and are occasionally referred to, but these are the works around which this book is written. The greatest weight has been placed on "Philosophy as Rigorous Science," *Ideas, Cartesian Meditations,* and *The Crisis of European Sciences and Transcendental Phenomenology.*

Husserl's life was centered in his philosophical activity. Although he lived through dramatic times, the drama of his career was inward; it consisted in the discovery of a new terrain of consciousness and of an extraordinary method for the disclosure of its scope and structure. The intensity of Husserl's intelligence, his passion for truth, and the ultimate seriousness of his endeavor attracted a significant band of students from many parts of the world who found in phenomenology the genius of its creator. To his students and colleagues, he represented philosophy in its incorruptible essence. But severity, as far as I can judge from both published accounts and personal association with a number of Husserl's disciples, was restricted to intellectual matters. In his individual dealings with his associates, Husserl was an interested, fair, and generous teacher and colleague. In a diary he kept in Freiburg in 1928, Professor W. R. Boyce Gibson (the future translator of Husserl's *Ideas*) writes:

I wish to set on record here how immensely I am impressed with Husserl's personality. He is wonderfully good to his students, takes endless trouble to make things clear to them. He is full of the significance of his work, but with nothing petty about him. . . . He has strong feelings, and it is chiefly—so I gather from his conversation—the tremendous effect of the war upon his Lebens and Welt-anschauung, his inability to see Reason at work in the world [he lost one son in the war and another was blinded in one eye] that makes him regard all Lebens-and-Welt-anschauungen as *Privat*, and concentrate on the Pure *Apriori* Reason of Phenomenology as the sole field in which one's faith in Reason can have its perfect way. He has a strong, great personality, simple, intense, devoted. He makes a perfectly excellent host, he is a good clear lecturer but particularly efficient as leader of the Seminar.[2]

At the time he wrote this, Boyce Gibson was not an impressionable young student but a professor in his late fifties. I hesitate to introduce other reports for fear of making them sound like testimonials. Phenomenology does not rest on the character of its founder, but philosophies do not write themselves, and the reader may find this glimpse of Husserl the man of some interest.

Boyce Gibson's passing reference to World War I is enough to remind us that, if the drama of Husserl's life was inward, that inwardness was invaded by immeasurable catastrophe. Even for those of my generation, for whom "the War" means World War II, the human devastation of the First World War is still felt. Husserl's loss was grave: "Wolfgang, Husserl's younger son, a brilliant student of the oriental languages, was killed in action before Verdun in 1916. . . . His older son, Gerhart, professor of law and philosopher of law, was wounded severely two times during the War."[3] But apart from the war, Husserl's life was far from placid. There was a period of profound philosophical

2. W. R. Boyce Gibson, "From Husserl to Heidegger: Excerpts from a 1928 Freiburg Diary," ed. Herbert Spiegelberg, *Journal of the British Society for Phenomenology*, II, no. 1 (January, 1971), 65. Also see Herbert Spiegelberg, *The Phenomenological Movement*, 2d ed., Vol. I; and Arion L. Kelkel and René Schérer, *Husserl*. Note: Full bibliographic information is provided in the footnotes of this volume only for works not included in the bibliography.

3. Herbert Spiegelberg, Editorial Preface to Boyce Gibson's "From Husserl to Heidegger," p. 78.

and professional discouragement in 1906 as well as the recognition, in the final years of his life, that Reason was threatened at its root, that Europe was suicidal. It is a measure of Husserl's historical discernment rather than philosophical self-doubt that he writes in 1935: "Philosophy as science, as serious, rigorous, indeed apodictically rigorous, science—*the dream is over*." [4] That his manuscripts survived the thirties and forties may give at least some solace to Husserl's readers. That phenomenology has survived and is being practiced is the final respect history has paid to one of its most penetrating philosophers.

The stress I have placed on the works of the middle and later years of Husserl's research and the weight I have given his philosophy of the life-world and of the crisis of Western man reflect my own interpretation of phenomenology. It is not Husserl the logician nor even Husserl the epistemologist who impresses me most, but the Husserl whose philosophy of transcendental subjectivity offers a theory of consciousness, world, and history. Although it would be easy to say that this view provides an existential dimension to phenomenology and despite the fact that I am more sympathetic to existential philosophy than many Husserlians, it would be inaccurate to consider this book as a plea for existential phenomenology. I insist on phenomenology as the grounding discipline, though I believe that its final results have existential implications. Where I have brought the two schools together, it has not been to integrate them but to identify certain common concerns. But whatever doubt may linger about an "existential" interpretation of Husserl, there is no question about the secondary status given to the *Logical Investigations* in this study. Those whose interest is in Husserl's logic and in epistemological problems relating to that logic will find little nourishment in my pages, while those who delight in the possible engagement (if never a marriage) between phenomenology and linguistic philosophy will find their revels unencouraged. It is not that I see nothing in Husserl's logic or that I find no credible connection between phenomenology and linguistic philosophy. Rather, it is that I read the early Husserl as a prelude to transcendental philosophy—precisely the turn which the admirers of the *Logical Investigations* think brought phenomenology to grief and which the votaries of linguistic analysis find offensive. I am

4. Edmund Husserl, *The Crisis of European Sciences and Phenomenology*, p. 389.

prepared to settle for what I have done; I have no wish to argue that the thinker presented here is the only, the "authentic" Husserl. No doubt there are as many ways to Husserl as there are serious philosophers willing to provide them.

It may be said that every manuscript contains two books: the one the reader finds and the one the author intends. With publication, the writer loses control over the former; it is even doubtful whether he retains dominion over the latter. It is my hope, nevertheless, that the reader will find what the author intends: an authentic approach to phenomenology.

Acknowledgments

I WAS BORN on Thanksgiving Day, and so giving thanks comes easily. W. H. Werkmeister introduced me to the study of Husserl twenty-five years ago. That study was continued and intensified several years later under Alfred Schutz. Indirect instruction came from the writings of (and occasional meetings with) Marvin Farber, Herbert Spiegelberg, Erwin Straus, Harmon Chapman, Fritz Kaufmann, and Dorion Cairns. Although I cannot formally qualify as his student, I consider Aron Gurwitsch to be one of my teachers. In all of my work in phenomenology, I have gone my own way—a way sometimes considered too existential to satisfy rigorous phenomenologists and too phenomenological to please committed existentialists. Whatever failings it may have, my approach to phenomenology is that of a "second-generation" Husserlian who is, paradoxically, the child of European parents, decisively American, and no less emphatically indebted to a philosophical tradition which still remains fugitive to American consciousness.

During 1971–72, when this book was written, I was a Senior Fellow of the National Endowment for the Humanities. I am grateful to the Endowment for their support. Those who have helped in the preparation of the manuscript of this book are also to be thanked: Phyllis Halpin and Charlotte Cassidy of Cowell College at the University of California, Santa Cruz. Mrs. Cassidy was my typist; no author could have had more responsible assistance. For bibliographical aid I relied on Joan Hodgson of the University Library. She gave expert and kind help. The editors and staff of Northwestern University Press have been properly demanding and agreeably understanding. Nicholas Natanson assisted with the proof and Kathy Natanson helped with the index.

Most academic authors have a list of colleagues to thank for reading a manuscript, for their criticisms and suggestions. We are told that if it were not for those critics, the author would have blundered more often than he has. My work has been solitary. One of the publisher's readers did raise a number of points which I found helpful, but apart from some very minor changes, this book is the one I originally submitted. My intellectual indebtedness is largely to my phenomenological predecessors and distinguished contemporaries who are dead. One of Husserl's students told me some years ago that Husserl preferred an audience of nonphilosophers for his books because they came to phenomenology with fewer prejudices and set positions; they brought freshness in place of technical expertise to the study of his ideas. That freshness I have found in the encouragement and criticism of the one reader I have relied on for advice, Lois Natanson.

M. N.

Santa Cruz, California
April 19, 1973

Edmund Husserl

Philosopher
of Infinite Tasks

1 / Introduction

PHILOSOPHY, THESE SULLEN DAYS, is somewhat a pensioner in the family of knowledge. Like an aged grandfather living on a legacy outstripped by the times, philosophy depends on the kindness of relatives who may take some pride in the aura of grandness which surrounds the old man but who help to maintain him more out of loyalty than devotion. Indeed, most of the grandfathers have died in the past generation, Russell and Jaspers most recently, but before them a larger band: Bergson, Whitehead, Dewey, Santayana. Apart from Heidegger, Marcel, and Sartre, there are few philosophers alive today who qualify for a magisterial role. The elders are not being replaced. Instead, there is a profusion of professors. Whatever esteem philosophy may have had in earlier times has been eclipsed by the demands of immediacy: the realms of politics, economics, and history do not seem to be much concerned with philosophy's ruminations. Although it has always been known that philosophy bakes no bread, it was assumed that it could occasionally supply a little yeast. In the natural and social sciences, the activity of the philosophers has been great, yet it is doubtful that most students of physics or of sociology have felt any substantial impact. Historians remain dubious about the legitimacy of the discipline known as philosophy of history, while people in literature are unsettled by the advances of aestheticians. There is a general sense of embarrassment when grandfather leaves his room to meet the guests. Who needs him? That, finally, is the question that comes to the surface, a piece of classical debris which insists on being noticed.

Where philosophy has penetrated the larger scene in modern times, it has come either through the force of older movements such as Marxism or traditional institutions such as the Roman Catholic church. An exception to this pattern has been existentialism, whose challenge has come through the celebrity of Jean-Paul Sartre and by way of literature and the theater. But even there, the distinctively philosophical roots of Sartre's thought have not caught the public eye, and among philosophers it has taken years for the recognition and appropriation of the Sartrean philosophy of being. And for all the pleas for mutual understanding between Continental and Anglo-American philosophers, there is still more isolation than there is genuine interchange. Philosophy remains more or less a stranger to the public, remote to the practitioners of the sciences, and a divided cause for the philosophers themselves. Although there has been a great deal of discussion regarding the methods of philosophy and the controversies between schools, one theme has been left aside: the station of philosophy. It is not the fashion in contemporary American and British circles to ask what philosophy is, to reflect on its mission, or to wonder what happened to its concern with wisdom. But there is one major exception to philosophy's indifference to itself: the phenomenology of Edmund Husserl. For our century, he is philosophy's primal grandfather.

At first glance, the work of Husserl would seem to offer only erratic support for the claim that he has brought philosophy back to the center of our world. For many readers, that first glance might very well prove to be a last look at phenomenology, for it all depends on where one happens to turn in his writings. The range is doubly bewildering: included are books on mathematics and logic, various "introductions" to phenomenology, discourses on such themes as time, and discussions of the sickness of Western man. Titles alone, however, are not a sufficient guide to the books. In fact, some of the writings on logic are concerned with the sources of our everyday world, while parts of the analysis of our cultural crisis are taken up with problems in what is ordinarily called the history of science. Moreover, the "introductions" to phenomenology prove to be bewilderingly complex and seemingly arcane exercises in advanced topics—introductions for those who are "beginners" in Husserl's special sense of that word but forbidding treatises for the novice. Even Husserl's essay on phenomenology for the *Encyclopaedia Britannica* was impenetrable for most users of that work. In recent years it has been replaced. If we add to all of this a reliance on a new vocabulary, a thick style only occasionally lifted by a thrusting passage, and a scarcity of illustration, we have a good case for arguing that, if technical philosophy is out of the reach of so many today, Husserl has done more than his share to make it so. Before explaining why what is apparent here is only apparent, I must turn to a further complication.

Although Husserl published a number of sizable volumes in his lifetime, he was not really a writer of books. He was the author of an encyclopedia of cognition, a vast history of consciousness, notes for which occupied the major part of his career. The fact is that the books he published were but a fragment of the manuscripts he wrote, many of which are in the course of being published by various editors in the complete works known as *Husserliana*. Husserl left some 45,000 pages of manuscript *written in shorthand*. The sets of books hidden in that staggering output constitute a philosophical glacier floating beneath the tip of the published work. Once again, it seems that everything about Husserl would lead us to believe that his thought would be the last to make a claim for involvement in the world or for bringing order out of the human and disciplinary fragmentation of our age. How can a thinker whose books are largely inaccessible and much of whose work is unpublished be said to be of vital interest to an audience other than specialists in phenomenology or students of contemporary European philosophy? Why is Husserl so much our contemporary? And how, finally, are we to understand the revitalization which his ideas have brought to almost all segments of the spectrum of knowledge?

Philosophy, for Husserl, is the search for radical certitude. It is the effort to locate in experience the kind of necessity which mathematics has, but a necessity which is a function of our life in the world rather than of the postulations and definitions of an axiomatic method. Beyond necessity which is involved in the world, Husserl was searching for a certainty of roots, of conditions which underlie experience and make it possible. How far can one go in such a search? Descartes believed that his meditations had uncovered an absolute ground for knowledge, one founded on the inescapable givenness of thinking which is evident even when one doubts such thinking. Husserl is very much a Cartesian, but, despite his debt to Descartes's method, he moves far beyond Cartesian philosophy in the development of phenomenology. Descartes, so Husserl believed, came close to the discovery of phenomenological philosophy but stopped short of the crucial insight. Philosophical methods and philosophical results are integral, and so a philosophy which does not attend scrupulously to its own methodology can never achieve its proper goal. More than any other modern thinker, Husserl insisted on the fundamental clarification of the grounds of philosophical inquiry, on making explicit philosophical method, and on illuminating the involvement of the thinker in philosophizing about the everyday world which he inhabits and whose demands embrace him. It is in the complex relationship between the philosopher and the mundane realm that the clue to certitude is to be found.

Appearances to the contrary, philosophy and daily life are strangers. Philosophy begins with a reflexive turn toward the everyday world, a turn which puts the philosopher in an odd relationship with everything else. Consider some of the themes which entertain the philosopher. He interests himself in the reality of his experience, in the question of how such experience is possible, how it can be known with good warranty, how it is possible for fellow men to know the same world he knows, and how our world is to be valued, its purpose or significance. Even with such basic problems posed, there are more fundamental issues. The reality of experience presupposes the being of the world about which inquiry is made. Prior to raising the question of its reality, *experience* is posited, recognized, admitted. And, perhaps, before "experience" there is a believing-in, a primordial acceptance of, reality as *there,* given in such absolute terms that the whole of belief reduces to a vast naïveté in which the individual and his experiential reality are seamlessly united. The reflexive activity of the philosopher must, if it is to be completely searching and unremitting, concern itself with such primordial belief. The alternative is to accept the world as problematic only at levels which already take for granted man's *having* a world at all and his natural engagement with the issues presented to him as problematic within the horizon of daily life.

Husserl's struggle for philosophical certitude begins with the recognition that it is only at the granite base of mundane knowledge and belief that a proper foundation is to be found for erecting a veridical philosophy. It is the radicality of that insight and the daring of that commitment which make it hard literally *to follow* Husserl's thought. A number of obstacles present themselves. Getting at an absolute foundation means that nothing can be assumed or borrowed on good faith from others, whether they are previous philosophers, scientists, or fellow men we ordinarily rely on. It will be necessary to begin strictly on one's own. In phenomenological terms, that will mean insisting on an egological standpoint in which reports from others are sifted and ultimately translated in the matrix of individual experience. The obstacle here is overpowering, for translation into first-person terms must be accompanied by a reconstruction of the individual's standpoint. What use is it to translate intersubjective terms into egological ones if the individual covertly takes for granted the legitimacy and efficacy of his being in *our* world? Furthermore, the language of traditional philosophy, no less than that of common sense, is inflected with a variety of assumptions and attitudes. There is no neutral ground on which to begin speaking about philosophical problems. Nor will the turn to a purely formalistic language do: ultimately any symbolic system of expression will have to be translated into someone's mother tongue. Logicians who discuss their work with colleagues may wrestle each other for control of the pencil or the chalk, but their most mordant "Now, if you please!" is uttered in English, in German, in Italian but not in the symbolic terms whose cogency they are disputing. Language itself becomes self-problematic to the philosopher hunting for certitude.

The difficulty of Husserl's language may now be appreciated. Part of the trouble with his style may indeed simply be Husserl's obscurity as a writer. All the philosophical exegesis in the world will not overcome a bad sentence. But the problem goes much deeper. Husserl utilizes language in a number of different ways. First, he introduces some new terms and uses old ones in novel ways. This, of course, is hardly remarkable in the history of philosophy, but for phenomenology the problem is posed in a rather peculiar way. Language itself is both a central part of the everyday world which the philosopher is to inspect and reconstruct and the instrument through which all description and analysis are presented. An obvious paradox arises for the phenomenologist: How is it possible to gain certainty by relying on an intrinsically uncertain instrument? There is a paradox beyond the paradox: Even if language is reliable for the philosopher, how can he communicate with equal reliability with the nonphilosopher? Husserl does not resolve these difficulties, but in trying to appreciate the reasons for the obscurity of much of his thought it is important to recognize that he is attempting to push language to the limits of philosophical as well as mundane acceptability. The linguistic borrowings evident in such phenomenological terms as *"epochē," "noesis," "noema,"* and *"hylē"* are efforts to relocate words less loaded with contemporary prejudice than many alternative synonyms but also reminders of conceptual sources in the Greek tradition, resonances in language which may yield a resurgence of meaning and linguistic courage in the face of fixity and stasis.

In addition to problems of achieving an egological standpoint and finding the language appropriate to phenomenology, Husserl was confronted with the aggravating task of locating the right starting point for his philosophical work. *Where* does the phenomenologist begin? If the search is for certitude, then the point of departure may have decisive implications for whatever results are gained. Determining a proper starting point, then, is itself a phenomenological issue. There are two interrelated undertakings involved in making a phenomenological start: first, there is the literal question of exactly where one should begin in pursuing phenomenological work; second, there is the disciplinary problem of how the total domain of phenomenological work should be charted. Deciding where one should begin presupposes some conception of the larger field of activity, and so both aspects of the situation tag along with each other whether one wishes to have them together or not. It is that combination of factors which makes for methodological irritation, for each time the phenomenologist picks up a specific theme for inquiry he knows that he is, tacitly at least, making a decision about the proper approach to the totality of phenomenological work of which that theme is merely a fragment. For Husserl, the problem was seen in its most intense form. He realized that the longest of lifetimes would not suffice for either completing a map of the terrain of the whole realm of phenomenology or for making a major start toward the actual working out of phenomenological descriptions and analyses. Nor was there any compromise possible between giving up the schematic view of the totality and completing at least some concrete analyses. In either case, all that could be done really involved efforts in both directions. Husserl found himself pulled apart any way he turned. What he did, in fact, was to accept the contradiction of his work and to persist in a struggle which offered no satisfactory resolution.

We are now in a position to understand the strange character of Husserl's philosophical career. He felt himself to be a wanderer in "the trackless wilds of a new continent," where he had "undertaken bits of virgin cultivation."[1] A philosophical Columbus, where was Husserl to begin appropriating the prize of discovery? If he were to spend his life completing the outline of the new world, to be its sovereign cartographer, he could hardly have time to examine its wealth of detail; if he sought to describe and analyze the treasure, piece by piece, he would have to give up the charts which could guide his successors. In fact, Husserl bled from wounds incurred by being impaled permanently on both horns of the dilemma. His writings bear witness to his predicament. On the one hand, he gave us an incredible wealth of detailed, close phenomenological analysis of concrete problems; on the other hand, most of his books were attempts to present a map of the new "continent" and to give the future voyager reliable instructions about how to make the journey for himself in an efficacious way. The image of discovery repeats itself in prophetic terms for Husserl, for he recognized that he was opening up a new route which his successors would have to travel. He writes: "The far horizons of a phenomenological philosophy, the chief structural formations, to speak geographically, have disclosed themselves; the essential groups of problems and the methods of approach on essential lines have been made clear. The author sees the infinite open country of the true philosophy, the 'promised land' on which he himself will never set foot."[2]

At one and the same time Husserl is immersed in concrete work and trying to provide a phenomenological rationale for that work: the result of the duality is a reappraisal of the meaning of philosophical beginnings. Put another way, phenomenology is a reflection on the meaning of philosophical activity, a search for its essential roots and its connections with the variegation of the experienced world. To be a beginner in Husserl's sense is to concern oneself with the history of the given in experience, with the career of consciousness in intimate relation to the given, and with the "archaeology" of all phenomena. Beginning means a perpetual effort, for there is no static achievement in philosophy in the sense of work once and for all done.

1. Edmund Husserl, *Ideas*, p. 23.
2. *Ibid.*, pp. 28–29.

Each person must go through his own philosophical performance, interrogate *his* experience, and come to terms with what
he can make of his fellow man's claims and pronouncements.
The burden of responsibility falls always, again and again, on
the concrete individual who has to find his point of access to
philosophy. The significance of an egological orientation becomes apparent here. There is no substitute for the individual's
own seeing. But it should also be clear that the ultimacy of an
egological ground does not mean that "seeing" is an easy or
automatic affair. The obligation of the philosopher to his contemporaries is to support their attempt to find the ground on
which phenomena become, in the strictest sense, *evident*. Rather
than being a mentor or guide in the classical sense of a companion who leads the novice, the phenomenologist strives to
give the initiate autonomy from the outset, to place him in
charge of himself, and to demand of him the same rigor he
expects of himself. Beginning, for Husserl, is the permanent
state of the genuine philosopher.

Perhaps we now have enough of an overall view of Husserl's
philosophical motives and intent to appreciate the bond that
unites him with a humanistic conception of philosophy. As we
have seen, all the appearances go against the thesis that phenomenology has an integral relationship with the world we
find ourselves coping with today, yet the reality beneath the
appearances tells another story. The opaqueness of Husserl's
language and style comes from an effort to elucidate the grammar of consciousness as well as the subtlety of prereflective
experience, not from an unwillingness to express himself forth-
rightly. The disequilibrium between his published work and the
deep vault of his manuscripts is the consequence of a persistent
effort to introduce the reader to phenomenology while practicing
phenomenology. And the return again and again to introductions
and beginnings is Husserl's way of assessing the bond between
the experiential world and the task of the philosopher. To search
for beginnings, for Husserl, is to see the actuality of historical
existence as the product of a generative process in which the
nature and meaning of events are encapsulated—"sedimented,"
in phenomenological terms—in the flow of time. What the ordinary man as well as the historian finds "present" in the world
of public events is history-laden reality. Any figure or occurrence
has within it and behind it a large range of pertinent phenomena. Unfortunately, the language of "within" and "behind" lends

itself to misinterpretation, as though the presence of the past in the present were like a set of Chinese boxes. The more exacting image comes from poetry, where a word or phrase comes to bear the career of its predecession in language in general and in the poem in particular. So too with mundane reality: the concrete given in experience tells the story of its roots and associations— its *situation*.

We shall return to all of these themes in the course of our study, where Husserl's ideas, terminology, and methodology will be given a more sustained and systematic treatment. For the moment, we are trying to get an overall clue to the nature of phenomenology as a method and as a philosophy. From the discussion of some of the problems of the accessibility of phenomenology and its relationship to the immediacy of the experienced world there emerges at least one consideration which might enable us to go on ahead—a base camp from which the explorations of higher reaches can be attempted: *Radical certitude is Husserl's goal; radical certitude must be phenomenology's method.* The person who strives for such certitude must turn to himself as the locus of ultimate rigor, for all of the translations made of history and of the deeds of fellow men in the worlds of spirit and politics must finally be made by the individual for whom reality exists to be comprehended. Past any cheap "subjectivism" and beyond all merely idiosyncratic attitudes, the egological structure of experience stands as the last criterion for philosophical accountability. Husserl writes:

> Anyone who seriously intends to become a philosopher must "once in his life" withdraw into himself and attempt, within himself, to overthrow and build anew all the sciences that, up to then, he has been accepting. Philosophy—wisdom . . . —is the philosophizer's quite personal affair. It must arise as *his* wisdom, as his self-acquired knowledge tending toward universality, a knowledge for which he can answer from the beginning, at each step, by virtue of his own absolute insights.[3]

From the foundation of radical individuality—the meaning of which we will discover later in the phenomenological doctrine of the intentionality of consciousness—Husserl will attempt to reconstruct the entire superstructure of knowledge. We are now able to glimpse the outlines of the whole enterprise:

3. Edmund Husserl, *Cartesian Meditations*, p. 2.

1. Phenomenology purports to be a "presuppositionless" philosophy. What is meant is simply the principle that nothing can be accepted by the inquirer unless he has scrutinized its character and implications and also recognized that it is a feature of experience. Strictly speaking, a presuppositionless philosophy is not a philosophy without assumptions; it is a philosophy in which assumptions are candidly admitted, examined, and accounted for. The obligation of the phenomenologist is to be fastidious in the inventory and analysis he makes of what is taken for granted by both common-sense men and theoreticians as well. Major examples of philosophical presuppositions include what Husserl calls the "general thesis" of the natural attitude: the tacit faith ordinary men have in the reality of their world, the assumption that the shared world of everyday life is indeed the same for all normal individuals, that whatever exists in our world has a natural history—a causal basis—that we can reasonably expect the world to continue in the future in much the same way it has in the past, and that value, symbolic significance, aesthetic worth, and religious commitment are elements of or associated with the mundane world they transcend. Such cardinal presuppositions of experience are not denied or cancelled out. How could they be? Rather, the phenomenologist attempts to discern their character and to locate their limits. Once "under control," assumptions may be appropriated for philosophical use.

2. Consciousness is the source and matrix of all phenomena. The very word "consciousness" is a stumbling block for most discussions of phenomenology because it is, quite naturally, taken most often in a psychological sense. Consciousness, psychologically understood, is a function of what happens in the brain. Taken in this way, consciousness is connected with "awareness" and stands in contradistinction to the "unconscious" or to the "subconscious." Most vital for the neurological perspective, consciousness psychologically conceived is an individuated affair because each person "has" consciousness in the same way that he has a brain. For Husserl, consciousness is to be understood in a fundamentally different way. Without denying the neurological aspect of consciousness, he maintains that it is in the structure and not the physical basis of consciousness that we can locate its essential character as the bearer of perceptual reality. In the operation of the mind, a mathematical computation holds equally good and true whether

the individual performing it thinks quickly or slowly, thinks to-day or tomorrow, thinks coolly or obsessionally. So too in every act of thinking there is a universal feature which helps to explain what the phenomenologist means by "structure": every act of thinking implies an object thought of. Thinking is necessarily thinking *about*. All other acts of perception, broadly understood, have a directional force: remembering, imagining, and willing point to or, as Husserl says, "intend" some object, something remembered, imagined, willed. In sum, consciousness is by its very nature always *consciousness-of*, and that is the kernel of the axial principle of phenomenology: the intentionality of consciousness.

3. Phenomena are objects of intentional acts. "Objects" here are not taken as real entities or events; they are whatever present themselves by way of the acts of perception. The being of the intentional object is of interest to the phenomenologist only insofar as he intends it "as real" or "as unreal." It is essential to understand that Husserl is not presenting a theory of "phenomena" in the Kantian sense. The phenomenologist is not dealing with "appearances" over and against "reality"—things as they are in themselves. He is concerned with his awareness-of all of the elements of his experiential life. Intentionality carries with it a reflexive dimension which distinguishes it from what otherwise might be thought of as simple, straightforward inspection of data—the kind of close, painstakingly accurate description of animals done by some naturalists. For the phenomenologist, the phenomena strictly understood are purely intentional in nature. Their reality is reality-as-intended and their contextual history is a feature of the world-as-intended. Put somewhat differently, phenomena are *meant*, not simply acknowledged in perception. In its most obvious sense, then, phenomenology is the science or discipline of phenomena as "meant" entities—meanings ordered and, indeed, constituted by the appropriate acts of consciousness. The discipline endeavors to comprehend the rationale of the entire domain of intentional meaning, to become the logos of the phenomena. We are led to the following conclusion: The reflexive life of consciousness is truly infinite in its reach and discloses an infinite horizon for the description and analysis of intentional acts and their objects.

4. Phenomena may be appreciated as essences. The word *essence* has a bad name in philosophy partly because ordinary parlance gives it the connotation of mystery. The "essence" of

something is an almost occult quality, a hiddenness of things. Husserl takes the opposite tack: essences are simply aspects or qualities of objects-as-intended. An older tradition speaks of "whatness" or "quiddity." Locating the object as thing or as intended phenomenon depends on the perspective of the inquirer. The phenomenologist believes that essences do not lurk somehow behind or within objects but are the object grasped in its intentional character, grasped *as* being this or that. Such graspings are potentially available to everyone. Husserl writes: "The truth is that everyone sees 'ideas,' 'essences,' and sees them, so to speak, continuously; they operate with them in their thinking and they also make judgments about them. It is only that, from their theoretical 'standpoint,' people interpret them away." [4] I prefer to speak of essences rather than essence because it is less misleading to the reader who might otherwise assume that for every thing there is an essence just as for every walnut there is the meat. In this view, essences are especially tough nuts to crack; those who weary of trying to break them take the concealed fruit on faith. To all of this Husserl objects vigorously. Essences are unities of meaning intended by different individuals in the same acts or by the same individual in different acts. The White House is essentially the same intentional object whether viewed earlier or later in the day, remembered or directly perceived or even imagined, today or last year. The "real" White House was once burned by the British army and the rebuilt White House is subject to fire, but the White-House-*as-intended* cannot be destroyed, its essentiality cannot be scorched.

5. Phenomenology demands its own method. It is clear that everything the phenomenologist is trying to do requires a vantage point which neither takes for granted the world that common sense subscribes to and is dominated by nor presupposes the orientation of natural science toward the reality of the events with which it deals. For the former, the world is *of course* real; for the latter, the reality status of the world as experienced by ordinary men is either a distinctively psychological problem or else of interest to philosophers. Husserl holds that believing-in-the-world is the most fundamental philosophical commitment with powerful consequences for any account of experience. Such

---

4. Edmund Husserl, *Ideen zu einer reinen Phänomenologie und phänomenologischen Philosophie*, sec. 22 (trans. Dorin Cairns in his article "An Approach to Phenomenology," p. 13).

believing is not shameful in some fugitive way—as though a blush should come to the cheeks of the epistemologist who has so believed. To the contrary, believing-in-the-world is the paradigm of normality. The philosopher's task is not to ridicule it but to understand it and to point out its implications. Any attempt to examine such believing will be prejudiced, however, by the philosopher's own believing unless he finds a way to free himself of the very attitude he seeks to elucidate. The most radical of all of Husserl's procedures is introduced at this point to meet the problem. It is called *epochē*, which means a restraint or suspension on the part of the philosopher with regard to his participation or complicity in experience. No concept in phenomenology is more difficult to grasp; none is more essential to the understanding of Husserl. At this stage in our discussion it is best to set aside the ramifications of epochē and restrict ourselves to a warning. Phenomenological restraint sets aside the individual's believing-in-the-world but does not cancel it or negate it in any way. To equate epochē with denial is to miss the point of phenomenology.

6. Phenomenology is especially concerned with prepredicative experience. Within the ordinary stance of man in the everyday world—the "natural attitude," in Husserl's language—things and events are experienced in typified form, not as concrete individuals but as types of individuals.[5] We see animals, birds, reptiles, cats, and fish before we pick out either kinds of animals or particular individuals in the class. And even, as Husserl points out,[6] if we mistake a whale for a fish, we are typifying the object. Acquaintanceship with types comes early in childhood, but most approaches to its logic attribute the whole of naming and recognizing to association and conditioning. But the latter presuppose an original experiencing whose logic phenomenology tries to disclose. The prepredicative sphere is made up of all perceptual intentions which help to establish our formal, self-reflective knowledge of the world. Before I characterize a scene as familiar or odd, as traditional or innovative, I have a passive or tacit grasp of the typically expected and even the utterly untypical. Experience in its prepredicative givenness is richly endowed with meaning. "Familiarity" is an example of the density of the prepredicative organization of experience. No one ever instructs us

5. See Edmund Husserl, *Experience and Judgment*, pp. 331–34.
6. *Ibid.*, p. 333–34.

about the familiar; we absorb it and build upon it "naturally." Yet the "natural" here is far from evident to the individual who makes use of it. As we shall see later, Husserl shows that the roots of the "familiar" are found in certain primordial assumptions about any element of experience: that continuity and repetition are the basal presuppositions for there being anything given as part of our day-to-day reality. The recognition of the importance of the prepredicative realm contributes to the enlargement of philosophical experience.

7. Phenomenology offers itself as the foundation of science. A number of misunderstandings must be avoided at this point. First, "science" should be translated as knowledge in the generic sense—*Wissenschaft*—and not taken to mean the physical sciences alone. Second, "science" includes the social sciences in its nuclear meaning, not as a liberal afterthought. Third, "foundation" must be understood in an epistemological sense: it establishes the ground of knowledge, not a panoply of postulates and rules for the formal construction of a discipline such as mathematical physics. That understood, we may say that phenomenology attempts to "found" science by clarifying the meaning of all basic terms of discourse in their relationship to intentional consciousness, as they are built up in the activity of the ego. "Thing," "event," "cause," "relationship," and "fact" are examples of the kinds of terms we call "basic." Formal definition of terms is insufficient for the phenomenologist's purposes; he tries instead to comprehend their sources in the life of the individual as each of us comes to grasp their meaning in the context of experience. Rather than a diversity of lives leading to a plethora of interpretative results, the phenomenological analysis of terms is carried out at the level of essential interpretation: it is not the actual event which interests Husserl but the event as an exemplar of its class or type. At the foundation of science there is a universe of meaning to be disclosed in terms of the possible being of its constituent data. Thus, *irreality*, the subjunctive dimension of experience, proves to be the true ground of knowledge. The task of the phenomenologist is to explore the range as well as the constitutive order of that ground in its dynamic aspect, i.e., as a living and developing realm of possibility.

8. Phenomenology is a philosophy of the life-world. We have already spoken of the "natural attitude" of man in the everyday world, a reality that he takes for granted as veridical and reliable for all practical purposes and a reality that he "lives"

directly through his aspirations and demands. The world of daily life is also the business world in which the transactions of men are handled and decoded. The small businessman may or may not have a profound grasp of economic theory, but he knows pretty much what needs doing in his corner of the market. The patron of the grocery store need have no insight into the theory of world trade to know that there is inflation. The unemployed have the right words for a period of depression, whatever their schooling. The long promenade of mundanity—infants, actors, morticians, belly dancers, and bureaucrats—possesses its own coherent system of explanation for anything that happens. Every interpretation is the product of a schema of explanation for both intimate and public events. At one and the same time, such schemata are naïve and highly sophisticated. A man who is wiped out in business may successfully go through bankruptcy. With or without the advice of lawyers, accountants, and friends, he may find his way through the requirements and loopholes of the law. *His* interpretation of what needs to be done, *his* evaluation of the advice others offer him, *his* decisions are ultimately the screen through which his action passes and is filtered. As with prepredicative experience, there is a complex logic at work in the activity of the bankrupt. His interpretative home is what Husserl calls the life-world, the domain of our unreflective, simply taken-for-granted being. The cardinal consideration here is that it is within the life-world that all projection of more specialized realms—the law, government, the professions—takes place, and it is the life-world itself which becomes philosophy's theme: the search for self-knowledge coincides with the illumination of mundanity.

9. Phenomenology is a defense of Reason. There is, Husserl insists, a teleology proper to human action: it must be directed toward its own completion within the larger network of the fulfillment of all consciousness in rational terms. The Reason in question here is the classical Greek model, and Husserl thinks of limited reason as being an infinitesimal portion of that ideal. But he also wishes to avoid the idea of reason as a scourge of the affections or as a mutilator of the integrity of the human creature. "Rationality," Husserl writes,

in that high and genuine sense . . . which in the classical period of Greek philosophy had become an ideal, still requires, to be sure, much clarification through self-reflection; but it is called in its mature form to guide our development. On the other hand we readily admit . . . that the stage of development of *ratio* represented by the rationalism of the Age of Enlightenment was a mistake, though certainly an understandable one.[7]

Reason, in its ideal sense, is protective of the reflective principle: for all consciousness there must be the possibility of turning back on itself, a lonely recoil in which the individual and the topic of his attention are united. In reflection ideas seek their limits of development and the individual becomes the one who sets aside occurrence in order to understand its source and goal. To discover oneself as a reflecting being is then to place in one continuum subject and object, reflector and reflected upon. It is not difficult to see that in these terms the elevation of thinking and analysis to the center of man's being is hardly rationalism in Husserl's sense. Indeed, Reason, in phenomenological philosophy, is a repudiation of the thesis that, through objective use of his mind, man may evolve into an autonomous and just being. Husserlian Reason is committed to the responsibility of man for sustaining and honoring philosophical reflection: the integral person seeking to know himself.

   10. Phenomenology is a critique of philosophy. Just as Reason leads necessarily to philosophy, so, for Husserl, philosophy is a clue to history. The European scene of Husserl's day, like our own, was fraught with unreason energized or demonized into a glorification of antireason. The sickness of Europe became, for Husserl, the image for a larger weariness which has beset man and which elevates irrationalism into a counterprinciple opposed to that of reflection. Paradoxically, philosophers in many quarters have contributed to the general malaise, whether their intent was to abet or stanch. Wherever relativism has been pursued the philosopher, like the historian, has retreated from the task of providing a unified account of man. The argument is that such "retreat" is in reality simply the necessary acknowledgment that necessity and universality cannot be found in what has been or in what is. We are left with fragments to care for, and even those gifts are destined in time to be replaced by others. Meanwhile, the search for absolutes is relegated to theologians who have undergone their own *crise de conscience*—academi-

7. Husserl, *The Crisis of European Sciences and Transcendental Phenomenology*, p. 290. Note: Here, as well as in other quotations from the *Crisis*, the translator's brackets have been omitted.

cians thriving on the "death of God" or wayward ministers trying to learn to pray again in a Godforsaken world. Philosophers have, for the most part, tagged along after relativism—history's whore—and relinquished the dream of the early moderns for a universal grammar of knowledge. Only parts and pieces can be managed: large horizons are out. I once heard a philosopher speak of a "package deal." It is pointless to make accusations here, but the point is that philosophy at one time represented the disciplined effort to wrest truth from knowledge and, in the process, touch wisdom. All of that is dead now and, Husserl asks, What has replaced it? Where are we? Where do we stand? Phenomenology assumes the responsibility for posing these questions because its reflective principle is vital to philosophy. Philosophical self-scrutiny is the essence of Reason and the credential of phenomenology.

Put together, our previewing of Husserl's conceptual terrain amounts to this: Phenomenology is a presuppositionless philosophy which holds consciousness to be the matrix of all phenomena, considers phenomena to be objects of intentional acts and treats them as essences, demands its own method, concerns itself with prepredicative experience, offers itself as the foundation of science, and comprises a philosophy of the life-world, a defense of Reason, and ultimately a critique of philosophy. Concealed in these thickets, as I have suggested, is a curious ambivalence regarding system-building and the establishment of authority. Husserl is, in principle, the master builder of philosophy, yet he insists on remaining a perpetual beginner; he spends his career trying to introduce phenomenology and yet its enigmatic quality remains; he celebrates the realm of essence but turns finally to the concrete world of everydayness; he urges us to remain faithful to the immediately given quality of experience only to reveal at last, as in the culminating act of a magician, that the life-world holds within it an infinite realm of transcendence. In the pages which follow we cannot hope to show the "real" Husserl or to present the "true" phenomenology. Instead we can only try to find a legitimate way into the complexity of his thought and to clarify those critical elements which serious reflection discloses. Inevitably, we shall find that phenomenology honors philosophy by seeking to return it to its original station as the source of our dignity and the guarantor of human Reason.

"NATURAL KNOWLEDGE," Husserl writes, "begins with experience . . . and remains *within* experience. Thus in that theoretical position which we call the 'natural' standpoint, the total field of possible research is indicated by a single word: that is, the *World*."[1] Within the natural standpoint (or natural attitude, as Husserl actually calls it) the "world" is tacitly accepted as "real," as having its "being" *out there*, and as being reliable enough for all ordinary pursuits. The words in quotation marks are not taken as problematic for common-sense men. *We* emphasize the odd status of "real" and "being" as, at some preliminary level, critics of experience, but the procedure is artificial. To the extent that we reflect on our status as beings in daily life, we stand at some distance from the current of everydayness. "Within experience," in Husserl's terms, means the orientation of any perceptual experience referring to the reality of the world. There is no way to grasp the world prior to reflection *when we discuss the natural attitude*, but that attitude is precisely prereflective and enmeshed in a naïve living of its own experience— a life immanently grasped as real. How is it possible to say anything about unreflected-upon life without introducing some alteration of it in the very act of analysis? The paradox is not an insurmountable barricade. If there were a qualitative gap between life and reflection such that, of necessity, the one always was fugitive to the other, then it would be impossible to do more than guess at the nature of raw experience. What makes the

1. Edmund Husserl, *Ideas*, p. 51.

case a different one is that the natural attitude includes reflection on its own activity. The exact character and scope of such reflection need interpretation.

If the greatest part of daily life is experienced in naïve terms and taken for granted as real, there are moments, at least, when the individual is aware that he is experiencing something in a particular manner. The most available examples involve an awareness *that* one is experiencing something: the typist aware that he is typing, the bird watcher self-conscious in the strict sense of that term, the conductor lucidly present to himself *as* leading the orchestra. A number of distinctions are needed before the illustrations will be of service. "Self-consciousness" can be misleading unless we restrict it, in the present context, to an attentiveness on the part of the individual to some phase of his activity which ordinarily goes on without notice. Thus, we are thinking of an ongoing involvement which suddenly comes into relief for the subject, rather than the quality of personality that characterizes the individual who is overly aware of his every move. Still further, the "suddenness" with which self-awareness occurs in our examples is worthy of note, for it means that self-consciousness is not being practiced or appropriated in some routine fashion but is a matter of happenstance. There is a spontaneity, then, in becoming aware that one is aware. Yet such spontaneity would appear to be a possibility of the natural attitude and so, in some sense, "within" its expression in daily life.

The irruption of a reflective self-awareness in the individual going about his business may strike him as odd or strange and is, most commonly, brushed aside or shaken off. When it persists, moods of an oblique kind are created through which the person makes his way back to his old self. The language is interesting: to "make his way back" the person needs to have strayed; to locate his "old self" he must possess criteria for recognition. The cause of mood shifts is not of interest to us at present, nor are we trying to work out the dynamic of movement from a taken-for-granted world to a self-inspected sphere, momentarily bizarre. The problem before us is the coincidence of an unanticipated reflective moment with the flow of mundanity as grasped in the straightforward appreciation of experience by the ego. I find myself aware of my own awareness *within* the actuality of the world. Now it should be understood that the examples I have given are reasonable enough as indicators of the sort of phenomenon in question here, but the individual's "having" of such moments is not restricted to discrete psychological units. While sitting an examination, I may indeed look around me at my fellow examinees and "suddenly" become aware of myself as "taking an examination." Such self-awareness is at the periphery of the illustration rather than its center. In truth, there is a sliding movement of self-consciousness throughout the individual's experiential day: a glancing, marginal, hinting intentiveness which points toward the world while announcing itself in flickering terms. The subtlety of "ordinary" experience is only partially caught in its variegation and complexity; what is most primordially cunning about the mundane is its capacity for pointing to itself at the same time that it manages the work of perception.

Underlying the moments of self-consciousness there is a continuous believing in the world, a nonself-conscious "faith" in the reality which encompasses the believer. The sleeper expects to wake, the dreamer to dream out his dream. Again, the language of mundanity invites inspection. "Expects to wake" translates into "accepts the continuity and sameness of experience." Of course, there is no point in the career of the individual when such acceptance is elicited or confessed. It is rather the case that every act of the person points toward the regeneration of the present. If the world is given as real, it is no less the case that consciousness posits it as real. Strictly understood, what presents itself to the individual as "real" should be taken as "what is given," not as that which is real. Reality is an added predicate to immediate experience, though it is ingrained in experience. To deny intentive expectation as a fundamental feature of mundane experience would be to propose instead a phenomenalism of sorts, to view the given as a tissue of presentations cohering in the moment of being apprehended but having no other unity or destiny. But phenomenalism is a distinctly technical position, not an achievement of common sense or an expression of the needs of daily life. The backdrop for entertaining the credibility of phenomenalism remains the world in which our movement takes place: the world-believed-in as it is relied on to sustain and outlast us. In these terms, mundane reality is necessarily comprehended as a final horizon for both reflection and action. Each time some facet of the world is perceived, our glance is carried along a path whose terminus is an essential "sameness," a possibility of experience going on in familiar terms. It would seem that there is no point of access to the natural attitude which is not already a part of its own structure.

Faith in the givenness of the world as real is the essential characteristic of the natural attitude. It is a believing that undergirds all discrete acts of perception, including overt positings of any object or event as "real." The words "faith" and "belief" are useful but also limited terms for the characterization of the natural attitude. We turn to them because it is hard to find more effective language but also because they are at least suggestive of the direct grasp that binds person and world. Husserl's own formulation of the problem of the natural attitude begins with an attempt to scan the philosophical outlines of the situation of man thrust into the world. He writes:

> I am aware of a world, spread out in space endlessly, and in time becoming and become, without end. I am aware of it, that means, first of all, I discover it immediately, intuitively, I experience it. Through sight, touch, hearing, etc., in the different ways of sensory perception, corporeal things somehow spatially distributed are *for me simply there*, in verbal or figurative sense "present", whether or not I pay them special attention by busying myself with them, considering, thinking, feeling, willing.[2]

The operative terms here are *immediately* and *intuitively*. By the first, Husserl means a presence to perception in which what is given is directly apprehended; by the second, Husserl understands the way in which consciousness grasps its object. Later we shall examine the notion of intuition more closely. For the present, a negative caution is necessary: intuition, for Husserl, has nothing to do with feeling, nor is it an occult power. Intuition is unmediated seeing, in the generic sense of the latter term.

The landscape of the directly given is not the whole of the natural attitude. To be sure, I am aware through my senses of a continuous world spread out before me, a world I trustingly take as given to my fellow men as well as to me and given in essentially the same manner. Although I recognize that cultures, languages, and historical epochs make for qualitative differences between groups of men, I also know that there are features universal to all societies. Everywhere and at all times children play, there are rites proper to maturation, marriage, and childbearing. The burial of the dead is commonly accepted as the responsibility of survivors. Viewing the world as basically one reality for all of us means that in the acts of perception—in knowing,

2. *Ibid.*, p. 101.

thinking, reflecting, and interpreting,—I accept the givenness of experience as intersubjectively and interculturally valid for all men. There is no "proof" which the ordinary man possesses for such a claim. Indeed, the question of proving his belief to be warranted does not arise in any fundamental way. Elements of experience may turn out to be dubious, and claims with respect to them may be disputed and even relinquished; the natural attitude persists. Nor should we be misled about the question of universality here. To have faith in the world as possessing universal features through which all men articulate their existence is not based on ethnological sophistication. Let us suppose that a band of hitherto unknown men was discovered in some remote clime and was studied for a number of years by a team of anthropologists, and that we were then informed that in the new race children never played, no rites were associated with maturation, marriage of any kind was unknown, and the dead were left to rot where they dropped. Would we then say that these were still human beings? If so, would it be fair to hold to our original conception of Man?

For the purposes of understanding the natural attitude—not for analyzing the problem of cultural relativism—we may say that the truth of the claim to universality implicit in the belief of common-sense men is irrelevant to the phenomenological status of the natural attitude. Whether or not their faith is warranted by anthropological or historical fact, men simply accept the givenness of an intersubjective reality in which essentially the same world exists for all of us. If doubts arise about the world, they make sense only over and against the frame of the world *within* which they present themselves. When something typically expected does not turn out to be the case, the individual more or less accepts the actuality as unusual, accidental, or perverse. In short, he turns from the given to something indirectly manifest: the structure of mundanity as faith holds it should be. Whatever the inconsistencies of experience, the natural attitude expects an underlying uniformity, a persistent texture. The bridge between what is given and what is anticipated is the indeterminate penumbra of association which surrounds perceptual experience. In a way, the "given" includes what is not directly perceived but merely apperceived. Husserl writes:

What is actually perceived, and what is more or less clearly copresent and determinate (to some extent at least), is partly pervaded, partly girt about with a *dimly apprehended depth or fringe of indeterminate reality*. I can pierce it with rays from the illuminating focus of attention with varying success. Determining representations, dim at first, then livelier, fetch me something out, a chain of such recollections takes shape, the circle of determinacy extends ever farther, and eventually so far that the connection with the actual field of perception as the *immediate* environment is established.[3]

There is, then, a situational aspect to immediacy. I take as real my fellow man's psychophysical existence and I believe that he experiences pain just as I do. When I see him wince, I know that he is hurt. But that knowing is set within a context: the grimace of the weight lifter may in purely anatomical and physiognomic terms be indistinguishable from that of a soldier being operated on under primitive conditions on the battlefield, but we perceive them differently. What we literally see and what we know about the two cases merge in the differentiation of the pain of extreme exertion and the pain of suffering. Of course, our reading of the situation may be mistaken. The weight lifter may be withstanding severe pain due to a sprained wrist. He should not be lifting weights at all. The soldier may actually have nothing more than a slight discomfort from what seems to us to be a major wound, but the sense of having failed to achieve his objective in battle may be an anguish. The newborn baby's smile comes from gas pains, not sociality. Without the fringes of experience, reality is bereft of meaning. It must be recognized, however, that in the ongoing nature of mundane experience, the context of any event is open and undecided in any strict way. The notion of "world" remains constant, my believing in the world remains fixed in its essential certitude, but the givenness of experience is permeated with undefined possibilities. As Husserl says, "An empty mist of dim indeterminacy gets studded over with intuitive possibilities or presumptions, and only the 'form' of the world as 'world' is foretokened. Moreover, the zone of indeterminacy is infinite. The misty horizon that can never be completely outlined remains necessarily there." [4]

It might seem that we are underrating the shrewdness of common sense. Surely, mundane life has its own serious doubts as well as occasional qualms. In daily life we search out

3. *Ibid.,* p. 102.
4. *Ibid.*

situations for their hidden implications, cast a lingering eye on people for their personal motivations, and adopt the motto: *Caveat emptor!* But the dubiety of these occasions is restricted. Something in the field of experience is being subjected to analysis, but the field itself is simply there. And even when the doubting refers to an entire domain or discipline, the world which includes all disciplines is left unchallenged. Both the world directly given and the world surmised or intended by way of allusion and connotation are prereflective grasped as real by the individual immersed in daily life. Any doubts, however serious and far-reaching, are tied to a primordial acceptance of everydayness. In a familiar but telling passage, Husserl says:

> I find continually present and standing over against me the one spatio-temporal fact-world to which I myself belong, as do all other men found in it and related in the same way to it. This 'fact-world,' as the word already tells us, I find to *be out there,* and also *take it just as it gives itself to me as something that exists out there.* All doubting and rejecting of the data of the natural world leaves standing the *general thesis of the natural standpoint.* "The" world is as fact-world always there; at the most it is at odd points "other" than I supposed, this or that under such names as "illusion," "hallucination," and the like, must be struck *out of it,* so to speak; but the "it" remains ever, in the sense of the general thesis, a world that has its being out there.[5]

This is Husserl's most decisive statement of the meaning of the natural attitude. A number of points must be noted. First, the reality I am part of in mundane terms—the "fact-world"— has no origin or source; it is simply "there" and always has been "there" for all of us. "There" is less a spatial than an epistemological term. It refers to a surrounding presence of things, events, and persons as well. Furthermore, "there" cannot be used in contradistinction to "here," for what is "there" for the individual in the natural attitude is the plenitude of all things insofar as they are conceived or *meant* as real. Second, the fact-world is an intersubjective community comprised of fellow men who at least tacitly treat experience as a shared reality, a mutual trust. Despite my bodily placement *here* I believe that you at the other end of the hall perceive our surroundings as "there" for both of us. The assumption which underlies the perception of the fact-world as possessing interchangeable perspectives (the converti-

5. *Ibid.,* p. 106.

bility of every "here" into a "there") is a vital feature of the natural attitude. We shall treat it more thoroughly a little later. For the moment, the point being emphasized is that the fact-world is accepted as shared prior to any analysis or argument. Third, any doubts we may have about experience fall into one of two fundamental categories: either we doubt some discrete facet of the world or else, somehow, we doubt the world itself. Some examples are needed to make this clear.

1. Piecemeal Doubt: We have the familiar instances of optical illusions as well as simple questioning of the truth of various claims. Thus, I doubt that the stretch of water ahead on the road is real. With the sun blazing and the road traversed totally dry, it seems unlikely that there should be water ahead. But my doubts may be unjustified. There may have been a sun shower a few minutes earlier, a sprinkler truck may have watered that portion of the road for some reason, or a truckload of bottled water may have overturned and flooded the stretch. If, when I drive through the "wet" part, the road proves to be dry, I decide that my doubt was warranted: I was subject to a mirage. If I see spots before my eyes, I may think that they come from staring too steadily into the sun, from floaters in the vitreous fluid in the eyeball, or from a detachment of the retina. If they persist or worsen I may decide to see an ophthalmologist. The doubts that I have, in any case, are limited to the functioning and health of the eyes. In principle, in all piecemeal doubting, I either know what will resolve the doubt or recognize that some course of action is appropriate for settling the problem. There is no doubt about this last statement.

2. Wholesale Doubt: Imagine someone who not only takes seriously Calderón's dictum that "life is a dream" but *lives* the torment of that utterance. If nothing is real, then it might seem we have resolved all doubts by committing ourselves to the thesis that the dream-world is certain. Yet that "certitude" proves to be evanescent if it, too, is a piece of the dream. Where does the dreamer stand if his dream is part of a total dream? Who, then, is the dreamer of the larger dream? If the cruelty of never being able to know the truth of the dream is accepted as indubitable, then the world whose reality was placed in question to begin with proves to be grounded in human suffering, which is life, not dream. And if that is so, what is the force of holding to Calderón's truth? In the end, wholesale doubt is a magnified form of piecemeal doubt. There is no Archimedean point on which to

place the epistemological lever of genuinely pervasive, total doubt. The final outpost of the natural attitude is what Husserl calls its "general thesis," the ultimate positing of "world" as a referential horizon for all experience.

Although the reality of the world may be affirmed by a self-conscious judgment—a seal of epistemic approval—it is rarely the case that the individual explicitly says or even thinks to himself: "The world is real." Believing in the givenness of experience is, for Husserl, a prereflective affair. He writes: "The General Thesis according to which the real world about me is at all times known not merely in a general way as something apprehended, but as a fact-world *that has its being out there*, does *not* consist of course *in an act proper*, in an articulated judgment *about* existence. It is and remains something all the time the standpoint is adopted, that is, it endures persistently during the whole course of our life of natural endeavour." [6] If there is no act proper, no deliberate positing of the general thesis, then it might seem that it is an unconscious or instinctual piety. This is not what Husserl maintains. The traditional differences between consciousness and the unconscious are grounded in distinctly psychological assumptions and categories. The map of the mind is drawn to a genetic scale. What is expressed in an individual's conscious or unconscious belief is a causal reflection of his concrete career. Moreover, the scope of awareness is restricted by a purely psychological viewpoint. The entire question of the nature of the general thesis demands a movement away from causal analysis toward a more neutral and discriminating approach to the character of consciousness.

To penetrate further into the meaning of the general thesis, let us imagine it at work in the life of common sense and typical experience. Here I am at the carnival, a brittle sticky apple in one hand and my other arm around Gwenda Lynn's waist. In the booths lining the midway are games of skill and chance, stands selling hot dogs and beer. The steam from a huge vat of sauerkraut covers the face of the hot dog man. Nearby, a dwarf stands on a heavy stool before a dark grid on which a pork-filled snake is being sizzled: CONEY ISLAND, the sign says, the longest wurst in carnival history, slithering in chopped onions. Each time the dwarf rearranges the heap of onions, he ends by cracking down the knife, edge perpendicular against the grid, to get

6. *Ibid.,* p. 107.

the last onion fragment off. Then he wipes his hands on a tarred apron and croaks the name of his meat, a bleating song which cuts under the cries of the other hawkers. In the distance the great wheel turns against the sky and the whiplashed shrieks of the coaster riders move out raggedly across the hum of the evening. It rained last night and the carnival grounds are still soggy in places. I guide Gwenda Lynn around the mire by pressing the heel of my palm against the lateral part of her back, leading her as if we were dancing. As we pass the dice cage, a man yells, "hot damn!" and I sink my teeth into a new side of the apple, suddenly especially white against the frozen red encasement of the jelly.

Walking, apple in one hand and girl in the other, the young man is poised in and against the flow of the evening. Without saying to himself—or even being able to say to himself—"here I am," he is present to himself through the sights, sounds, and fugitive kinesthesia of the moment. Looking-at means seeing the canopy of the penny-pitch attraction set above the cotton-candy sign. Hearing the barker's cry means attending to it over the come-and-go roar of the roller coaster. And sensing the girl's stepping toward the puddle means that a continuous awareness of bodily movement flares into a tiny signal of danger. In all of these sensuous realms what is seen, heard, and felt persists like an originless pulse. There is no adjective adequate to the complexity of its presence: "conscious" is an indicator but should not be understood as deliberate; "aware" points to a root attentiveness but is not synonymous with alertness; "percipient" helps us to grasp the range of its insistence but should not be tied to the senses as organic instruments. Perhaps the closest we can come to an adequate terminology is to speak in phenomenological terms of an *intentiveness* which is the essence of the general thesis. In ordinary parlance, to intend is to plan, to have in mind—a preparatory notion. As it is used in phenomenology, intending refers to a turn of consciousness toward its object, a grasping of direction. Rather than involving design and forethought, intending is presupposed in all acts of consciousness. Later we shall present a full discussion of the doctrine of intentionality which Husserl advances, but for now it is important to clarify the root of the general thesis.

The intentiveness at issue here is protoperceptual and involves a coincidence between particular acts of consciousness and the thematic continuum of awareness within which they are manifest. The girl is aware of an arm around her waist but not necessarily conscious of it at all times. The pressure of the hand at her back is both known and felt, but between the moments when knowledge and feeling are activated there remains constant the presence of the world as *there*, oneself in that world, and the possibility of being touched *again*. Each discrimination of consciousness points back to its intentive source. Avoiding mud means continuing the activity of walking but making a sharp turn in a new direction. That it was always possible to go left instead of straight ahead is hardly considered an accomplishment, yet that seemingly trivial potentiality indicates the tension of consciousness toward alteration and transition. The presence of possibilities of choice and decision mirrors an underlying "willingness" of the ego. For Husserl, the primordial believing in the world which characterizes the natural attitude undergirds each self-conscious aspect of experience and reveals itself in what we have called the presence of the world to the ego. It is in the variegation of experience that such presence is revealed, for the world is alive with predicates of urgency and worth. The carnival scene may be considered exhilarating or tawdry, but in some way it attracts or repels. Even those who are left untouched by it one way or the other recognize it as garish or empty. To an old carney it may be taken for granted as routine existence, but he knows soon enough what is missing in town. Familiar or exotic, the world burns with its own presence.

Although the general thesis remains the root of the natural attitude, the root thrives in a soil of interrelationships. Of fundamental importance to an understanding of the natural attitude is the placement of the human body in the world. It is obvious to common sense that each of us has a body which occupies space. It is perhaps a bit less evident that there are two ways of regarding the body: from the standpoint of the observer (perceiving the body of another person) or from the standpoint of the actor (my awareness of my own body). As an observer, I locate your body as *there*, at some distance from where my body is, i.e., from *here*. Yet it is no less true that "there" and "here" are convertible terms, mobile identifications, through which our orientation in the world is established. As Husserl writes,

By free modification of my kinesthesias, particularly those of locomotion, I can change my position in such a manner that I convert any There into a Here—that is to say, I could occupy any spatial locus with my organism. This implies that, perceiving from there, I should see the same physical things, only in correspondingly different modes of appearance, such as pertain to my being there. It implies, then, that not only the systems of appearance that pertain to my current perceiving "from here", but other quite determinate systems, corresponding to the change of position that puts me "there", belong constitutively to each physical thing. And the same in the case of every other "There." [7]

Once again, it is necessary to remember that pointing out features of the natural attitude does not mean that men in daily life are self-consciously aware that naïve life *has* structure. It may well be the case that most of us never happen to think about the "there" and "here," yet we utilize the implications of those structures in our mundane lives. The same "intentiveness" which is at work in the general thesis also underlies the individual's sense of spatial placement which makes of any possible scene a "there" for his "here." A simple illustration will serve to make the point. When we wish to point out something to a companion during an excursion, we ask him to look over there. "Where?" he asks. "To the right of that blue building," we reply. "I don't see a blue building." "It's just beyond the white church." "All right, I've got the church, now what?" "Well, to the far side of the church you'll see the covered bridge." "Yes, that is remarkable. There can't be many left in this part of the world." Now if our companion had failed to see the bridge, we could have given him still further clues to its location. Failing everything else, we might ask him to change places with us. Whatever the outcome of that maneuver, both of us know that there is some point to it and that, more importantly, in the exchange of places, what had been here for me will become here for my friend, the same here I formerly held. The epistemological problems involved in the possibility of such an exchange and the philosophical questionability of two individuals sharing the "same" here are unrecognized by common sense. The langauge of "same" and "different" and even of "here" and "there" seems artificial if insisted on too rigorously. For ordinary men in actual daily life it is assumed that places can be exchanged, that what is here for me can also be here for you, that the "same" here means nothing more than the sharability of any location in the world.

7. Edmund Husserl, *Cartesian Meditations*, pp. 116–17.

For the most part, of course, we do not literally exchange places with people when we try to get them to see what we see. The transaction of exchange is carried on in subjunctive or hypothetical fashion. "Were you to be standing where I am, you would see the churchyard directly before you" presupposes not only that the prospect is essentially the same for anyone standing in this place but also that were my fellow man—the Other, as he has come to be called in philosophical discussion—to point something out to me, he too would assume that were I to stand where he is I would see what he wants me to. To be sure, there is some knowledge of perspective which every person has, along with a wealth of past experience to rely on—situations involving past exchanges of position. We should be wary of simple reductions here, for, apart from the fact that any earlier exchange would still have to be accounted for philosophically, there is a danger in arbitrarily turning away from a complex phenomenon. I expect the Other to see what I see. The full illumination of that deceptively simple statement demands caution and adroitness. Expectation includes a protolinguistic and protoconceptual dimension. In visualizing the exchange of places, we focus first on the individuals moving from here to there, but there are no less significant secondary considerations in the shift. As my friend comes over to where I am so that he can be here, I turn aside to make way for him. Both of us turn toward each other so that he can slide into the chair I occupied. As he brushes by me I extend my hand to help him into the seat. At the same time, I steady myself by holding on to the back of a neighboring chair. The bodily accommodation achieved by these twistings is an intersubjective entertainment of subjunctivity. The "were" of each movement of the body is replied to by a complementary "were," through which the Other assures me that what I am doing is acknowledged by him.

There are many preconceptual interrelationships in everyday life which presuppose the same intentiveness we have seen at work in the example of exchangeability of positions. Indeed, some of the discussions of the theme come from unexpected sources. From a behavioral standpoint George H. Mead developed the notion of a "conversation of gestures" which is carried out at a bodily level.[8] The feints and moves of the wrestler or boxer are

8. See George H. Mead, *Mind, Self and Society: From the Standpoint of a Social Behaviorist,* ed. Charles W. Morris (Chicago: University of Chicago Press, 1934), pp. 14 and 63.

shared meanings in an ongoing bodily conversation. Men working together speak a language of common labor in moving, lifting, pushing, heaving, and resisting. They know what they are doing, of course, but that knowing is by no means equivalent to the pattern of labor. Heaving all together hoists the anchor, but the heaving includes a rhythm of pull, retention, and pull, with the imminent peril of a rushed return of the weight of the chain if pressure were suddenly relinquished. The moment of mutual attainment when the anchor has been successfully lifted another foot is a satisfaction of the common effort rather than a statistic of seamanship. The roots of a primordial form of communication are spread through the soil of sociality. We are in touch with each other before formal interchange is established. In the phenomenological tradition, Alfred Schutz refers to the precommunicative ground of social interaction as involving a "tuning-in relationship," examples of which are such interrelated activities as "the relationship between pitcher and catcher, tennis players, fencers, and so on; we find the same features in marching together, dancing together, making love together, or making music together. . . ." [9] The intentiveness which underlies precommunicative life is an axial feature of the natural attitude even though it remains undisclosed, for the most part, in the course of everyday life. It is in the thematization of that intentiveness that phenomenology achieves its distinctive mark: the phenomenologist brings to explicit givenness the otherwise immanent reality of precommunicative experience.

In addition to bodily placement, there are other aspects of the natural attitude to which Husserl gives serious attention. He finds that naïve believing-in-the-world involves two interpretative modes of intention—"idealizations," in phenomenological terminology—which are at the basis of perceiving experience as continuous and orderly. They constitute the phenomenological ground of habituality. Although the context of his discussion is that of the ideality of logical structure, Husserl gives us the following description of continuity and repetition:

> We have *not yet taken into consideration all the idealizations* that play a universal role for a pure analytics. I mention in addition only the *fundamental form "and so forth,"* the form of *reiterational* "infinity"; never stressed by logicians, it has its subjective

9. Alfred Schutz, *Collected Papers*, Vol. II, *Studies in Social Theory*, p. 162.

correlate in *"one can always again."* This is plainly an idealization, since de facto no one can always again. Still this form plays its sense-determining role everywhere in logic. One can *always return* to an ideal significational unity or to any other ideal unity. . . .[10]

"And so forth" (which I have called continuity) signifies the openness of any series perceived or imaginable. The quotation from Husserl is set in the matrix of mathematics, where, as he points out, "given any cardinal number, *a*, one can always form an $a + 1$; and in this manner, starting from 1, form the 'infinite' series of cardinal numbers."[11] But, as he also says, "and so forth" (and related "categorial formations") has a great role to play "even in the sphere of preconceptual objectivations."[12] It is helpful for our purposes to recognize that the mathematical context Husserl has chosen for the presentation of continuity and repetition is not the sole form in which these concepts can be located. To the contrary, mathematics is one among many illustrative frameworks through which we may understand what he has in mind. We shall turn to other, more experiential grounds.

The openness of any experiential series means that anything given is presented through a horizon of potentially infinite continuity. Perceiving a man running implies background, purpose, and the margin for adding new interpretative elements as they appear or are suggested by the scene. Thus, the man is seen as jogging, as fleeing, as chasing, as training for a track event, as running after a wind-blown hat, as doing a scene for a movie, or as participating in a surrealistic happening. In each placement of the running man, we find these elements of continuity: first, the kicking legs and thrusting chest point toward some object, some goal, whether it be a place or a state of physical well-being; second, the movement of the runner points back to some earlier period of decision or resolve; third, the interpretation of the activity remains open because there is a qualitative gap between what the observer makes of the runner and what the runner means or intends by his action. We shall come back to this last point later. The "openness" being claimed in our example is tied to the interpretative horizon through which the runner is viewed.

10. Edmund Husserl, *Formal and Transcendental Logic*, pp. 188–89.
11. *Ibid.*, p. 189.
12. *Ibid.*

We do not have a movement circling back on its own impulse but rather a *significative* activity to which more and more meaning may be granted. Limited as the illustration may be, it permits us to recognize the ongoing character of perceptual interpretation. We expect something *more* in the eye's translation of a fleeting figure than is allowed by the bare data of pumping arms. It is somewhat like listening to a story: "The man was running." "He was running because . . ." "As he ran . . ." We may continue the story by supplying the regalia of motivation and incident, but, however the story is clothed, it remains open for emendation and expansion.

"One can always again" (which I have called repetition) is, as Husserl said, the "subjective correlate" of "and so forth." Any typical act can be repeated in principle. If X can be added to, X can be repeated. The act of addition contains within it the possibility of returning to whatever one commenced with. The utility of simple tools in daily life is based on the possibility of repetition as a structural principle of everyday experience. Having learned to use a scythe, the farmer expects that each time he picks up that implement, holds it in the proper position, and swings it in that stiff, threshing rhythm he will be able to mow tall grass. If the blade is recently sharpened and the farmer executes his movement in traditional fashion, the grass is expected to fall. Any failure in the procedure must be due to its mechanics. Even before there is any thought of trouble, there is the tacit certainty that what worked in the past will continue to work in the future. When Husserl speaks of "one can always again" as an idealization, he is referring to the a priori status of typified expectation. Each empirical instance of using a tool in a routine way presupposes a nonempirical assumption: that routine use is always possible and that it will produce standard results. Testing the tool does not mean testing the idealization its use exemplifies. Within the natural attitude, an impairment of use may occasionally occur; a failure of structure would mean a negation of everydayness, a nihilation of order within life.

Continuity and repetition are conditions necessary for the possibility of experience. In being able to go on to or come back to, the individual is immersed in a world which is reliable and supportive. But the movement toward and return to are concerned with general or essential features of the given, not with concrete, personalized unities of meaning. The immediately presented given—this slanting aspect of the portrait on my wall—

can be grasped again and regained in typically the same way. Immediacy, in these terms, offers the certitude of essential rather than actual presentation. It is in the fundamental *possibility* of being able to regain the experiential world from moment to moment that the source of reality is to be found. Although the passage is embedded in phenomenological concepts we have not yet had an opportunity to examine, the following statement by Husserl should be considered carefully:

> Every evidence "sets up" or "institutes" for me an *abiding posses-sion*. I can "always return" to the itself-beheld actuality, in a series of new evidences as restitutions of the first evidence. Thus, in the case of evidence of immanent data, I can return to them in a series of intuitive recollections that has the open endlessness which the "I can always do so again" (as a horizon of potentiality) creates. Without such "possibilities" there would be for us no *fixed and abiding* being, no real and no ideal world.[13]

For the natural attitude, there is a thematic quality to the flow of experience: in *familiar* form, the parade of consciousness is marshaled and executed. The same baton twirlers, the same trumpeters, the same drum majors, and the same spectators carry on the spectacle. For all of them, what is anticipated and desired is the reperformance of a traditional march. The band members may seem younger, the uniforms vary, the music played changes, but participating and watching remain constant. In Husserl's terms, permanence is a function not of actuality but of possibility. What this means with regard to the natural attitude is that having some spread of perceptual experience before us at any moment is to have intentive awareness of the sameness of the objects and events both with respect to their history and their future. The caps and capes of the marchers are typical of brass bands; they renew their past exemplars at the same time that they project next year's version. Seeing the strut of the drum major is witnessing the stylized persistence of memory and expectation cohering in direct perception. The *thematic* aspect of the movement of consciousness concerns the grounding of the elements of perception and the question of their reality status. For Husserl, "fixed and abiding being" refers to the central impulse of the general thesis of the natural attitude, the ascription of reality to the parade of consciousness. What in-

13. Husserl, *Cartesian Meditations*, p. 60.

tentiveness points toward is tacitly held to be valid beyond any legitimate doubt: the world persists and can be regained from moment to moment in essentially universal form. The natural attitude assures the validity of our world by establishing and reinforcing its transpersonal reference.

The "horizon of potentiality" which Husserl speaks of goes beyond its application to repetition. Indeed, one may generalize the notion of "horizon" in phenomenological philosophy to signify any stance or line of access in terms of which experience presents itself. What is presented is always seized from some perspective, the range going from epistemological to cultural placement. In these terms, the natural attitude both is a fundamental horizon and includes horizons. There are two ways of trying to expand on the concept of horizon: by turning to the way in which horizon is phenomenologically constituted or by catching it at work in perceptual experience. At this stage in our examination of Husserl's thought, it might be prudent to consider the practical dimension. Horizonal perception, far from being an esoteric doctrine, is implanted in common sense. It is possible to see this, but not that, side of the building; it is impossible to hear a requiem mass sung all at once—instantaneously; one must wait for a wound to heal; and to get from here to there it is necessary to pass an in-between somewhere. Reality presents itself in aspects, profiles ("adumbrations," Husserl called them) that reveal the unity of the object or event in gradual ways. Thus, when we speak of experience as "presenting itself" what we mean is that some facet of the totality of the occasion "shows" itself and, in turn, reveals a further segment of the whole. But if the whole necessarily unfolds in perspectival facets, then how do we arrive at knowledge of the whole? Before trying to answer that question, some others come to mind: Is it true that wholes are necessarily grasped piecemeal? If so, is that a psychological truth about the limitations of the individual or an ontological truth about the nature of reality? Even if it is true that the audience cannot hear a mass all at once, would it be possible for the composer to hear it that way? Mozart is a case in point.

In his *Principles of Psychology*, William James includes the following extraordinary footnote:

Mozart describes thus his manner of composing: First bits and crumbs of the piece come and gradually join together in his mind;

then the soul getting warmed to the work, the thing grows more and more, "and I spread it out broader and clearer, and at last it gets almost finished in my head, even when it is a long piece, so that I can see the whole of it at a single glance in my mind, as if it were a beautiful painting or a handsome human being; in which way I do not hear it in my imagination at all as a succession—the way it must come later—but all at once, as it were. It is a rare feast! All the inventing and making goes on in me as in a beautiful strong dream. But the best of all is the *hearing of it all at once.*" [14]

Even allowing for Mozart's genius, it is difficult to make sense of his claim to hear "all at once" what in human terms demands a temporal succession. One can only suggest that Mozart hears the way God sees. Yet the composing process does begin with "bits and crumbs" and not with a fully realized unity. Why not with the finished product? If there is a heavenly transcension of temporal succession, why not an equivalent movement in the building up of a composition? I confess that Mozart bewilders me and that I can offer no answers to the questions he raises. His is a limiting mystery for a more nearly human world in which men come to know reality through successive adumbrations. If the clue to understanding Mozart's gift of hearing lies in a psychological or neurological analysis, then we must relinquish any hope in the present context of grasping what it is to hear "all at once." We are thrown back on the earthly ground of perception in which ordinary men come to wholes by way of parts. Yet even that statement needs clarification.

In seeing another person, I am aware of a certain side of his body. It is his back or profile that I watch as he moves across the room. The portion of a face that reveals itself to the perceiver is surely regarded as more than a circumscribed patch of nose and forehead. The aspect seen is "part of" the face in the sense of presenting the unity "face." To see the curve of the left portion of the mouth as "part of" the full mouth is to see it in its intentive character, as "pointing" to the full-featured face. The part shows itself, then, but as directed toward the whole it, for the moment, represents. Were we to take things strictly as they are given, in their precise and restricted manifestation, we would see, instead of faces, collages of sectors of eyebrow, inches of

14. William James, *Principles of Psychology*, (New York: Henry Holt, 1893), I, 255.

cheekskin, two or three caps of tooth, and a brief measure of tongue. To say that these anatomical fragments add up to a human face because we somehow put them together by some conceptual-perceptual arithmetic or because we are "conditioned" by past experience to expect hair, skin, and enamel to go along with men and women is to negate the force of the natural attitude, whose truth is that we do not perceive fragments but each other. There are times, of course, when the part as part is attended to for special purposes. Doctors, beauticians, morticians, and those engaged in sensitivity training may at times scrutinize moles as moles. Within the flow of everyday life, however, we respond to faces, to fellow men. And in perceiving the part we are transported to the whole. The movement requires no special talent. As Sartre writes:

> The human face cannot be taken apart. Just watch an enraged man calming down; his lips soften, a smile begins to form, just as a drop of water does, on the lower part of his angry face. Is it probable you will then talk about local disturbances? Or will it occur to you to add them all up? Only the lips moved, but the whole face smiled. And besides, anger and joy are not invisible events of the soul which I may only guess at from certain signs; rather they dwell in the face just as the reddish-green color dwells in this foliage. To see the green of leaves or the sadness about a mouth, we need no apprenticeship.[15]

Just as the face carries with it its own transcendence, as Sartre says, so the diverse profiles through which reality presents itself bear their own form of transcendence. They point always beyond themselves to the hidden frame of unity they participate in or disclose. Faces are the commencement of persons presenting themselves to the world. Whatever they reveal or hide is indicative of the transcendence of all human signification: the pointing beyond itself which establishes any adumbration of the human being as expressive of his own identity and unity. The world of which persons are part is then coherent because, literally, anything which is perceived is grasped as part-of or as continuous-with or as indicative-of some further and larger totality. The world itself becomes the ultimate horizon through which we are able to act as common-sense individuals in the

15. Jean-Paul Sartre, " 'Faces,' preceded by 'Official Portraits,' " trans. Anne P. Jones in *Essays in Phenomenology*, ed. Maurice Natanson, pp. 159–60.

natural attitude. Any concrete given is presented over and against the background of its history, its familiarity or strangeness, its potential for continuity and repetition. Through the intentive character of experience we are returned again and again to the infinite horizon of *world* as such.[16] It is especially important to remember that, within the natural attitude, there is no conscious recognition by the individual that objects and events intend some larger unity of which "world" is the ultimate horizon. What is "natural" about the natural attitude is the spontaneous complicity of consciousness with its orientation. That spontaneity deserves a final word before we turn to its phenomenological examination.

In the traffic of everydayness, I trust not only my senses but what my senses report: the flesh and stone existence of the things perceived. There is no biographical moment when such trust can be said to arise, nor is there for the individual a patterned memory of the trials and experiments which led up to it. "For as long as I can remember" is the phrase that first comes to mind when one reflects on the surety of common-sense faith in the reality of the world. But the notion of "origin" is a misleading one when it comes to the natural attitude. In a certain sense, it may be said that the believing in the reality of the world has no beginning, just as consciousness itself has no "start." The psychoneurological history of consciousness involves a tracing out of the genesis of the nervous system and the brain. There it is possible to speak of stages in the development of the central nervous system in the embryo. But consciousness in its structural aspect is not a function of the body; it is, as Husserl has shown, an autonomous creation, sustained by its own dynamic. The simplest of analogies must suffice for illustration at the moment. The ratiocination of the mathematician undoubtedly has a physical aspect: enough damage to the cortex will hamper or destroy his capacity to do mathematics. Moreover, the swiftness with which an individual mathematician does his work varies, as does the way in which he gets his ideas. It is said of Helmholtz that scientific insights came to him as he came to a rise on the path of the walk he regularly took, just at the time his cigar was going well. Now none of these contingencies is pertinent to the validity or importance of science itself. Without

16. Cf. Ludwig Landgrebe, "The World as a Phenomenological Problem," pp. 38–58.

a healthy brain the mathematician may be unable to function, but the regularities of geometry are independent of the brain. Without cigarettes and coffee, the mathematician may be too nervous to concentrate, but algebraic theory has nothing to do with stimulants. So too, though in different and more subtle ways, with the status of consciousness: its logic is free of its physical moorings and resides not in the space of the body but in the timelessness of essence. The moment this becomes clear, we are no longer in the natural attitude.

3 / The Phenomenological Attitude

THE TURN TO THE PHENOMENOLOGICAL ATTITUDE is beset by some genuinely difficult methodological problems, but there are also some unnecessary complications that are not philosophical but simply imaginary. The misunderstanding of phenomenology is not altogether unrelated to the pervasiveness of the natural attitude. It might be prudent to introduce Husserl's new orientation by first indicating a few initial misconceptions which often prevent its appreciation. The basic block amounts to this: it is falsely supposed that in shifting from the natural to the phenomenological attitude the individual is ordered to abandon ordinary life and enter a conceptual monastery. There, in a solipsistic cell, the novice is expected to contemplate essences and chew his transcendental cud. While the real world goes on, the phenomenologist resides in timeless, historyless seclusion. The more sophisticated versions of the same claim retain at least one belief—that the phenomenologist "leaves" one realm to "enter" another. The imagery is inevitably spatial: one world is exchanged for another. It will be of enormous help to the reader if he will set aside the idea that phenomenology involves a departure from mundane reality. The world presented in the natural attitude is neither denied nor abandoned; it is, instead, reconstructed. How that comes about, we shall presently learn, but there will be little progress made in understanding Husserl if we think of him as the potentate of an insulated realm.

Another misapprehension of phenomenology is that it is still another introspectionist doctrine, carrying with it all the traditional weaknesses and dangers of subjectivism: the purely idiosyncratic reports of the individual; the lack of intersubjectively warranted criteria for verifiability; the assumption that psychological states of mind are indices of objective states of affairs. It is ironic that phenomenology should be charged with being a species of introspectionism, for Husserl's entire effort was to undercut the subject-object dualism established by Descartes and embraced by much of the naturalistic tradition of the nineteenth and twentieth centuries, just as it was his mission to refute the very "psychologism" which underlies the introspectionist's viewpoint. There is no inner searching the phenomenologist goes through, nor is there an acceptance either of the idea that what might be found by rummaging through one's mental closets is of legitimate philosophical interest. Husserl's tendency is in a different direction. If anything, his philosophy is "extrospective," moving toward phenomena as objects, in the broadest sense, of perceptual acts. The "glance"—to use Husserl's language—of the phenomenologist is directed toward what is presented in experience, not toward a repository of mixed sensations within the psyche. The only way to account for the persistence of the accusation of introspectionism in connection with phenomenology is that the term itself has been abused, turned first into an epithet and then into an anachronism. To defend Husserl against the charge of introspectionism does not mean that introspectionists are philosophical lepers. The simple fact is that whatever the credits or liabilities of introspectionism may be, phenomenology operates in a qualitatively different dimension.

Further, there are those who regard Husserl as a metaphysician and consider metaphysics outmoded. Again, the criticism is badly misplaced, for it was Husserl's concern to develop a philosophy which was neutral with respect to the classical wars of the metaphysicians. Quite apart from the question of the status of metaphysics in contemporary philosophy, phenomenology is not concerned *in its fundamental orientation* with the nature of the reality it describes and analyzes. Ultimately, Husserl conceived of phenomenology as providing a new point of access to the problems of traditional metaphysics, but before such a grand extension is possible, the principles of phenomenology must be systematically clarified and justified. What Husserl actually did in his lifetime was to struggle to get philosophy established on firm ground, to assure its rigor of method, and to make it accountable for the full range of its application to human experience. The emphasis, the central intent, has to do with *phenomena,* not with transcendent being or ultimate reality. Since Husserl's phenomena, unlike Kant's, have no noumenal, "behind the given" corollary, they are not topics for metaphysical investigation. It is possible, of course, to say that metaphysics may be defined in other ways, that it may be conceived as the exploration of categories or of structures necessary to the formation of a world. There need be no quarrel with such assessments of the proper role of the metaphysician. All that needs to be said here is that phenomenology concerns itself with existence and ultimacy only insofar as it tries to provide a *path* to reality. It does not pretend to be metaphysics; even less does it claim the status of a world view. Those who expect of Husserl a revelation of the "essence" of reality, in the sense of its final meaning, will be disappointed. Such vows are not to be counted among phenomenology's promises.

Finally, phenomenology has frequently been said to be antiscientific, substituting intuition for empirical inquiry or as a replacement for the canons of received scientific method. Nature, so the critics say, has not been given due respect by the phenomenologists. In place of empirical investigation, Husserl has put together still another system of philosophical idealism—an effort to weave the fabric of reality out of the filament of ideas. Has it been altogether in vain that Husserl repeatedly denied such a representation of phenomenology? "Our phenomenological idealism," he wrote, "does not deny the positive existence of the real . . . world and of Nature—in the first place as though it held it to be an illusion. Its sole task and service is to clarify the meaning of this world, the precise sense in which everyone accepts it, and with undeniable right, as really existing. . . ." [1] More broadly, phenomenology and science cannot conflict if both are properly understood, because the latter deals with matters of fact whereas the former is concerned with the realm of possibility, not with reality but with "irreality." There is no competition between phenomenology and science for the same domain of knowledge. Most important, Husserl never claimed to have developed an alternative method for explaining the facts of nature or the neuropsychological basis of mind. Most bluntly put: the phenomenologist does not deal in facts. The way in which one finds out how the brain functions is through mastering the anatomy and physiology of that organ and by pursuing

1. Edmund Husserl, *Ideas,* p. 21.

experimental and clinical research. The phenomenologist has no professional competence qua phenomenologist in determining the histological features of nerve cells. Microscopy and related disciplines must be relied on for such determinations. Husserl was trained in science and retained a strong respect for its achievements. He also knew, however, that the philosophical grounding on which science rests was closed to scientific method and that the critique of that grounding was an inescapable responsibility for a philosophy committed to self-scrutiny.

Any appreciation of the positive nature of the general phenomenological attitude must begin with the relevance of the natural attitude not only for everyday life but for philosophy and science as well. Science, in the generic sense of knowledge, shares some of the fundamental assumptions of the mundane world. The philosophical position which brings the causal-genetic orientation of science into view is termed "naturalism" by Husserl. It may be defined most simply as the interpretation of man as a qualitatively continuous part of nature. It follows that the methods of science, understood as ideally represented by the natural sciences, are the proper instruments for exploring the reality which human beings share: the social world, with its manifold cultural and historical horizons. Man's consciousness of that world is understood as a product of, as well as a part of, the same nature interrogated by scientists. It follows that, for naturalism, consciousness consists of faculties and acts which are embodied by the physical world and which are considered to be events in or facets of the natural order. Husserl writes:

Naturalism is a phenomenon consequent upon the discovery of nature, which is to say, nature considered as a unity of spatio-temporal being subject to exact laws of nature. With the gradual realization of this idea in constantly new natural sciences that guarantee strict knowledge regarding many matters, naturalism proceeds to expand more and more. . . . The natural scientist has the tendency to look upon everything as nature, and the humanistic scientist sees everything as "spirit," as a historical creation; by the same token, both are inclined to falsify the sense of what cannot be seen in their way. Thus the naturalist, to consider him in particular, sees only nature, and primarily physical nature. Whatever is is either itself physical, belonging to the unified totality of physical nature, or it is in fact psychical, but then merely as a variable dependent on the physical, at best a

secondary, "parallel accompaniment." Whatever is belongs to
psychophysical nature, which is to say that it is universally determined by rigid laws.[2]

The naturalization of consciousness proceeds along three
broad fronts: first, the "history" of consciousness becomes an
evolutionary process in which mind comes into being as a bio-
logical event and in which ideas are generated out of contingent
neurological circumstances. Second, the logic of mind—the laws
of reasoning, for example—is founded on material conditions
in nature. Strictly speaking, there is no longer a logic of reason
but a physics of the brain. Third, consciousness naturalized is
consciousness relativized. Since every event in nature is contingent on the circumstances in which it is actualized, meaning,
purpose, and value become functions of individual or historical
fortuities. In the end, even the laws of nature may be comprehended as statistical probabilities. The large result of naturalism
is the relativization of reason. And with that result comes a
double paradox: If a philosophy whose decisive orientation is
scientific ends in relativism, in what sense can it be considered
scientific? If science is understood as a species of relativism, on
what grounds can it establish its own claim to truth? Even if
its conclusions are presented as propositions with as high a
degree of reliability as an evolutionary method can presently
manage—and in some fields that degree is indeed impressive—
how is it possible to gauge the philosophical value of a body of
knowledge whose foundations are as yet uncertain and whose
significance is unresolved? What may work for the solution of
concrete problems in chemistry or biology is unsatisfactory in
principle for the establishment of science as science. Pragmatic
devices may be unavoidable in the pursuit of knowledge within
the focus of empirical inquiry, but the ultimate defense of
pragmatism rests on something other than a further piecemeal
procedure. At some point the analysis of philosophical stances
must come back to the fundament of philosophy itself. For
Husserl, relativism is not one more philosophical position but
the denial of reason to cope with its own genius.

The impact of naturalism has been felt most strongly in
psychology, where, according to Husserl, the entire approach of
the discipline has been affected by its tacit commitment to a

2. Edmund Husserl, "Philosophy as Rigorous Science," in his
Phenomenology and the Crisis of Philosophy, p. 79.

philosophical position which accepts the world as real and which assumes that mind is something connected with the body as part of the real world. It is the naïveté of such assumptions which Husserl points to as the clue to the philosophical character of naturalism. The question is not whether psychology is wise in building upon naturalistic principles but whether it has given judicious consideration to the philosophical problems involved. For the most part, psychology is uninterested in the reality of the world it analyzes: the philosophical themes of epistemology and metaphysics are of no initial concern to the psychologist who takes the world he inhabits as simply *there*. The unenthusiasm for philosophy is characteristic not only of naturalistic psychology but of science generally. "All natural science," Husserl writes, "is naïve in regard to its point of departure." [3] But naïveté is not identical with neutrality. On the contrary, by "naïve" Husserl means unreflectively accepting the world as real and as being what it appears to common sense to be. Rather than being a lack of philosophy, naïveté is a hidden philosophy, at least in elemental form. In other terms, the philosophy of common sense may be called "naïve realism." When psychology is grounded in philosophical naïveté, its placement of the psyche is "in" the world or "in" egos which are empirically present as incarnate fellow men. In all of these interpretations, the psyche is denied autonomy. Husserl writes:

It is the task of psychology to explore this psychic element scientifically within the psychophysical nexus of nature (the nexus in which, without question, it occurs), to determine it in an objectively valid way, to discover the laws according to which it develops and changes, comes into being and disappears. Every psychological determination is by that very fact psychophysical, which is to say in the broadest sense . . . that it has a never-failing physical connotation. Even where psychology—the empirical science—concerns itself with determination of bare events of consciousness and not with dependences that are psychophysical in the usual and narrower sense, those events are thought of, nevertheless, as belonging to nature, that is, as belonging to human or brute consciousnesses that for their part have an unquestioned and coapprehended connection with human and brute organisms. To eliminate the relation to nature would deprive the psychical of its character as an objectively and temporally

3. *Ibid.*, p. 85.

determinable fact of nature, in short, of its character as a psychological fact.[4]

The physicalistic interpretation of consciousness carries with it the unstated directive: Look to the connections! Given some awareness or state of mind, the immediate question is, What produced it? The question itself deserves some consideration. When we look to causal conditions for an account of the state of affairs, we regard the latter as "produced," as the outcome of antecedent states of affairs. In one direction of explanation, the preceding conditions amount to other states of consciousness—motivations, intentions, reasons. If someone calls out my name, I turn toward him expecting a greeting, an inquiry, a request, or a conversation. If none of these ensues and there was no mistaken identification, I assume that the caller decided not to go on with what he had in mind, that for reasons I may not understand he is silent, or that he is playing games. If such behavior persists, I may think that he is eccentric or disturbed. In any case, I expect that calling my name out presupposes design on the part of the Other—design connected with a coherent network of intelligence and reflection. In another direction, however, the state of affairs may be taken as referring to the individual occasion which embodies it. My name called out, in these terms, leads back to the specific person who spoke, to his concrete psychophysical state of being at that time. Rather than referring to antecedent conditions as other states of consciousness, we are led to the empirical nature of actual events. Causality, then, has two interpretative impulses: we may turn to consciousness as pointing to further aspects of consciousness or we may look upon consciousness as itself an actualization of nature. In both cases, psychology moves in a naturalistic orbit, for reference to antecedent states leaves moot the question of how *those* states are to be understood. Within the naturalistic horizon of explanation, the answer must eventually turn on the embeddedness of the mental in the physical.

The naturalization of consciousness reveals the physical grounding of mind in still other ways, most notably in the relationship between psychology and logic. Husserl, in effect, maintains that "psychologism" is the naturalization of logic. By psychologism is meant the attempt to found logic on psychological

4. *Ibid.*, p. 86.

grounds. More precisely, it is the substitution of an extralogical criterion for validity. Not only does logic rest on psychological foundations, it may be defined as an arm of the corpus of psychology. Husserl quotes John Stuart Mill as a spokesman for the psychologism of the nineteenth century. "Logic," Mill writes, "is not a Science distinct from, and coordinate with, Psychology. So far as it is a science at all, it is a part, or branch, of Psychology; differing from it, on the one hand as a part differs from the whole, and on the other, as an Art differs from a Science. Its theoretic grounds are wholly borrowed from Psychology and include as much of that science as is required to justify the rules of the art." [5] To conceive of logic as a branch of psychology is to make reasoning synonymous with thinking and to understand the latter as a specified activity of the brain. The most extreme statement of this kind of reductionism is attributed to the nineteenth-century zoologist Karl Vogt: "The brain secretes thought as the liver secretes bile." [6] The result of psychologism is, for Husserl, the destruction of the autonomy not only of logic but of philosophy itself. By making logic part of psychology, psychologism in turn makes psychology the foundation of philosophy. Husserl sees the consequences as devastating and assumes the responsibility of refuting psychologism. That refutation has since become a classical chapter in the history of modern philosophy.

We will not review the details of Husserl's arguments against psychologism. His concern is to demonstrate the a priori status of logic, its independence of empirical fact, its privileged interest in necessity, and its restriction to form, not content. How one thinks, why one thinks, and the similarities and differences in individual thinking are fundamentally irrelevant to the question, What is the formal structure of logic? There are certainly legitimate ways in which the how, why, and variableness of thinking may be studied, but the disciplines properly concerned with these problems are at once outside of logic and presuppose logic. Anyone who either agrees or disagrees with any of these statements must, in the very act of identifying them, tacitly invoke the laws

5. John Stuart Mill, *An Examination of Sir William Hamilton's Philosophy* (London: Longman, Green, Longman, Roberts and Green, 1865), pp. 388–89 (quoted by Husserl in *Logical Investigations*, I, 90–91. J. N. Findlay translates the quotation from Mill from German back into English. I have given the original).
6. Quoted by Henry W. Johnstone in *What is Philosophy?* (New York: Macmillan, 1965), p. 17.

of logic. Without the Law of Identity—that *A* is *A*—it would be impossible to suggest that there is anything to discuss. At the same time, the laws of logic are universally necessary conditions of reasoning and not claims of a remarkable degree of probability. Husserl writes:

> The Law of Contradiction does not tell us that one must *surmise* that one of two contradictory judgments is true, one false, the mood *Barbara* does not tell us that when two propositions of the form "All A's are B's" and "All B's are C's" are true, it is to be *surmised* that a corresponding proposition of the form "All A's are C's" is true. And so generally, and in the field of mathematics as well. Otherwise we should have to treat it as an open *possibility* that such a surmise would fail to be confirmed by an extension of our ever limited horizon of experience.[7]

To take seriously the notion that, given the laws of Aristotelian logic, a valid syllogism with true premises may possibly have a false conclusion is to offer an addition to the story of the three fools: our fourth fool, having mastered the rules of plane Euclidean geometry, persists in drawing triangles in the hope that, besides equilateral, isosceles, and scalene triangles, he will someday find a fourth kind.

Important as his analysis of psychologism is for logic, Husserl has a broader theme in mind in his treatment of necessity. The ultimate implication of the reduction of logical laws to empirical contingencies is the relativization of knowledge. With such relativization truth becomes a function of fact, a variable in the life of mind. As Husserl says: "Psychologism in all its subvarieties and individual elaborations is in fact the same as relativism, though not always recognized and expressly allowed to be such." [8] The form in which Husserl takes up the large problem of relativism is historical. It is in the *Weltanschauungsphilosophie* of the late-nineteenth and early-twentieth centuries that he picks up the central problem of historicism. It is true that every effort to pose and analyze human problems is set within some historical context and involves some set of categories which, in a sense, are also grounded in the history of thought. It is possible, I would say, to speak of a "horizontal" dimension of criticism in which the relatedness of problems and history (in

7. Edmund Husserl, *Logical Investigations*, I, 99–100.
8. *Ibid.*, p. 145.

the broadest sense) may be explored in systematic terms. Thus, phenomenology in Husserl's sense came into a world preceded by the contributions and influence of nineteenth-century versions of naturalism. The relationship between phenomenology and naturalism involves some reference to the historical context in which they appeared. There is a legitimate set of problems involved here. But there is also a "vertical" dimension to all criticism: besides the matter of relatedness there is also the distinctively philosophical question of how the truth of these positions is to be ascertained and appropriated. Whatever may have been the conceptual-historical situation in which naturalism and phenomenology originally arose, what truth is there to their claims?

It would, I suppose, be obvious that evaluating the work of a mathematician may be done quite apart from reviewing the economic, sociological, or psychological reasons which led him to become a mathematician. Yet very strong arguments have been advanced by such thinkers as Dilthey to show that in the case of philosophical work, the philosopher is caught up in the swirl of historical change and development. Philosophical systems are not immune to the determinate influence exerted by the impulse of the age; they, too, are affected by the world they seek to comprehend. Husserl turns to a statement by Dilthey as a point of departure in presenting an analysis of historical relativism:

> The theory of development (as a theory of evolution based on natural science, bound up with a knowledge of cultural structures based on developmental history) is necessarily linked to the knowledge of the relativity proper to the historical life form. In face of the view that embraces the earth and all past events, the absolute validity of any particular form of life-interpretation, of religion, and of philosophy disappears. Thus the formation of a historical consciousness destroys more thoroughly than does surveying the disagreement of systems a belief in the universal validity of any of the philosophies that have undertaken to express in a compelling manner the coherence of the world by an ensemble of concepts.[9]

Husserl does not dispute the factual truth of the clash of systems in philosophy's history. He does ask whether *in principle* the

9. Dilthey, as cited in Husserl, "Philosophy as Rigorous Science," p. 124.

contradictions and disputes of the philosophers are an essential attribute of philosophy itself. The problem of relativism is ultimately the problem of what philosophy should be, not of what it has been.

Husserl maintains that philosophy and history are concerned with quite different objects: ideas and facts. The two are, of course, related in a variety of ways but have qualitatively different conceptual grounds. New discoveries in empirical science cannot in principle change the status of philosophical truth, though they might lead to the posing or reposing of philosophical questions in a new manner. It is well known that for generations textbooks in logic used the proposition "All swans are white" as an example of a factually true assertion. The discovery of the first black swan must have shocked the publishing world, but it had no effect on the designation of "All swans are white" as an affirmative universal categorical proposition. The existence of black swans was irrelevant to the hypothetical implications of the traditional proposition. With or without black swans, it remains the case that if "All swans are white" is true, then "Some swans are not white" is false. But the logic manuals had always also said that if "All swans are white" is false, then "Some swans are not white" is true. The empirical truth or falsity of propositions has nothing to do with the logical relationship between contradictories. But the situation in logic is not the same as in the physical or social sciences, where, it would seem, there must be a more intimate relationship between ideas and facts. For Husserl, the distance between philosophy and history remains decisive. He writes:

> The science of history, or simply empirical humanistic science in general, can of itself decide nothing, either in a positive or in a negative sense, as to whether a distinction is to be made between art as a cultural formation and valid art, between historical and valid law, and finally between historical and valid philosophy. It cannot decide whether or not there exists, to speak Platonically, between one and the other the relation between the idea and the dim form in which it appears. And even if spiritual formations can in truth be considered and judged from the standpoint of such contraries of validity, still the scientific decision regarding validity itself and regarding its ideal normative principles is in no way the affair of empirical science.[10]

10. *Ibid.*, p. 126.

A fundamental point is at issue in Husserl's insistence on the independence of philosophy from history. What he is saying is that any account of where ideas come from, how they develop, and what their relationship is to the sociocultural world in which thinkers of ideas live, still does not touch the matter of the ideas themselves, their normative as well as logical character, their status *as* ideas. History can neither affirm nor refute philosophy because its resources are this side of philosophical discourse. The historian deals with the truth status of fact, not with the status of truth. Husserl writes:

> How . . . is it to be the historian's task to decide as to the truth of given philosophical systems and, above all, as to the very possibility of a philosophical science that is valid in itself? And what would he have to add that could make the philosopher uncertain with regard to his idea, i.e., that of a true philosophy? Whoever denies the ideal possibility of a philosophical system as such, must advance reasons. Historical facts of development, even the most general facts concerning the manner of development proper to systems as such, may be reasons, good reasons. Still, historical reasons can produce only historical consequences. The desire either to prove or to refute ideas on the basis of facts is nonsense.[11]

If, in these terms, the history of philosophy has been a seesaw of competing thinkers, the ideas at issue are untouched by what historians make of philosophers' quarrels. Perhaps a better way to put it is to say that philosophy as it has hitherto been practiced contains an inner form, a nuclear landscape which is the source of genuine philosophy, of philosophy, in Husserl's phrase, as "rigorous science." The achievements of genuine philosophy remain independent of historical criticism. As Husserl says, "If criticism proves that philosophy in its historical growth has operated with confused concepts, has been guilty of mixed concepts and specious conclusions, then if one does not wish to fall into nonsense, that very fact makes it undeniable that, ideally speaking, the concepts are capable of being pointed, clarified, distinguished, that in the given area correct conclusions can be drawn. Any correct, profoundly penetrating criticism itself provides means for advancing and ideally points to correct goals, thereby indicating an objectively valid science."[12] To take the most severe line, philosophy as rigorous science is a task to

11. *Ibid.*, pp. 126–27.
12. *Ibid.*, pp. 127–28.

be undertaken rather than an accomplishment we inherit from the past. "I do not say," Husserl argues, "that philosophy is an imperfect science; I say simply that it is not yet a science at all, that as science it has not yet begun."[13] The transition from philosophy as concept-baiting to philosophy as science comes about, then, through a critique of relativism in all of its forms. In place of relativism Husserl proposes a discipline which is designed to establish philosophy on certain grounds and to return the philosopher to the nuclear source of his activity. That discipline is phenomenology.

In one way, the phenomenological attitude consists in attending to awareness of experience. Not the experience straightforwardly seized but reflection on the experience is the phenomenologist's concern. Holding to this truth will help us to avoid the temptation to translate the phenomenological attitude into an esoteric realm divorced from the real world. Anticipating our discussion of phenomenological method, it may be said now that the turn from the natural to the phenomenological attitude is a shift in the direction of one's interest, not in the abandonment of one world for another. There is but one world, though there are different ways of attending to it. In the natural attitude, as we have noted, the individual lives spontaneously in his perception of what there is; in the phenomenological attitude, he makes of his perceptual life an object of inquiry. In Husserl's language, perceptual experience is thematized by the phenomenologist. How is this possible? Before we can try to answer that question, it is necessary to pose a more rudimentary one: How is it possible for the individual ever to leave the natural attitude? Put differently, How is it possible for man to know that he is in the natural attitude? The answer, I believe, consists in the interpretation of the meaning of primordial doubt or wonder. Apart from the classical claim of the Greeks that philosophy begins with wonder, it may be suggested that when wonder takes hold in everyday life, it includes a decisive element of doubt. There is a fundamental dubiety undergirding particular instances of doubting in mundane terms. A closer look at this suggestion may be helpful.

There are many modalities of doubt. I may doubt your word, doubt your judgment, doubt some prediction, doubt some statistics, doubt some experimental or clinical report, doubt the

13. *Ibid.*, p. 73.

sagacity of a decision, doubt the existence of God or the coming of the Messiah. However slight or grave the topic of doubt may be, in the cases we have listed the doubting is directed toward some object or state of affairs by or from a source which is not itself included in the doubting—the doubter himself. In the natural attitude, the doubter is somewhere at the time he does his doubting. He is lolling on the sofa, in the garden with his foot on the spade, making his way out of the stock exchange, tying his apron in the laboratory, dozing at his desk, or trying to keep from gagging in the dentist's chair. Not only is he somewhere, the doubter is engaged in an activity which he does not ordinarily attend to within the scan of his doubt: lolling and gardening are not themselves included in the doubting. Further-more, the doubting itself is tacitly oriented *in the world,* for there is nothing remarkable to the doubter about his doubting. The right to doubt, like the right to privacy, is a free man's in-heritance, but the former is distinguished from the latter by its internal power and independence. Yet the nature of doubting as a gift of the natural attitude remains a mystery. Doubt seems to come "naturally," but it is not clear what that really means. At the center of the problem of the status of doubt in the natural attitude is the conviction of the individual that doubt is indeed possible, that the world permits doubting. Such permission pre-supposes an immanent suspension of primordial doubt.[14]

Just as there is never in the life of the individual an explicit decision to believe in the world, so there is no equivalent mo-ment in his biography when he decides to suspend all doubt in the reality of his experience. We are speaking of the systemic character of belief and doubt rather than their natural history. Doubting presupposes believing something believed; believing presupposes that doubting has been, in the terminology of Husserl, "bracketed." There is no chronology at issue here, no chicken-or-egg riddle. The danger in taking belief and doubt as activities of the ego is that the psychological instead of the structural features of such activities is stressed. What interests Husserl is the formative character of belief. My "accepting" the world as real is noticed *after* the acts of perception and judg-ment which predicate reality of the world have been fulfilled. Yet all the time I perceived the scene about me as real, I

14. Alfred Schutz calls such suspension "the epochē of the natu-ral attitude" (*Collected Papers,* I, *The Problem of Social Reality,* 229).

entertained no doubts about its reality. In prepredicative terms, experience is "lived" as real. I "expect" my next footstep to hit upon continuing pavement. I move along, swinging my arms and propelling my legs in the activity called "walking" without self-conscious decisions from moment to moment about where to place my feet. As I see the turn in the path ahead, I feel the quickening of the atmosphere, hear the baying of a distant hound, and suddenly become aware of my tongue. At the time such experience is lived, there is no awareness of the horizons of selection and continuity which may later be delineated. The path may lead to a tryst, the sharpening of the air may remind me of hog-butchering, the hound may put me in mind of a story by Faulkner, and my tongue somehow make me think of a red icicle. At the moment we are concerned with, however, these thoughts and associations are potential, not actual. They are *not* activated but positioned, as it were, for possible use.

The immanent suspension of primordial doubt is the obverse side of the general thesis of the natural attitude. The suspension assures the indomitable faith of everyday man in the actuality of his world and helps to explain his refusal to take seriously the philosopher's arguments about realism and solipsism. Such discussions are recognized as clever and entertaining but not as part and parcel of the truth of daily life. Yet philosophy *does* arise, there *is* wonder, and we do have recourse to the kind of radical reflection which Husserl proposed. Despite the apparent insularity of common sense to primordial doubt, daily existence swarms with possibilities, among them the self-illumination of mundanity. It would seem that some point of leverage is needed to bring the natural attitude into view. Philosophy may not be able to pull itself up by its own bootstraps, but it can provide a point of access to the natural attitude through a radicalization of the meaning and method of fundamental doubt. With the elaboration of the nature of epoché—the phenomenological suspension of belief—Husserl takes the first and most important step in the constitution of the phenomenological attitude.

The radical suspension of belief in the world and the decision to refrain from building upon the posits or results of the special sciences are the preliminary conditions for the employment of phenomenological epoché. Husserl describes the procedure:

> *We put out of action the general thesis which belongs to the essence of the natural standpoint,* we place in brackets whatever it

includes respecting the nature of Being: *this entire natural world therefore* which is continually "there for us", "present to our hand", and will ever remain there, is a "fact-world" of which we continue to be conscious, even though it pleases us to put it in brackets.

If I do this, as I am fully free to do, I do *not* then *deny* this "world", as though I were a sophist, *I do not doubt that it is there* as though I were a sceptic; but I use the "phenomenological" *epoché*, which *completely bars me from using any judgment that concerns spatio-temporal existence.* . . .

Thus *all sciences which relate to this natural world,* though they stand never so firm to me, though they fill me with wondering admiration, though I am far from any thought of objecting to them in the least degree, *I disconnect them all, I make absolutely no use of their standards, I do not appropriate a single one of the propositions that enter into their systems, even though their evidential value is perfect, I take none of them, no one of them serves me for a foundation*—so long, that is, as it is understood, in the way these sciences themselves understand it, as a truth *concerning the realities* of this world. *I may accept it only after I have placed it in the bracket.* That means: only in the modified consciousness of the judgment as it appears in disconnexion, and *not as it figures within the science as its proposition, a proposition which claims to be valid and whose validity I recognize and make use of.*[15]

Few concepts in phenomenology have led to as much misunderstanding as epoché. The chief problem seems to be that it is interpreted as signifying the denial or, somehow, the cancellation of reality. A number of terms, some suggested by Husserl and his followers, others by critics of phenomenology, have been employed to translate "epoché": "suspension," "disconnection," "abstention," "setting aside," "canceling," "placing in abeyance," "bracketing," "putting out of action," "withholding assent," "denial," and "elimination" have all been utilized. Of this group, the terms which carry the least danger of misapplication are "placing in abeyance" and "withholding assent." This does not mean that the others are wrong or even that the abeyance and withholding are necessarily correctly understood. What is crucial is not which word is used but how that word is conceived and interpreted in the context of Husserl's work. It is not hard to see what is confused about many of the accounts of epoché offered

15. Husserl, *Ideas,* pp. 110–11 (I have transliterated the Greek word for "epoché" and also modified the translation at one point).

by critics of phenomenology and sometimes by expositors. First, epochē is thought of as having to do with a striking out of reality, a denial somehow of the actuality of the world. Second, it is not infrequently assumed that suspension is a kind of psychological breath-holding. Third, epochē is conceived as a means of re- moving the phenomenologist from one world to another. All of these ways of approaching the meaning of epochē are misin- formed and misleading. Worse, they psychologize precisely what Husserl sought to redeem: the *believing* which undergirds the natural attitude.

Positively understood, epochē is a method the phenomenolo- gist employs to place in relief what common-sense men take for granted: their acceptance of the world as real—what is termed "existential belief," that is, belief in the existence of what sensa- tion and cognition report. To place in relief means first of all to attend to that believing, to make it manifest, to inspect it in its own right. Moreover, the emphasis is put on the believing, not on the facticity of what is believed in. Withholding assent means refraining from positing existence or nonexistence of some object or event in experience. It does not mean thinking or saying that the object or event is or may be real or illusory, true or false. With the performance of epochē the real world does not change in any way, nor does the phenomenologist undergo any type of transformation. Everything continues as it did before, with the decisive exception that the world which hitherto had been straightforwardly accepted as real is no longer viewed *in terms of* or *on the basis of* the general thesis of the natural attitude. Husserl writes:

> The world experienced in this reflectively grasped life goes on be- ing for me (in a certain manner) "experienced" as before, and with just the content it has at any particular time. It goes on ap- pearing, as it appeared before; the only difference is that I, as re- flecting philosophically, no longer keep in effect (no longer ac- cept) the natural believing in existence involved in experiencing the world—though that believing too is still there and grasped by my noticing regard.[16]

Another misunderstanding of epochē presents the phenom- enologist as a recluse of his ego. With the abstention from ex- istential positing, it is assumed that all that is left to the in-

16. Edmund Husserl, *Cartesian Meditations*, pp. 19–20.

dividual is the pulsation of his own consciousness: a residuum which no longer has any connection with reality either as a psychological or as an ontological affair. The trouble here is that Husserl has never suggested that placing one's believing in the world in abeyance means that what is so placed is neglected, let alone denied. Nothing is denied in epochē and nothing is forgotten. Instead, what had hitherto been simply accepted as "obvious"—so obvious, in fact, that it went beyond the barest notice or mention—is now recognized reflectively as a performance of consciousness and subjected to analysis. While that analysis goes on, the phenomenologist remains as much in the world as he ever was, retains all of his interests and knowledge, and persists in his human concerns. The only change (and it is a crucial one, to be sure) is that he reflects selectively on what he had hitherto simply lived, though both the reflecting and the living continue, side by side, in the life of consciousness. Rather than a residuum of nothing, the world in its entirety is retained and, if you like, regained. "This universal depriving of acceptance," Husserl writes,

> this "inhibiting" or "putting out of play" of all positions taken toward the already-given Objective world and, in the first place, all existential positions (those concerning being, illusion, possible being, being likely, probable, etc.),—or, as it is also called, this "phenomenological epochē" and "parenthesizing" of the Objective world—therefore does not leave us confronting nothing. On the contrary we gain possession of something by it; and what we (or, to speak more precisely, what I, the one who is meditating) acquire by it is my pure living, with all the pure subjective processes making this up, and everything meant in them, *purely as* meant in them: the universe of "phenomena" in the . . . phenomenological sense.[17]

It might appear that despite the claim of radicality for phenomenological epochē, the procedure is, to some extent, followed in nonphenomenological circles. In fact, it might be asked whether some form of suspension is not practiced in everyday life. No doubt, there are many situations in which the reality of an imputed motive may be self-consciously set aside in favor of attending to the performance of a person. Even in professions such as psychiatry where "why" questions are hardly shirked, there may be a circumscription of interest in the "what" of a

17. *Ibid.*, pp. 20–21.

patient's behavior. These are limited cases, of course, and do not reflect either the stance of mundane existence or the methodology of the professions. But enough has been suggested to catch the point: there are times when, for various purposes, the individual may choose to set aside what he ordinarily takes for granted. Is it the case that within the limits of what has been suspended, a true epochē has been made? Without examining the details of the examples we might use for illustration here, it can be said that limited epochē in the sense of restricted suspension of belief, or doubt, does not touch the phenomenological problem, whatever interest and validity it may have on its own score. The radicality of Husserl's epochē consists in both its scope and its rigor. Limited suspension still leaves the bracketed object *within* the world; i.e., believing in its reality as bounded by the rest of the world remains unchanged by anything less than epochē. What is presented may indeed be strictly attended to in limited suspension, but the horizon of the presentation is naïvely followed. It is as though a movie set of a gold rush town were set up and taken with complete seriousness and involvement by the actors. For the purposes of the scene being shot, the actors may "lose" themselves completely during a barroom brawl, yet the "reality" of the saloon remains, the solidity of its furnishings must be reckoned with, and the presence of the actors is a reminder of the being of fellow men in the world.

The rigor of epochē consists in the effort to make no use whatever of the testimony of others in confronting the givenness of experience. Such discipline is painfully difficult to achieve, for one's natural impulse is to hold on to the support which history and community offer. There is a desolation in refusing to build on what others have accepted, and there is a loneliness in confronting a world egologically constituted. Such root feelings may nevertheless be overcome through discipline and forbearance. The more demanding task is to achieve rigor in practice. The use of epochē does not carry with it any automatic insurance about results. The phenomenologist may find that in practice he has not succeeded completely in refraining from ascribing existence to some aspect of his experience. That he can recognize such relative failure is noteworthy, for it means that in making phenomenological descriptions and analyses, the investigator has control over his material. He is able to see that here or there he has slipped back into the natural attitude or has failed to maintain his stance in strict accordance with the demands of epochē. At the same time, it is important to realize that there is no internal contradiction in Husserl's claim that the phenomenologist can control his own procedure. The objection can, of course, be made that whether he is conscious of it or not the epochist—to coin a term—continues to believe in the reality he has bracketed. If the word "unconscious" is used strictly in this context, then it would be hard to know how it can be determined that belief continues to operate. If the word is intended in a fairly loose sense, however, then it must be understood that beyond stringent inspection and scrupulous care, there is nothing human beings can do to assure compelling results. No philosophy can claim to be free in principle from the possibility of error; no philosopher can elevate himself to the throne of infallibility. But error can be acknowledged and fallibility can be admitted. The question then is how one proceeds with the business at hand. Epochē remains the methodological commencement of an unremitting assault on the peak of certitude.

The phenomenological attitude leaves standing everything included in the natural attitude, but it brings to the fore man's *consciousness-of* the world and its contents. Beyond that very considerable accomplishment, the achievement of the phenomenological standpoint makes possible the self-inspection of phenomenology's procedures. Here we come to the crux of the difference in the two attitudes. Common sense is closed to itself. Whatever its many insights, it has no perspective on itself. Phenomenology not only attends to its own methods in the narrower sense of refining its tools, it has as an unavoidable obligation the task of building its own philosophical edifice with its own resources and evaluating its work from the foundations up. Epochē is vitally important to phenomenological method, but it is not the whole of that method. Starting with the need for placing in abeyance the general thesis of the natural attitude, the phenomenologist recognizes that the location and examination of the realm disclosed initially by epochē requires a more complex machinery than we have indicated so far. There are a number of reasons for that recognition. First, the bracketed world remains an intersubjective achievement. It must be determined what role the pure ego plays in the constitution of a shared reality. Second, the bracketed world has its own history. It is necessary to learn what relationship exists between the force of history in the natural attitude and the sense of history intended by the ego. Finally, the grounding of the ego itself needs clarification. If the natural attitude is built out of the plurality of persons who sustain the social world, the phenomenological attitude must be able to account for that possibility. Given sociality, how is it possible? That question is the inevitable responsibility of phenomenological inquiry. It characterizes the distinctively transcendental dimension of Husserl's thought and leads to an extension of epochē to the primordial ground of subjectivity. It will be the task of Husserl's theory of phenomenological reduction to carry out the exploration of the transcendental realm which epochē discovers.

4 / Phenomenological Method

THE RADICALITY OF PHENOMENOLOGICAL METHOD is both continuous and discontinuous with philosophy's general effort to subject experience to fundamental, critical scrutiny: to take nothing for granted and to show the warranty for what we claim to know. The continuity is best seen in Husserl's indebtedness to Descartes. As with Cartesian doubt, phenomenological doubt places in question everything which is posited by consciousness. Indubitable knowledge, what Husserl refers to as "apodictic" knowledge, is sought as the basis for erecting philosophy as "rigorous science." But where Descartes's method carried with it a metaphysical apparatus involving the role of God in the assurance of objective nature and extended and thinking substance, Husserl's procedure sets aside questions of this order and moves along a metaphysically neutral path. Moreover, Husserl, unlike Descartes, is not searching for a propositional keystone on which to build the arch of philosophy. "I think, therefore I am" may be an emblem by which to recognize the method of radical doubt, but it is not in itself a satisfactory basis for constructing a rigorous science. Descartes's dream of a new science, a universal formalism or grammar of knowledge, failed to achieve its goal. The empirical sciences today are hardly a testimony to the fulfillment of Descartes's mission. What is needed, Husserl says, is a return to the critical inspiration of the *Meditations*, its egological radicality, without being tied to the content of Descartes's essay. Philosophy in our time has splintered itself into competing factions which have lost all sense of their original purpose and which have replaced the ideal of wisdom with the goal of piecemeal acquisition. Husserl calls for a return to the original force of Descartes's vision as a way of overcoming the contemporary fragmentation of philosophy:

> Cannot the disconsolateness of our philosophical position be traced back ultimately to the fact that the driving forces emanating from the *Meditations* of Descartes have lost their original vitality—lost it because the spirit that characterizes radicalness of philosophical self-responsibility has been lost? Must not the demand for a philosophy aiming at the ultimate conceivable freedom from prejudice, shaping itself with actual autonomy according to ultimate evidences it has itself produced, and therefore absolutely self-responsible—must not this demand, instead of being excessive, be part of the fundamental sense of genuine philosophy?[1]

Although Husserl allies himself with the spirit of Descartes, he is not simply a Neo-Cartesian. In fact, it may be said with justification that phenomenology begins where Cartesianism leaves off.[2] The central difference between the two is that for all their disciplinary brilliance, the *Meditations* are encapsulated in an inadequate conception of subjectivity. More cautiously stated, the full radicality of an egological standpoint was missed by Descartes just as he came to the brink of the discovery of the potential prize of his meditations: the full domain of transcendental consciousness. Descartes's "I think, therefore I am" was proclaimed under the assumption that upon its back the whole of philosophy could be carried. What he failed to see was that the "I" of that dictum was the hero of the story of consciousness and that the "I" demanded the most profound attention, the most exhaustive analysis. For such analysis to be possible, the method of radical doubt had to be submitted to an equivalently searching scrutiny. Descartes utilized a technique whose full significance he failed to explore. Blinded by his own genius, he missed a world beyond the world he discovered. Husserl hopes to rectify this failure:

> Unlike Descartes, we shall plunge into *the task of laying open the infinite field of transcendental experience*. The Cartesian evidence —the evidence of the proposition, *ego cogito, ego sum*—remained

1. Edmund Husserl, *Cartesian Meditations*, pp. 5–6.
2. Cf. James Street Fulton, "The Cartesianism of Phenomenology," pp. 58–78 and Aron Gurwitsch's review of Fulton's essay in *Philosophy and Phenomenological Research*. Also see Ludwig Landgrebe, "Husserl's Departure from Cartesianism."

barren because Descartes neglected, not only to clarify the pure sense of the method of transcendental epochē, but also to direct his attention to the fact that the ego can explicate himself *ad infinitum* and systematically, by means of transcendental experience, and therefore lies ready as a possible *field of work.*[3]

Starting with a Cartesian impulse, then, Husserl goes on to win his own distinctive position in the attempt to draw the final consequences of the meaning of epochē. The door to which epochē is the key opens to an entire realm of subjectivity which Descartes barely touched. It is to the description and analysis of the structure and constitution of that realm that phenomenology is devoted. The larger method (to which epochē is the clue) of phenomenology is called "reduction" and is one of the most difficult concepts to grasp in all of Husserl's work. Understanding reduction is made even more complicated by the fact that there is more than one kind or level of reduction. One commentator locates at least six levels of reduction in Husserl's writings.[4] I shall not enter into such a typology here for a variety of reasons. More is to be gained by restricting the discussion to certain fundamental distinctions essential to the utilization of phenomenological method. The main thing is to comprehend what reduction itself means. Most simply, reduction refers to a radical shift in attention from factuality and particularity to essential and universal qualities. More exactly, reduction is the movement from the believingness of the natural attitude to the domain of transcendental subjectivity. With this preliminary approximation, rough as it is, we come to two species of reduction which I shall take as definitive for the full range of phenomenological method, even though certain important distinctions of level and function will have to be sacrificed in the name of both simplification and intelligibility. The turn from fact to essence will be called eidetic reduction. The movement from believingness to transcendental subjectivity will be called phenomenological reduction.

Before turning to an account of each of the reductions, it might be useful to see them at work through illustrations, restricted though the latter must be at this point.

A. As I write these lines I am looking out over a view of the city. In sight are the rooftops of the neighboring houses, their

3. Husserl, *Cartesian Meditations,* p. 31.
4. Quentin Lauer, *The Triumph of Subjectivity,* p. 50 ff.

chimney stacks jutting upward; some of the fences surrounding yards are visible, part of a school building can be seen, there are many trees about, and, in the far distance, a part of the bay can be glimpsed. I know who lives in some of the houses in the line of my vision, the kinds of trees around me, the style of the environing architecture. Although I cannot see the tracks, I hear the whistle of the railroad train a mile or so away. Each time I look out the window, I see once again the same sight, the same buildings and foliage. I know that they are reliable features of my prospect, part of my world. Now, in eidetic reduction, I choose to attend to the scene in a different way. I set aside the actuality of the houses and the details of their ownership and history. The house across the way has a mortgage, a roof in need of repair, and a freshly painted door. I concern myself only with its being there for me as a something seen and a something noticed. The mortgage drops away; the roof presents itself as a patchwork; the door gleams bluely. That Haskall lives next to Immerbind no longer is part of my viewing—that knowledge has been set aside. I see rectangular and oblong stretches of multicolored shapes. The train whistle is a plaintive sound, piercing the quietude to which it recedes. Depending now on what I wish to do as a descriptivist and analyst of the scene, I may attend to those patches *as* houses, *as* water, or *as* Mrs. Mayhew standing in the driveway, calling her cat.

B. Perhaps what is set aside in eidetic reduction is becoming clear, but it is no less important to note what has not been altered: there is still the "I" who looks out over the view; there is still the past of that "I," its history; there is still the scene set within the world which surrounds and includes it; and there is the history of that world, *our* history as beings who share the world. Bringing all of these subtle elements into clarity is the first requisite of phenomenological reduction, and refraining from positing and building upon those primordial grounds is the goal of that ultimate reduction. Rather than a discontinuity between the first and second reduction, there is a vital relationship: phenomenological reduction must be preceded by a turn from fact to essence. Now looking out my window, "I" (the observer —no longer I the concrete individual with a unique biography) am conscious of a flow of perception (which may be said to include remembering and anticipating as well as seeing, hearing, and other present awarenesses) of "objects" and "events" taken as counterparts of the perceptual acts directed toward them. The "objects" in question are not taken to be part of anything else (unless they are overtly intended as "part-of-the-world"), nor are they held to be there for others as they are for the observer (unless, once again, they are specifically intended as "there-for-others"). Finally, the *becoming* of the world as a historical reality and of the ego as the product of a psychological genesis is bracketed. The essentiality given in the eidetic reduction is now translated into a realm of pure possibility—*phenomena*, in the strict Husserlian sense—in which origin is noted but not utilized. For me as observer, there is presented the window scene as a unity of intentional awareness of colors, sounds, shapes, masses, outlines, and horizons. The patchwork taken-as-roof or as-neighboring-roof is merely given a claim to being real, tagged, as it were, with an identification which otherwise may be disregarded (just as, in this instance, it is possible to appreciate an exquisite antique for its own sake by choosing not to look at the price tag or even to mutter to oneself: "That must be worth at least ten thousand dollars.") Lost in the sheer appreciation of the presentation, the phenomenological observer finds himself present to himself. The scene comes to an originary clarity in that moment of phenomenological coincidence.

Related to the first reduction is the method of free variation in fantasy, as Husserl calls it.[5] It is possible to imagine a window scene and to change, add, and detract certain elements from the view: in place of the rooftops, meadows; instead of water a golf course; rather than a school building a cemetery. A number of different kinds of questions are implicit in such variation. We are asking what is invariant in the object or the event (as imagined), what the minimal conditions are for something to be presented or represented, and what alterations in some aspect of what is fantasied can make a change in the thing imagined. There is obviously a great diversity in the way in which free variation can be carried out. On the surface, we have a procedure which would seem to be a psychological experiment, one whose results would have as wide a range of reliability as the number of individuals carrying it out. On closer inspection, however, it may be seen that the method of free variation is not directed toward concrete objects as such but toward the possible exemplification of types of objects. The geometer and the chess

---

5. See Edmund Husserl, *Experience and Judgment,* pp. 340 ff., where the translators use "imagination" rather than "fantasy."

player are tacitly practicing elements of eidetic reduction. The concern with types rather than tokens (with triangle as such and not the illustration of a triangle in the textbook), with the subjunctive rather than the actual—these are indicative of a mind dealing with essence, not fact. The roots of such essentiality are to be found in the natural attitude, where the individual knows in a general way what something is or should be but may, on occasion, accept or project a somewhat different form of the same thing. Preparing for an interview, we may rehearse in imagination the script we have prepared. A variety of responses may be imagined to alternating sets of questions. In all of this, however, the status of both individual and world remains unclarified. With eidetic reduction in the strict sense, the natural attitude begins to come into view.

Free variation is carried out in fantasy, and since it has no reference to the facticity of the empirical world, its results are binding not on things but "unthings," not on reality but "irreality." Eidetics is a discipline of the fictive. Aron Gurwitsch has given an exceptionally clear statement of the matter:

The process of "free variation" is carried out in imagination. All the forms which originate from each other by way of transformation and variation play their roles as, and *only* as, possible varieties, i.e., as possibly contrivable in imagination. This holds without exception for every member of the series generated in the process under discussion. It also holds for the member from which the process starts, even when the member in question happens to be a real occurrence. For the process of ideation to apply to an object given in actual experience, the latter object must be subjected to what Husserl occasionally calls "eidetic reduction." By eidetic reduction, the real existent is divested of its actuality, of its existential character, its spatio-temporal determinations from which it derives its individualization, and of all those characters that accrue to it on account of its integration into the real world. Every real existent can be regarded as an actualized possibility. Under the eidetic reduction, the fact of its actualization is considered as immaterial, and, hence, is disregarded. What is encountered as a matter of fact, is "irrealized"; i.e., considered as to its imaginableness and not as to its actuality, it is transformed into a "pure possibility" among other possibilities. From the status of a real existent, it is transferred to that of an example or exemplar lending itself to "free variations" and thus becoming apt to function as starting point for an infinitely open series of possible (i.e., imaginable) varieties. Eidetic reduction is obviously a necessary condition for a real existent to play a role in ideation. Only possibilities can find insertion into a process whose very purpose is to yield a survey of what is possible in a certain domain.[6]

In the case of the irrealization of the particular, we start with something existent and then take it as an example of a type. In the natural attitude we read public signs as guides and instructors to exits and offices. We may, however, regard the sign *as* sign, as itself the instrument or, if you like, the bearer of its greetings. At a still further remove, we may entertain possibilities in imagination which have only an indirect or quite remote connection with real events. Fiction is an exercise in the eidetic attitude. Even the reader engages, to some extent, in the kind of fantasying at issue here. He is free to construct episodes and characters for the unwritten second part of *Felix Krull.* And even where Mann has promised that a character in the first part shall be encountered again, the reader as fictivizer may, with eidetic warranty, contradict the author and explain to *his* reader why Mann's promise could not be kept. Of course, in fiction the existence of the characters is a problematic affair. It is odd to suggest that such "existence" may be set aside in favor of possibility. Perhaps we should speak of literature as possibility of the second degree: possibility of possibility. It does make sense to say that in fiction there is a reality defined by the characters themselves, a world constituted by Krull's intrigues no less than by Mann's intentions or the reader's trust. One may take an event in the story—Krull's medical examination for military service—as a reality-within-the-fiction which may be subjected to free variation. Did Krull have no other choice but to simulate an epileptoid condition? Is there a reasonable ground for suggesting that Mann's hero might have turned to another disguise? If so, would Felix Krull have become a different character? The answers to such questions are not matters of convention but products of a conception of fictive reality. The resources of the method of free variation are immense despite the fact that the most rigorous employment of eidetic reduction remains at qualitative distance from transcendental subjectivity. Yet everything encountered at the first level will have its corollary illuminated through phenomenological reduction.

Our approach to the meaning of phenomenological reduction

6. Aron Gurwitsch, *Studies in Phenomenology and Psychology,* p. 383.

will be crablike, for a direct assault tends to minimize the complexity of Husserl's most subtle achievement. A veteran phenomenologist once told me that it took him years to master the phenomenological reduction. Some students, on the other hand, report that they are able to understand the reduction in twelve minutes. Although I doff my cap to such feats, I must confess myself to be among the slow learners. A number of related approaches are necessary, in my judgment, to get a sense of the range and implications of phenomenological reduction. The bracketing of the general thesis of the natural attitude has already been stressed. To this should be added a suspension of belief in the historical dimension of experience. In the natural attitude we know that the world came into existence aeons ago, that there have been past civilizations, and that there is the history of modern man. Our language, religion, mores, and culture are all historically grounded. To bracket history, then, is no small feat. It must be remembered that the phenomenologist's effort is at once both more modest and more daring than the effort to set aside history. What Husserl is after is a new point of access to historicity, to consciousness-of historical experience. As long as what is perceived in the natural attitude is grasped as history-bound or history-tinged, phenomena are placed in a philosophically slanted light, they are assumed to be something rather than seen as something. The essential point is that objects and events are not apprehended in neutral fashion in the natural attitude. Depending on what questions one tacitly takes for granted, the world is interpreted one way or another. If one does not think or choose to ask about the purpose of an artifact, its historical significance as well as its function is thereby interpreted in negative or even false ways. Refraining from postulating a significance to objects may be a form of immanent choice rather than a mode of abstention. Concomitantly, the expression of choice in the act of deliberate interpretation may uncover historical meaning. R. G. Collingwood gives an example of this in archaeology:

> The many archaeologists who had worked at the Roman Wall between Tyne and Solway had never, I found, seriously asked themselves what it was for. Vaguely, you could of course call it a frontier defense, and that it was to keep out the tribes beyond it. But that will no more satisfy the historian than it will satisfy an engineer if you tell him that a marine engine is to drive a ship. How did it work? Was it meant to work, for example, like a town-wall,

from the top of which defenders repelled attacks? Several obvious features about it made it quite impossible that any Roman soldier should ever have meant to use it in that way. No one seemed to have noticed this before; but when I pointed it out in 1921 every one who was interested in the subject admitted that it was so, and my counter-suggestion that the wall was meant for an "elevated sentry-walk" was generally accepted.[7]

In the natural attitude, then, perceiving a ruined wall as evidence of the Roman presence in Britain may mean anything from thinking of it as a bit of "history" to considering it to be a fortification with a specific purpose. In phenomenological reduction the bracketing of history means rendering either naïve believing or self-conscious analysis explicit to reflection. In both cases, the investigator refrains from committing himself to the historical reality at issue and attends only to the presentative aspect of his consciousness-of what is experienced. This procedure carries with it an "interior" corollary: the history of the individual investigator—his biography—is set aside for purposes of phenomenological inquiry. To be sure, he continues to "have" a history in the mundane sense, but the dynamic of that history is held up for accounting. Every stage in the becoming of the individual brings its own force to bear on the character of any one experience. When and under what circumstances Husserl is read may have decisive importance for whether his thought is pertinent to the individual. What ordinarily is called "psychology" here has a more rudimentary aspect: the "I" of the person must be released from the "we" which binds it. Phenomenological reduction is a movement from the "I" as a communally grounded reality to the ego as a source of what is ultimately the individual's *own*, his "ownness," in Husserl's language.[8]

It is easier to speak of a "purely egological sphere" than it is to secure one. In the natural attitude I may decide to restrict all judgments to what I know firsthand. Yet what I know firsthand includes a wide range of perceptions, including memories and anticipations, which are oriented toward fellow men, toward what others have done in the past, and toward the imagined responses others will give to my actions. Objects on their own have intersubjective implications. Rigorous as I may try to be in

7. R. G. Collingwood, *An Autobiography* (Oxford: Oxford University Press, 1939), pp. 128–29.
8. See Husserl, *Cartesian Meditations*, pp. 92 ff.

pondering this brick or stone, I see it as having come from somewhere, as having been made by someone, or as something another person may heft and use. The reference to people does not
so much invade my thoughts as it turns out to be an original
inhabitant of consciousness, a strand of the fabric of the mundane self. That reference must be examined more closely, for it
includes the suggestion of "otherness" as well as the straightforward meaning of having reference to other individuals. When
I perceive an object as other-related I comprehend it, at a prepredicative level, as perceivable by others as well as having been
made or deposited by somebody else. The otherness of such perception involves a tacit claim to the mutual accessibility of the
object perceived. In these terms, seeing the stone is seeing it *as*
seeable by others. Phenomenological reduction is concerned with
the explication of the intersubjective impulse hidden in the apparent privacy of perception.

The communal or shared character of the natural attitude
also includes a causal element. The object perceived is presented
along a causal horizon: it was made by someone, harvested by
someone, left by someone, or affected by someone. In a different
direction, an event is understood as resulting from a change in
climate, in geological formations, or some other aspect of nature.
Language and customs bear the imprint of their connection with
what other people—our ancestors—have done. In a sense, anything perceived in mundane life is empowered or infused with a
dynamic of its own: the object looks back to what produced it.
We are speaking of causation as a quality of daily life rather
than a technical concept in the methodology of the natural
sciences. For men in everyday situations, events are bound by a
causal chain to antecedent conditions and motivating forces. A
man seen prostrate on the sidewalk of a city street may be viewed
in a number of ways, depending on one's own situation and interests. For a casual passer-by, the man may be regarded as the
victim of an accident, of a sudden illness or seizure, as a drunk,
a drug addict, or a dead man. The heap of flesh and clothes on
the sidewalk got there for some reason. It is not enough to say
that the man is on his back because he suddenly decided to rest
or because he fell asleep. We may, of course, be deceived. The
crumpled figure may prove to be a police decoy, an actor doing a
film scene, or someone being initiated into a fraternity. In all of
these cases the motive becomes clear; we see the individual do-

ing something *because* of something or *in order to* achieve something.[9] In any case, the figure is seen in context, as part of a larger scene and as related to some schema of explanation not directly given in the appearance of the body. Perception is tagged with references to causal conditions and coded with temporal implications. The more one inquires into the "given" in experience, the more one comes to appreciate its complexity. Causation gives to events a *tensed* richness, a world origin.

Besides the natural history of the world there is a phenomenological history of experience, a rootage not only to events but to the formation of the "world" which includes them. Just as events are presented over and against a horizon of their antecedent conditions, so "antecedence" itself involves a source or origin. Part of the difficulty in grasping the meaning of "origin" in the phenomenological sense is that thinking in the natural attitude is so deeply inflected with the assumption of causation that any appreciation of a more fundamental meaning of source is blocked. If anything experienced is grasped in context, then it is necessary to ask how context itself comes to be organized and, indeed, possible at all as a regulative feature of the natural attitude. The search for origin is a historical endeavor in which consciousness is the matrix of all becoming. "History," in this sense, is not already a manifestation of a causal order but itself the source of human action. The phenomenologist's task is to trace out and reconstruct the path of originary constitution through which the world comes to be world-for-me. If history, intersubjectivity, and causation are bracketed, then historical becoming, as a search for origin, may be understood as a theme for transcendental inquiry—a theme opened up by means of phenomenological reduction. Beyond a stiffening of methodological requirements for a "purified" description of immediate experience, the phenomenological reduction is a qualitative radicalization of reflective consciousness. As Fink has observed, "The 'phenomenological reduction' alone is the basic method of Husserl's phenomenological philosophy. It is the epistemological 'way' . . . which leads beginning philosophical reflection to the 'thematic' domain of philosophy; it grants us 'access' to transcendental subjectivity and it includes within it all of

9. See Alfred Schutz, *The Phenomenology of the Social World*, pp. 86 ff.

phenomenology's problems and the particular methods associated with them." [10]

Tersely put, in phenomenological reduction what we know about the world and what we take for granted about experience are scrutinized in terms of a purely egological standpoint whose own origin and becoming are thematic problems for self-analysis. The movement is from naïveté toward apodicticity. Husserl summarizes the procedure in the following way:

> Instead of living naïvely in experience, . . . and subjecting what we experience, transcendent nature, to theoretical inquiries, we perform the "phenomenological reduction". In other words: instead of naïvely *carrying out* the acts proper to the nature-constituting consciousness with its transcendent theses and allowing ourselves to be led by motives that operate therein to still other transcendent theses, and so forth—we set all these theses "out of action", we take no part in them; we direct the glance of apprehension and theoretical inquiry to *pure consciousness in its own absolute Being*. It is this which remains over as the "phenomenological residuum" we were in quest of: remains over, we say, although we have 'Suspended' the whole world with all things, living creatures, men, ourselves included. We have literally lost nothing, but have won the whole of Absolute Being, which, properly understood, conceals in itself all transcendences, "constituting" them within itself.[11]

In these terms, the prize of "Absolute Being" is won when the phenomenologist stands in relationship to the field he surveys in reduction no longer as an empirical self in touch with the world but as a phenomenological observer concerned with the "world" as the intentional correlate of transcendental subjectivity. Our language has thickened. Is there a simpler way to understand the reduction?

It would seem that if Husserl has discovered a methodological procedure for arriving at the analysis of pure consciousness in a completely trustworthy fashion, he would be able to set forth the steps involved so that anyone seriously wishing to follow him would be enabled to do so. Yet it would appear that for every instruction Husserl issued, he changed his mind a number of times, declared alternative possibilities, retracted his original

10. Eugen Fink, "The Phenomenological Philosophy of Edmund Husserl and Contemporary Criticism," pp. 75–76.
11. Edmund Husserl, *Ideas,* pp. 154–55.

formulation as unsatisfactory, and found himself at cross purposes with his own demands. Considering the centrality of phenomenological reduction for the entire enterprise of Husserlian philosophy, the mechanism and meaning of reduction are far from clear. Although he wrote a great deal about phenomenological reduction, Husserl does not set out the entire problem and procedure once and for all in unequivocal and completely accessible terms. The surface reasons for that failure are not hard to find. First, Husserl did not come to the concept of reduction full grown; it developed over a period of years; second, in the search for greater rigor, he sought to refine his method and was inevitably led to change and, in a sense, experiment; third, with the recognition of the vast realm possible to phenomenological philosophy, Husserl came to appreciate the need for the achievement of a method which would be equal to the task which phenomenology set for itself. In short, when we speak of phenomenological reduction, we are pointing to philosophy itself rather than some limited technique. What started as a methodological concept becomes the problem of philosophy striving to ground its own reflective capacity.

The distinctively philosophical character of the reduction may help to explain its obscurity and opaqueness to some who are otherwise sympathetic to Husserl's intellectual mission yet find phenomenological reduction a mystery. Understanding Husserl means more than reformulating the propositions of his position; it means invading that position and seizing it from within. The performance of phenomenology may be described in the natural attitude but it cannot be grasped in that way. As Fink says, "It would be incorrect to treat the reduction . . . as an easily summarized mental technique, the various forms of which could be easily given, a technique which traverses natural-psychical paths and which, given the appropriate instructions could be performed by every scientifically educated person, as if it were simply a matter of bracketing the 'natural concept of the world' in order to place acts of both theoretical and practical consciousness of the world out of play." [12] Just as philosophy is a possibility of the natural attitude, so reduction is a potential of mundanity. But the movement from the natural to the phenomenological attitude is a radical shift in being *positioned* in reality. Making

12. Fink, "The Phenomenological Philosophy of Edmund Husserl and Contemporary Criticism," p. 113.

the shift is not equivalent to describing the elements involved in the transposition from one attitude to another. Once again Fink has given a subtle account of the problem:

Every discussion of the phenomenological reduction, no matter how incomplete, finds itself faced with the unavoidable difficulty of being compelled to speak about it as if it were an activity of knowledge which it is always possible to perform, and which from the very start lies within the horizon of our human possibilities. In truth, however, it does not at all present a possibility for our *human* existence. The unfamiliarity of the reduction is therefore not only an unfamiliarity with it as a fact, but is also an unfamiliarity with its possibility. Although we also say that all talk about a particularly difficult kind of knowledge quite remote from our everyday knowing (for example, the knowledge of physics) presupposes *actually having been involved with it* (precisely for the reason that it does not belong to the everyday familiarity we have with our knowing and experiencing), a discussion of the reduction not only signifies an appeal to its actual performance, but also imperatively requires the performance of an act which places us beyond the horizon of our own possibilities, which "transcends" our *human* possibilities. The unmotivated character of the phenomenological reduction (the absence of any worldly problem which could serve as its real motive) expresses the reduction's unfamiliar nature in a similar way. Because it is the suspension of the "natural attitude" it cannot appear within this attitude and it therefore must be unfamiliar. The reduction becomes knowable in its "*transcendental* motivation" only with the transcending of the world. This means that the reduction is its own presupposition insofar as it alone opens up that dimension of problems with reference to which it establishes the possibility of theoretical knowledge. This strange paradox of the beginning of philosophical reflection finds expression within the fundamental perplexity into which all attempts to explicate the phenomenological reduction fall. Unmotivated and unfamiliar with respect to its possibility, every exposition of the phenomenological reduction is in a unique way false.[13]

The paradox of explaining the reduction would seem to be analogous to the problem of trying to understand Freudian psychoanalysis without undergoing analysis oneself. It comes to

13. *Ibid.*, pp. 104–5. This article was explicitly endorsed by Husserl, who wrote in the Preface to it: "It contains no sentence which I could not completely accept as my own or openly acknowledge as my own conviction" (*ibid.*, p. 74).

this: to understand the reduction, one must perform it. And as with psychoanalysis, one must not only go through it himself but must have a "good" analysis. Yet it would be false to say that only those who have gone through a successful analysis understand Freud. It would be cavalier to dismiss MacIntyre's study of *The Unconscious* or Ricoeur's interpretation in *Freud and Philosophy* because both authors state that their books were written without benefit of personal psychoanalysis. The truth is surely quite different: It *is* possible to overcome the paradox of having to possess a truth before one can recognize it as truth. The problem is an ancient one in philosophy. In its phenomenological form, however, we may say that it reveals two aspects. First, there is the problem of motivation: how can the inquirer within the natural attitude ever come to orient himself to a radically different world-stance? Second, having performed the reduction, how can the phenomenologist communicate his results? Perhaps it is possible now to begin to appreciate some of the obstacles to a straightforward exposition of Husserl's method. Even if there were no historical alterations in his doctrine, even if a complete formulation of reduction were possible, and even if the phenomenologist's language were simple and crystalline, there would still remain the transformation itself: the experiential movement from the world as the ultimate horizon of our being to the "world" as the transcendental correlate of the pure ego. The paradox of reduction lies in the peculiar traffic between two worlds: the world in its historical becoming and the becoming of the world in transcendental consciousness.

There have been almost as many interpretations of the phenomenological reduction as there have been expositions.[14] Without restricting the lines of criticism to specific writers, we may recognize three large claims that have been made about the reduction: it is ambiguous; it is philosophically obscure; and it is ultimately unattainable. Although it has deeper reaches, the charge of ambiguity includes Husserl's alterations in the meaning of so basic a concept as epochē. In the spectrum of meaning

14. See, for example, Rudolf Boehm, "Basic Reflections on Husserl's Phenomenological Reduction"; Richard Schmitt, "Husserl's Transcendental-Phenomenological Reduction"; Klaus Hartmann, "Abstraction and Existence in Husserl's Phenomenological Reduction." For discussion by Husserl, see *The Idea of Phenomenology, The Paris Lectures,* and *Erste Philosophie* (1923–24), Part II: *Theorie der phänomenologischen Reduktion.*

assigned to it, epochē signifies at one extreme a narrowly construed act of restraint and at the other extreme is almost synonymous with phenomenological reduction. Nor will a fixing of
time or periods in the development of Husserl's thought suffice
to rid the reduction of all ambiguity, for even at the end of his
career Husserl was still struggling with the attempt to reach
absolute certainty through reduction and came to speak of the
final step as "phenomenological-transcendental reduction." The
result of all of these shifts in terminology is that someone trying
to follow Husserl's method is put on a rather tortuous road, one
which winds back on itself and in which markers and signs con-
found the traveler. The criticism of ambiguity is legitimate, but
its truth is limited to inadequacies of presentation rather than
internal confusion. Most important, such ambiguity can be overcome by careful exegesis and resolved by insightful reflection. It
may well be, of course, that only the most diligent travelers will
persist, but then phenomenology is not for everybody.

The second criticism goes beyond problems of terminology
and change of emphasis. It concerns the substance of what is
philosophically in question in reduction. There seems to be
something recalcitrant to exposition in the effort of Husserl to
express the meaning of reduction. There are several ways to
translate that recalcitrance. It may be thought of as the ineffabil-
ity of reduction, the ultimate insulation of the phenomenologist
within the reduced sphere. But another interpretation is possible:
reduction may be thought of as a means for getting on with the
larger question of transcendental subjectivity. The obscurity of
the means should not, on this account, prevent us from appreciating the legitimacy of the ends. In fact, there is a certain in-
evitability in the inverse relationship between means and ends.
It has been suggested that in all great philosophies it is possible
to distinguish between fully realized and merely preparatory concepts.[15] If this distinction is granted, the obscurity of the reduction becomes understandable as a methodological barrier rather
than an intrinsic philosophical defect. It might also be remembered that disadvantages sometimes carry with them unexpected
resources. The philosophical obscurity of the reduction demands
of the inquirer that he perform the reduction as *his*, that *he*
orient himself within its confines. The turn to *self*-responsibility

15. See Eugen Fink, "Les Concepts opératoires dans la phénoménologie de Husserl."

is a gift of what otherwise might be considered philosophical isolation. Within the orientation he must find for himself, the investigator is free to further, if not complete, the transformation of phenomenological reduction into philosophy.

The final criticism has to do with the possibility in principle of performing the reduction in a truly rigorous way. A fully realized reduction would mean that the world has been made an object for transcendental subjectivity and that its becoming is explored by the phenomenological observer. But then where is the empirical ego? And who is it that puts the observer to work and takes note of his reports? Moreover, the act of reduction would seem to presuppose a psychological event in the psychophysical world. How can the reductionist escape the claims made on him by nature? Husserl struggled hard with the problem of the various selves or egos involved in reduction and emerged with what can only be called a proliferation of egos. In any case, he failed to find a clear and continuous line of advance in the analysis of the pure ego. What seems to haunt his efforts is the semblance of the self in the otherwise autonomous realm of transcendental subjectivity. The search for purity always seems to be hindered by some contaminating psychological aftereffect. Thus, in Merleau-Ponty's words, "the most important lesson which the reduction teaches us is the impossibility of a complete reduction. This is why Husserl is constantly re-examining the possibility of the reduction." [16] This statement has been picked up in phenomenological literature and repeated without too much reflection on Merleau-Ponty's purposes in the context in which it appears—a preface to a study of the phenomenology of perception in which Husserl's thought is given a dialectical placement as a point of departure and return for Merleau-Ponty's own ruminations. Also, the succinctness and critical punch of the statement tend to assure its popularity. Since the criticism strikes at the philosophic core of phenomenology, Merleau-Ponty's claim must be examined with some care.

Performing the reduction and perfecting the phenomenological work done in the reduced sphere involve different considerations. It would seem that Merleau-Ponty denies in principle that a complete reduction can be made. What he does, however, is to support that contention by evidence drawn from Husserl's

16. Maurice Merleau-Ponty, *Phenomenology of Perception*, p. xiv.

struggle to refine phenomenological performance within the reduced sphere. That is somewhat like saying that no man can lift a thousand pounds, only to find a strong man who does lift that weight, and then exclaiming, "Yes, he lifted it, but did you notice how he trembled?" Husserl's continued dissatisfaction with reduction came not from any internal inconsistency or fault in the concept but from the incredible difficulty in carrying out the reduction in rigorous fashion. The lure of the natural attitude is like a powerful undercurrent, pulling even the strongest swimmer off his intended course. Nor is there any assurance granted the phenomenologist that his work is beyond error. Husserl himself was perennially dissatisfied with his results, turned again and again to stricter formulations of his reports. Reports of work done within the reduced sphere are most certainly subject to criticism: they may be partial, incomplete, inexact. In evaluating the problem of how faithfully the reduction may be carried out, it is essential to know from whose standpoint the judgment is made—that of the phenomenologist or that of the critic in the natural attitude who tries to make sense of the phenomenologist's reports and claims. Meaningful criticism of the reduction can come only from one who has attempted phenomenological work rather than tried to make sense of phenomenology purely by inquiring into the implications of its theses. This does not mean that in order to criticize the reduction one must perform it; rather, criticism demands that one make an experiment on one's own, that the critic strive to move as far into the phenomenological attitude as he can manage, and that he base his response to Husserl on firsthand inspection and reflection rather than on positional or theoretical claims. In these terms, the question is not whether the critic has performed the reduction but whether he has dismissed its legitimacy solely on the basis of what he deems to be impossible or unacceptable. Ironically, the phenomenologist is daring the empiricist to look through the telescope.

In the case of Merleau-Ponty, of course, the situation is different. Here is someone who has done phenomenological work, who understands the problems from within, but who insists that reduction eludes Husserl because, in principle, it cannot be tamed. Some creatures simply cannot be captured alive or, if captured, die swiftly. Reduction would appear to be a wild notion, a concept out of control. But this is to psychologize Husserl. How the inquirer struggles within the reduced sphere is ultimately irrelevant to the nature of his activity qua phenomenologist. For Merleau-Ponty, the aspirant is always thrown back into the world, into the upsurge of existence, but for Husserl existence must be regenerated in terms of its own history in consciousness by tracing out its origin. The terms which connect with each other here are phenomenological observer and world as a transcendental correlate. The terms which are bracketed are empirical ego and empirical world. But it is in the dynamic of the relationship between "observer" and "world" that the meaning of the reduction comes through. Fink's formulation is subtly precise: "The true theme of phenomenology is neither the world on the one hand, nor a transcendental subjectivity which is to be set over and against the world on the other, but the *world's becoming in the constitution of transcendental subjectivity*." [17] Before it can be justly said that reduction is ultimately impossible, it is necessary to devote as much concrete effort to "proving" that claim as the phenomenologist devotes to doing the work of reduction. Surely, "proof" is not an operative term in this context. Merleau-Ponty is saying something quite different than his words might indicate. I would interpret him this way: Husserl's struggle with reduction cannot be resolved on transcendental ground; the *world* persists in its own renewal; concrete existence pulsates within and despite the reduction because man finds himself again and again within the force of an existence of which the general thesis is merely a clue. In effect, *existence* is rediscovered by Merleau-Ponty at the center of phenomenology. The irrealization of experience, the rendering of the world as strange, the forfeiture of fact for essence all become in Merleau-Ponty's translation the recovery of existential paradox in the recesses of phenomenological method. In these terms, the failure to achieve complete reduction becomes in Merleau-Ponty the victory of the existential dimension in phenomenology. He writes: "All the misunderstandings with his interpreters, with the existentialist 'dissidents' and finally with himself, have arisen from the fact that in order to see the world and grasp it as paradoxical, we must break with our familiar acceptance of it and also, from the fact that from this break we can learn nothing but the unmotivated upsurge of the world." [18]

In a later chapter we shall discuss in some detail the

17. Fink, "The Phenomenological Philosophy of Edmund Husserl and Contemporary Criticism," p. 130.
18. Merleau-Ponty, *Phenomenology of Perception,* p. xiv.

relationship between phenomenology and existentialism. For the moment, there is one point that cannot be deferred: the "I" who performs the reduction is not, for Husserl, the "I" who lives in the natural attitude. Of course, the two "I's" are not strangers to each other, for every distinction that can be made at the transcendental level has its corollary at the level of the natural attitude. But the "I" which operates in the transcendental sphere sees in unmediated fashion. That seeing is what Husserl terms "intuition," and if it be argued that such intuition is necessarily impure, blemished by the very existence it seems to apprehend, then it must be asked how such impurity is detected. Is the intuition of imperfection itself imperfect? But it is not only a logical paradox that one confronts if Merleau-Ponty's line of criticism is pursued; the very relocation or reinvolvement of the concrete person with his existential situation becomes no less paradoxical than the denial of pure intuition. Inserted again in the upsurge of existence, the concrete individual finds himself returned to familiar ground: the hectic, innovative extravagance of mundanity, being-in-the-world, is the familiar absurd, the same twinge of existence, the old chaos. Hurled into the facticity of the world at some unspecifiable moment of its becoming, I find myself *there;* yet the existential turn only succeeds in bringing back into view the very questions Husserl sought to illuminate through reduction: presence in and to a world, *world* as a horizon for human being, becoming itself as transcendental origin— all these are the distinctively phenomenological themes locked in existence and presupposed in any effort to illuminate concrete existence. In the end, Merleau-Ponty's criticism of reduction turns back on itself. If the lesson of reduction is that reduction is impossible, that lesson can only be learned through reduction. Instead of abandoning the reduction, Merleau-Ponty, in a final irony, reclaims it existentially: "Far from being, as has been thought, a procedure of idealistic philosophy, phenomenological reduction belongs to existential philosophy. . . ." [19] Either this means that a flawed reduction is proper to existential philosophy or that existentialism ultimately demands its own phenomenological foundation, for which an integral reduction is the necessary prerequisite. Merleau-Ponty does not resolve the ambiguity; he builds on its dialectical implications. What he leaves us with,

19. *Ibid.*

however, is the sense that method is an inescapable problem for existential thought.

Husserl's own conception of method is entwined in philosophical reflection. As long as epochē and reduction are thought of as steps in a routine, their meaning will remain opaque to the most earnest student. No doubt a severe reversal or shock to consciousness is involved in Husserl's way of seeing. The security of the natural attitude is not only threatened but doubly exposed, for it is both withdrawn and revealed. It would be a mistake to interpret "reversal" and "shock" in psychological terms. There may indeed be a moment of crisis in the mind of the individual for whom the world is rendered "strange" in reduction, but such a reference, as we have seen, can apply only to the psychological "I." The "I" of the reduced sphere is the ego before whom the world arises; it is the "I" of origin. At the same time, it is the "I" of direction, the ego pointing toward the world in its own functioning. And with the recognition of the purposive activity of the ego, there comes into focus what had been there unannounced throughout our inquiry: the intentiveness of consciousness, its propulsion toward the world it constitutes. The final gift of phenomenological method is the announcement of the intentionality of consciousness.

5 / Intentional Consciousness

PHENOMENOLOGICAL REDUCTION leads the inquirer from the mundane world of man with fellow man to the purely egological sphere of consciousness. The movement is from a psychological to a transcendental interest: from an empirical to a transcendental ego. Along with phenomenological reduction the transcendental ego is one of the thorniest notions in Husserl's writings. It is a complex concept and there is no simple way to explain it that I know of. At the same time, it is central to any understanding of phenomenology. As a first approximation, let us say that the transcendental ego is the matrix of consciousness in its ideal or purely possible aspect. There is a progression of a sort in three steps: first we have the actuality of consciousness in its psychoneurological facticity—thinking going on here and now; second, there is the eidetic or essential character of that thinking—its character apart from any here-and-now reality and independent of brain function; third, it is possible to consider the essential character of that thinking as itself an exemplar of transcendental subjectivity. With the third step we arrive at the transcendental ego. As a second approximation, we may consider the meaning of facticity in a broader fashion. The inquirer who turns from actuality to possibility is still rooted in a historical facticity; *his* ego still participates in the unfolding of *our* sociality. It is that complicity of the self in history and, more subtly, the tacit but pervasive intersubjective intent of what is usually called *personal* life which phenomenological reduction strives to undercut. With the thematization of the historicity of the ego, reduction is able to bring into relief the status of the transcendental ego. But these approximations tend to lean upon the meaning of reduction instead of advancing the argument of phenomenology. True as they may be, something more is needed to understand the form and content of transcendental subjectivity: that something more is the doctrine of the intentionality of consciousness.

It is time to make explicit what has been indwelling throughout our discussion of phenomenology thus far: the essence of consciousness is its directionality. All perceptual acts, according to Husserl, have one dominant characteristic; they point toward, or intend, some object. Thus, all thinking is thinking *of* something; all willing is willing *of* something; all imagining is imagining *of* something. Perception is not a state but a mobile *activity*. In its essential dynamic, perception (which we are taking in the widest possible sense) projects itself toward its intended object, but that object is not to be understood as a "thing" but rather as the correlate of its accompanying act or acts. The being, or what is often called ontological status, of the object of an intentional act is to be regarded under the sign of epochē, and with reduction the materiality, causal nexus, value, and meaning-for-others of the "object" are bracketed. What remains is the object *as meant,* regarded purely in terms of its givenness to the precise extent that it is given and solely in the manner in which it is given. The philosophical placement of the nature of givenness is of decisive importance to phenomenology. We come quickly to a divergence in path between Husserl's conception of intentionality and the descriptive stance of a psychology also bent on enunciating the givenness of the elements of psychic life, apart from their genetic and causal history. Intentionality is not descriptive psychology. The field of intentionality opened up by distinctively phenomenological research is a radicalization of the entire psychological sphere which nevertheless remains in the most intimate touch with the development of the empirical ego. Husserl writes:

> It would be much too great a mistake, if one said that to follow this line of research is nothing else than to make *psychological descriptions* based on purely internal experience, experience of one's own conscious life, and that naturally, to keep such descriptions pure, one must disregard everything psychophysical. A great mistake, because a *purely descriptive psychology of consciousness* (though its true method has become understandable and available only by virtue of the new phenomenology) is *not itself*

transcendental phenomenology as we have defined the latter, in terms of the transcendental phenomenological reduction. To be sure, pure psychology of consciousness is a *precise parallel* to transcendental phenomenology of consciousness. Nevertheless the two must at first be kept strictly separate, since failure to distinguish them, which is characteristic of *transcendental psychologism,* makes a genuine philosophy impossible. We have here one of those seemingly trivial nuances that make a decisive difference between right and wrong paths of philosophy.[1]

If descriptive psychology "reads off" its objects, phenomenology insists on the reflective turn which distinguishes what is simply given from what is intended-as-given. The reflective moment involved here signifies a restriction of interest to what is meant rather than to what is, to that which is pointed to in perception and not the perceived things themselves. There are four elements under discussion: (1) the real thing; (2) the actual perception; (3) the thing as meant; (4) the intentional act which presents the thing as meant. The first two items are characteristically psychological; they presuppose the natural attitude. It should be remembered, though, that "psychological" is not a synonym for superficial or a term of dismissal. Quite to the contrary, Husserl insists on the importance of the psychological domain and develops the discipline of phenomenological psychology. It is possible to do phenomenological work within the natural attitude, though the true radicalization of results demands reduction. Too often it is assumed that the phenomenologist has a quarrel with the natural attitude. That misses the point. It would be closer to say, following Yeats, that out of the philosopher's quarrel with the natural attitude comes analysis; from his quarrel with himself comes phenomenology.

The last two items on the list lead us to intentionality proper. Some new vocabulary is needed at this stage. Husserl introduces the words "noema" and "noesis" to stand for the intentional object and the intending act. In large characterization, "noema" refers to the object polarity of intentional structure and "noesis" to the subject side. Thus, noema is the referent of noesis. The duality is central to the meaning of intentionality. We may approach noema by an example. Seeing faces is the most common yet interesting feature of everyday life, where most of the people we see are never heard, addressed, touched, or discussed. In the

1. Edmund Husserl, *Cartesian Meditations,* pp. 31–32.

parade of mundane perception, faces are at least apt to be noticed, however fleetingly in most instances. In taking note of a
face, I see it in a certain perspective, from some distance or
proximity, in clear or muted light, with strong or weak eyes.
I may see the same face again and again within a fairly short
time interval. In the subway, for instance, I may ride on a car
with a stranger opposite me for thirty minutes. Let us say that
a stout woman holding a large shopping bag is presently sitting
across the aisle from me. My casual glance rests on a face turned
upward, as though its owner were searching the train roof for a
message. There appears to be a great deal of flesh around the
lower part of her chin and throat. I wonder if she suffers from
goiter. The shopping bag sits between her feet, steady despite the
occasional lurching of the train. From time to time, she looks
down to see if it is safe, adjusts the burden, and returns her gaze
upward. After ten minutes of riding, the pattern of seating has
changed and my companion moves over to accommodate a family that wishes to sit together. Now I see the lady obliquely. Her
profile is thrusting, her nose clamors, a dark fierceness presents
itself in place of the relative placidity of the face seen full view.
As the train passes through a tunnel the lighting shifts. In the
subway twilight, my lady's profile is softened, her glance retreats
into meditation, and by the time we pull into the station her face,
like mine, has fused with the city in the brittle unavailability of
a personless privacy.

Through a number of acts I see the same face. The conditions under which the acts operate vary considerably, yet I am
directed toward the same face. The lady seen full face or in
profile is seen as the same person. The glance which saw her a
few minutes ago and the one that catches her now both reveal
one and the same individual. The changes in light, vantage
point, and time do not affect the identity of the object intended.
Insofar as I see her face now, from this particular place, precisely in this light, I intend the lady as noema, as the object of an
intentional act. Quite apart from who she is and where she is
headed, the lady becomes someone *meant* as profiled in this way.
It must be noted that the noema is no part of the act in the sense
of being contained in it. In the course of a few minutes neither
I nor the lady may move in any appreciable way. I may close my
eyes and reopen them to find her the same. The acts through
which I attend to the noema vary; the intended object remains
invariant. Furthermore, the noema is not restricted to the present

tense. Sitting in the train I may recall the lady after she has gotten off. To the extent that I remember her *as* the face seen and noted, I reinvoke, as it were, her noema. Also, I may choose perhaps to imagine what she would be like sitting across from me still, in that pose of scrofulous adoration. The imagined lady, the remembered lady, and the perceived lady are one in the noematic unity of intentionality. And in that identity a critical feature of the noema is revealed: the lady *as meant* is immortal; she cannot be stung by a hateful look, badgered by vile elbows, or scolded by language. Neither is that immortality comforting, for the lady cannot be given affection or support. To the extent that we are concerned with what is presented to perception in its intentional aspect, the noema is that *sameness* which makes it possible for us, in the natural attitude, to enjoy a world of familiar, repeatable, and expectable events. Sameness—identity —is the prize of intentionality.

Noematic identity may be illustrated in the case of reference, where quite dissimilar statements nevertheless point to the same person. The author of *An Essay on the Foundations of Geometry,* the individual at issue in the case of *Jean Kay* v. *the Board of Higher Education of the City of New York,* the recipient of the Nobel Prize for Literature in 1950, and the subject of a memoir published in 1970 by Rupert Crawshay-Williams—all are Bertrand Russell. Despite the differences in emphasis, the same person is intended whether the reference be to his authorship, academic history, awards, or status as a biographee. So, too, it might be said that the many more casual references in daily life to an individual point toward the same person even though they may be concerned with distinctly different aspects of his being. The same individual is designated by his social security number, his tax return, his marriage license, his hospital record, his military service, and his church membership. The concept of social role offers the widest latitude for illustrating the way in which the same person may at one and the same time stand in quite different relationships to members of his family, his friends, business associates, political allies, as well as to more fugitive strata of the social world: strangers, unknown ancestors, and future descendants. In all of these realms, there is a distinction to be drawn between the real person in his actual existence at some moment in history and the person *as intended, as meant.* But the person as meant may be known only through one facet of his being. How is movement beyond the noema to the unity of the person possible? What is the phenomenological connection between identity and unity?

Intending an individual as one and the same despite the changes and variations in his career means that the identity at issue is open to continued references. Knowing that Russell wrote the book on geometry, I may learn that he joined Whitehead in writing *Principia Mathematica* and that he also wrote works on mathematical logic. Still further, I may come to regard him as a philosopher and read the many books he wrote on the problems and history of philosophy. Even more, I may appreciate him as an essayist, polemicist, letter writer, and follow his dabbling in fiction. With each new development, I not only add to my knowledge of Russell but come to broaden the meaning he has for me as an intentional referent. So, too, with what I learn about him from other sources. Reading the autobiography and letters of George Santayana, I come to see Russell in a new way. In turn, reading Russell on Santayana, I come to deepen my grasp of both men. Rather than a mere accretion of fact, what I gain from moving further and further toward an appreciation of the man is an expansion of the concatenation of noematic references—Russell, one is tempted to say, as an intentional construction built up from noematic constituents. In these terms, the additional information I gain is referred to the same person, but that sameness is an expanding unity in which every new item is translated into an intentional claim: Russell *as* logician, *as* philosopher, *as* teacher, *as* man of letters. Had I known Russell intimately, my range of reference to him would be greater but also more intensified. In point of fact I never met him, though I did attend a talk he gave in a huge lecture hall. The memory I have of him adds nevertheless to the intentional correlate we have been discussing: I remember the night twenty years ago, in New York City, when a small man with a great head amused his audience by announcing that he would not speak on the topic announced, something to do with poetry, because he had never written any poetry. From the distance of the balcony, it was still possible to see Russell's glee in bedevilment, and I remember the happy feeling I had, in leaving the auditorium, that we were contemporaries. Now in reading his autobiography or the books about him, I may, in phenomenological terms, intend him as the individual I saw in New York—that glimpse giving me a tiny point of access to the public figure. We have said nothing about the "real" Russell.

The other side of noema is noesis. As the correlate of intentional acts, the noema is the object side of consciousness. If we turn, however, to the act structure, we come to the phenomenological aspect of knowing, the subject side of consciousness. Russell perceived, Russell remembered, Russell imagined may involve the same noema, but the acts of perceiving, remembering, and imagining are qualitatively different noetic structures. Let us turn to a new example. A savage crime has been committed, the murderer found guilty by the jury. Let us suppose we had a translation of the judgment each juror made in agreeing to the verdict. The following patterns emerge: "The accused is guilty means I have attended to the evidence carefully, sifted the testimony of the witnesses, reflected on the arguments of the lawyers, heeded the instructions of the judge, and on balance have come to my conclusion"; "I am repelled by the animality which is threatening our institutions and have no tolerance for coddling criminals"; "Who knows what innocence or guilt is? All you can do is follow your instincts"; "My brother was killed by some hoods. In court, I saw his face again, pleading with me to keep that sort of thing from happening to others. I voted for the future." Now let us set aside the question of motivation and consider the nature of the various judgments. In ideal terms, they would reduce to: guilt as the determination of a juridical procedure; guilt as a projection of fear; guilt as the outcome of feeling; and guilt as the response to personal recoil. The verdict in all of these cases is identical but the judgments are quite different in meaning. The first is rooted in the law and sets aside questions of the crime rate, the future of society, and the implications of a verdict of guilty on potential offenders. The second is responsive to the present and critical of how justice is done. The third is atemporal and discounts both judge and judged in favor of passionate insight. The fourth is Janus-faced; the accused confronts the juror with an equally unhappy actual past and possible future. Whatever the "why" of their decision, the "what" of their individual judgments varies significantly and yields a true noetic diversity despite the noematic unity of the verdict itself.

The jury example goes beyond the logical characterization of judgment and, for that matter, oversteps Husserl's account of noesis, but it does lead to a larger phenomenological theme, that of the constitution of meaning. Apart from the particular biographical and psychological circumstances of the jury member whose brother was murdered, it is possible to examine the form of his response in its intentional structure: judgment based on ulterior considerations. Under the latter rubric may be placed all cases of decision in which the facts of a situation are offset by deeply held personal convictions, loyalties, or attitudes. Within that classification, we would have to specify a narrower category involving intense emotional response centering about a traumatic event in the life of the individual judging. In any event, it is possible to turn to the structure of such judgment apart from rehearsing the actual experience of the juror. The reasons for his voting as he did presuppose psychological actuality; the noetic character of such reasons is the subject matter of phenomenological inquiry. As I have said, a larger conception of judgment is at issue when we consider noesis. But what stands forth most importantly in this approach to judgment is the opportunity of showing its constitutive history. The formal structure of judgment has its dynamic; it is not to be understood as a desiccated mold. In the end, noesis must be understood in its active relationship to noema. The separation between them is legitimate, necessary, yet artificial—a matter of distinguishing rather than separating. Noesis and noema imply and demand each other.

We have gained enough of an understanding of the elements of intentionality to appreciate the radical sense of Husserl's conception of experience and meaning. Joining forces with two other phenomenological terms will advance us still further: essence and intuition. When, in the phenomenological attitude, I attend to the object *as meant* in strictest terms, I concern myself with essence. In the reduced sphere, I intend the noema. Essence (or *eidos* as Husserl also calls it) is seized in unmediated form: its enjoyment is called intuition. We might contrast, for a moment, the experiencing of an empirical object in the natural attitude with the intuition of essence. The real thing is seen as *there*, as being what it appears to be, as being there for others as well as for me, as having been placed there at some time or as having some natural history which accounts for its presence, as having value and purpose, and as having a place in the general scheme of nature—being subject to the laws of physics, for example. But there is a less abstract sense to empirical perception. The thing I perceive is *there* before me in its full embodiment and givenness as a thing, something real because its presence cannot be gainsaid, something objective because its objectness confronts me. Admittedly, something had been read into empirical experience (or read out of it) in these formulations, yet the basis for such a reading seems to be an option of the natural attitude. When that option is picked up, reapproached, and reassessed in phenomenological terms, the essence of bodily givenness, of incontrovertible presence, and of inescapable objectivity is made available for inspection and description. Intuition, far from being a dark trembling in the willow of the epistemological dowser, is the most straightforward and available of all procedures: seeing unencumbered by knowing.

The language of essence and intuition has not served Husserl's cause as well as more neutral terms might have, but then the philosopher is always faced with a thankless choice: if he retains traditional terms but uses them in unorthodox ways he is subject to misunderstanding; if he abandons the received vocabulary in favor of neologisms, he is accused of obscurantism. Nor will the effort to provide definitions of terms settle matters. Philosophical language suffers from an internal disorder, an incapacity to accept an ultimate circularity in expression. For some that failure keeps them from following what they otherwise think might be made clear; for others, philosophy's unwillingness to take for granted the terms into which something is being defined is its intellectual conscience. Misleading and bothersome as they may be, "essence" and "intuition" are words which also carry with them some benefits. Essence stands opposed to facticity and to particularity. To be concerned with essence is then to attend to the factic aspect of experience in an oblique way: to see the factic *as* specified and fragmented in the details of existent experience. Intuition is set off from perception in its hypothetical and implicative dimensions: states of affairs themselves, not surrogates or replicas of them, are intuited. In a way, the language of essence and intuition is so familiar it has become archaic. The phenomenologist is returning to the world from which mundanity has become estranged. He is saying: "See and listen once again." In an age of perceptual blockage and encumbrance, such advice must indeed seem singular. And at a time when philosophical style inclines to the ramblings of Dick and Jane, phenomenological language appears grotesque. It is a question of where genuine simplicity lies and also of what power language has for shocking us back into experience.

With intuition and essence we are able to comprehend the subject matter of intentionality. "Phenomena" in the rigorous Husserlian sense of the term may now be elucidated. The phenomenon is the intentional object, understood as the noetic-noematic correlate of the acts which intend it. The terms "noema," "essence," and "intended object" are different ways of posing the same reference to a state of affairs given in the perceptual immediacy of intuition. As the logos of phenomena, phenomenology is the discipline which seeks to identify, describe, and analyze the formal and constitutive elements of intentional consciousness. In these terms, phenomenology is the science of intentionality. However, this description must be taken as provisional, for all essential analysis requires a grounding in transcendental subjectivity, a grounding revealed in phenomenological reduction. What must be added to our portrayal of the phenomenon is its noetic rootage in a constitutive history of the ego. It would be a misreading of phenomenology to assume that pure description and analysis make up its total responsibility. Husserl writes:

> The phenomenologist . . . does not inquire with merely a naïve devotedness to the intentional object purely as such; he does not consider the intentional object only straightforwardly and explicate its meant features, its meant parts and properties. If that were all he did, the intentionality, which makes up the intuitive or non-intuitive consciousness itself and the explicative considering, would remain "anonymous". . . . When the phenomenologist explores everything objective, and whatever can be found in it, exclusively as a "correlate of consciousness", he does not consider and describe it only straightforwardly and only as *somehow* related back to the corresponding Ego and the *ego cogito* of which it is the *cogitatum*. Rather, with his reflective regard, he penetrates the anonymous "cogitative" life, he uncovers the *definite* synthetic courses of the manifold modes of consciousness and, further back, the modes of Ego-comportment, which make understandable the objective affair's simple meantness for the Ego, its intuitive or non-intuitive meantness. Or, stated more precisely, they make it understandable how, in itself and by virtue of its current intentional structure, consciousness makes possible and necessary the fact that such an "existing" and "thus determined" Object is intended in it, occurs in it as such a sense.[2]

"Constitution" is a fundamental but problematic term in Husserl's vocabulary. It may be understood in a number of ways. First, constitution refers to a logic of the building of meaning, a

2. *Ibid.*, p. 47.

process through which the meaning we find in experience has come to be established and organized in its particular manner. Given any phenomenon, it is possible to trace out the way in which it has come to be formed. Second, constitution may be understood as a self-generating dynamic of consciousness. The German language lends itself to some ambiguity here: *sich konstitutieren* may be translated "constitutes itself" or "is constituted." [3] Nor will the context always give an unequivocal determination of which expression is proper. The ambiguity, in fact, goes beyond language; it leads to a third sense of constitution. At times Husserl writes as though the constitutive process were one of world-creation and as though consciousness built up not only the order of meaning but the nature of reality. Once again, ambiguity is not to be taken as a necessary sign that Husserl's doctrine is unclear. As with some other notions we have discussed, different accents of meaning are best appreciated by recognizing the evolution of phenomenological thought. That the creative sense of constitution is stressed most fully in Husserl's transcendental idealism is interpreted by some commentators to indicate the unacceptable direction phenomenology takes when it ceases to be a theory of meaning and becomes a philosophy of being. It is not necessary to accept all of the implications of philosophical idealism to recognize the particular placement of Husserl's version. It must be kept in mind that he explicitly disassociated himself from both traditional idealism and realism. Although the positive features of phenomenological idealism remain unclear, it may be suggested that their ultimate significance turns on the nature of phenomenological reduction.

The language of reduction suggests a separating off and the attempt to arrive at a purified residuum. There are some dangers in that interpretation, for as we have seen, nothing is lost in reduction. Regarded in a different way, reduction involves a recursion of consciousness on its own movement. It has been pointed out that the word "reduction" taken in its strict etymological sense means a *return* or a leading back. [4] It is not necessary to tie Husserl to literal meaning to appreciate the impor-

3. Cf. Robert Sokolowski, *The Formation of Husserl's Concept of Constitution*, p. 216.

4. See Herbert Spiegelberg, *The Phenomenological Movement*, I, 133, and cf. Eugen Fink, "The Phenomenological Philosophy of Edmund Husserl and Contemporary Criticism," p. 126.

tance of that suggestion. In terms of constitution, the recursion of intentional consciousness may be traced out by identifying and illuminating the elements and stages of experience. What is grasped in its fulfilled manifestation in the natural attitude must be traced back intentionally to its sources in transcendental subjectivity. The relationship between objectivity and subjectivity is crucial here. The phenomenological position maintains that the source of objective states of affairs *as bearers of meaning* is to be found in the intentional ground of intentional consciousness. Thus, the determination of the geological age of the solar system is a problem for natural scientists, but the comprehension of the relative "oldness" of the earth by human beings whose history on it is quite recent in terms of geological time is a problem for human subjectivity. What relationship is there between the individual's sense of time and the time of the astronomers? If I am told that ten billion years from now the sun will have burned itself out, how do I begin to grasp such a figure in human terms? The various analogies I may make in order to get at least an image of that period of time are at best remote and ineffective instruments of imagination. I may as soon picture eternity as ten billion years. The preacher in *A Portrait of the Artist as a Young Man* says of eternity:

> Imagine a mountain of . . . sand, a million miles high, reaching from the earth to the farthest heavens, and a million miles broad, extending to remotest space, and a million miles in thickness: and imagine such an enormous mass of countless particles of sand multiplied as often as there are leaves in the forest, drops of water in the mighty ocean, feathers on birds, scales on fish, hairs on animals, atoms in the vast expanse of the air: and imagine that at the end of every million years a little bird came to that mountain and carried away in its beak a tiny grain of that sand. How many millions upon millions of centuries would pass before that bird had carried away even a square foot of that mountain, how many eons upon eons of ages before it had carried away all. Yet at the end of that immense stretch of time not even one instant of eternity could be said to have ended.[5]

Granted the infinite distance between ten billion years and eternity, Joyce's bird is as credible for the one as for the other. The trouble lies not with the act of transmission but with the

5. James Joyce, *A Portrait of the Artist as a Young Man* (New York: Viking, 1964), p. 132.

million-year pause between flights. How is *that* time period to be grasped by the mind? One knows what the numbers mean but not what the passage of time signifies for consciousness. Fundamentally, the problem is one of what is sometimes called inner time or temporality. Since the activity of consciousness involves its own temporal dimension, the structure of the world as the correlate of intentional acts is necessarily related to and affected by the order of its constitutive history. Phenomena, for Husserl, are historical in essence because they are products of a genesis of intentional meaning. Turning to the constitution of phenomena is searching for their origin in consciousness. What we said earlier about origin should be emphasized here. Phenomenology concerns itself with the *becoming* of the world in transcendental subjectivity. One aspect of that becoming is distinctively temporal, for experience is not simply a blind accretion of impressions and information but the selection which consciousness makes of the resources potential to the formation and renewal of a world. An imperfect analogy may provide some help. Just as it is possible for the individual to retrace the incidents and associations of his own career, so it is possible for the transcendental observer to return to the formal elements of his temporal progression. Origin is the intentional aspect of temporal recursion. Husserl is alive to the possibilities of phenomenological genesis. He writes:

The question of the essence of time leads back to the question of the "origin" of time. The *question of the origin* is oriented toward the *primitive* forms of the consciousness of time in which the primitive differences of the temporal are constituted intuitively and authentically as the originary . . . sources of all certainties relative to time. The question of the origin of time should not be confused with the *question of its psychological origin*—the controversial question between *empiricism and nativism*. With this last question we are asking about the *primordial material of sensation out of which arises Objective intuition of space and time* in the human individual and even in the species. We are indifferent to the question of the empirical genesis.[6]

6. Edmund Husserl, *The Phenomenology of Internal Time-Consciousness*, p. 28. We will not concern ourselves with the problematic but potentially rich concept of "sensation" in phenomenology. For a critical assessment of Husserl's views on the subject, see Harmon M. Chapman, *Sensations and Phenomenology*.

The *becoming* of the world has its source in inner time but it also is grounded in the matrix of the pure ego. We are dealing with different facets of the concept of origin, yet that concept remains elusive. Once again, we turn to the meaning of origin. Within the natural attitude, it is acknowledged that an event, a situation, or a person may be misunderstood if it or he is seized or interpreted in too narrow a focus. One cannot be certain of a reliable explanation of an event without making sure that a rather full placement of the event is provided. "Reading" faces is a notoriously hazardous enterprise: as often as not, the "criminals" turn out to be judges and the "psychiatrists" prove to be patients. The photographic eye is as uncertain as any observer's glance: it stills the hectic flush of experience in adumbrations which sometimes hide as well as reveal the truth. What appears to be a laughing face is the contortion of extreme pain; what appears sinister is innocence caught in a trick of lighting. Mechanical impressions no more than human sensibility can be trusted to translate the expressive world unless the situation or framework within which the smile appears or the cry is heard or the complaint is lodged is explored and penetrated. The appreciation of context in the natural attitude is an immanent turn to origin. The point is simply that the available surface of an event is a product, the outcome of a process, a history, which is the rootage of experience. When the surface is cut off from its productive source, the result is a denial of meaning, a scanning of appearance bereft of foundation.

Within the phenomenological attitude, origin implies a source for direction, a locus from which the movement of consciousness arises. The discipline of origin consists in tracing out the itinerary of consciousness in its constitutive history. Here it would be misleading to think of origin as a causal determinant. One tends to transform the temporal process into a time sequence in which a primordial event sets a causal chain of events into motion. With causation bracketed in the reduced sphere, the phenomenological notion of origin is free of sequential ordering. Instead, attention is turned to the flow of intentionality as consciousness reveals itself in a multitude of perceptions, judgments, rememberings, and anticipatings. To get at the origin of such a flow is to elucidate the mesh of acts and syntheses which constitute the experiential world. Again, an imperfect analogy may help to clarify an idea. Just as the phenomenologist in search of origin moves from the surface event to the

constitutive strata beneath it, so the painter, in an obverse movement, builds his surface by painting over again and again an
emergent form. And just as experts can remove layers of over-
painting and return a work to an earlier state, so the origin-
seeker can move back in meaning from the given to its formative
antecedent stages. In the course of such a regression, there is no
point at which one may stop and say, "*Here* is the origin we were
looking for." That would be to misconstrue the entire procedure.
In searching for origin the phenomenologist is trying to reconstruct the activity of consciousness in its complete integrity. Origin, like phenomenological *beginning*, is copresent with the life
of consciousness.

Finally, origin represents an absolute ground for Husserl, a
founding structure supportive of everything else. The search for
a presuppositionless philosophy, the development of a radical
method of doubt, the instruments of reduction, and the attempt
to build philosophy as rigorous science all include a passion for
certitude, a deliberate effort to locate an ultimate bedrock for
the construction of knowledge. To the extent that all of these
aspects of Husserl's thought involve a return to secure foundations, true beginnings, there is the urge to absolutivity as the
essence of origin. Phenomena, unlike gods, are not self-generating; they point back to where they have come from and to how
they have traversed their constitutive path. What is absolute
about them is their status for consciousness as intentional objects. That absoluteness, however, is not a function of belief in
the ordinary sense, for in transcending the psychological dimension of the general thesis of the natural attitude, the phenomenologist is concerned with the essential character of an
intentional correlate rather than the individual bond between
believer and believed-in. As a person I may claim final certitude
for my belief, but any appeal for the explanation of that certitude is translated into a recital of its fervency and depth: "I
know it could not be otherwise" means "I feel it could not be
otherwise." For Husserl such "knowing" and "feeling" are contingencies of a psyche in the world, clinging to the supports of
the natural attitude. Phenomenological certitude rests not only
on the in-person givenness of intentional objects but on the manner in which that givenness has been secured. Phenomenological
results are arrived at in a phenomenological way: substance and
form are integral. But the appeal to method is a call to origin.
The unity of the empirical ego—the mundane life of the individ-

ual—carries the story of consciousness in the world forward to the unity of the person. The order of intentional consciousness leads back to its essential source in the transcendental ego, a recursion we have termed origin.

If the empirical ego is the actualization of the individual's possibilities, the transcendental ego is the matrix of all possibility within which the career of one person is itself imaginable. As the final ground of intentional consciousness, the transcendental ego is universal. Access to it comes by way of the individual, but the transcendental ego is as close to The Absolute as Husserl comes. Accordingly, transcendental subjectivity cuts across the traditional boundaries of the ego and presents itself as valid for any possible ego. How is Husserl able to move from the ego to the alter ego? How does phenomenology deal with the problem of intersubjectivity? The answer comes in the fifth of the *Cartesian Meditations*, where Husserl traces out the constitution of the alter ego.[7] In its barest outline, the argument moves along the following path: With the reduction, the ego attends to what is distinctively *his* and arrives at a world whose relevance and meaning for others have been bracketed. Reference to fellow men and their history undergoes transformation into my unique intentional life. The primordial object encountered in this sphere of true privacy is my body, to which I have access from "within" through kinesthesia and which is subject to my control. From the same reduced standpoint, I encounter my fellow man not as a physical object—a thing of a certain mass occupying a certain amount of space—but as another body or, as we would ordinarily say, as another human being. Just as I am aware of my body from within, so I intend the body of the other as being available to him from within. There is a vital difference, however, in the way in which I come to be aware of my own body and that of the Other: my body is here, whereas the body of the other is there. Yet I intend the other's there as being here for him, just as I experience myself as being there for him and assume that he grasps that there as a here for me. Within the transcendental sphere, the heres and theres are identical, and the attribution of bodily placement in the world is the consequence of an intentional process whose source is the pure ego. The other is not restricted in this way to a figment of my transcendental consciousness but is granted full objectivity in his

7. Husserl, *Cartesian Meditations*, pp. 89–151.

interrelationship with me in what might be termed a transcendental community. That objectivity is disclosed in egological terms and cannot be understood apart from them.[8]

It might be objected that Husserl has established a sealed-in domain of transcendental subjectivity in which every reference to other selves and to the objective world must perforce remain locked into the reduced sphere. How does one get beyond himself? What is the point of connection between the transcendental and the real? In intentional terms, to say "real world" is to say "world-meant-as-real." We have already pointed out some of the differences between the "real" and the "meant-as-real." Phenomenology rests on the distinction between them. Yet there is also an intimate relationship between reality and intention, for the only way in which we come to know the real is by intending it as real. In the claim to objectivity there is an especial nexus between the real and claims made about what is there for all of us. Let us say that in illuminating the phenomenological presuppositions involved in the experience of a fellow man, I come to recognize that in perceiving his body as *his*, in perceiving him as there, in apprehending him as a psychophysical unity *like* me, I am aware in some undeniable sense of his actual presence in the world as a real person existent among other real persons in an ultimately real world. That awareness is in fact simply the force of the natural attitude. Within the reduced sphere it has become thematized so that it now stands out. What I have done is to make the general thesis of the natural attitude an intentional object. Is it fair now to say that I have internalized it phenomenologically so that its objectivity is somehow altered or lessened? The privileged position of consciousness, for Husserl, is that it always provides the point of access to whatever presents itself as real, objective, or for that matter, illusory and subjective. By grounding intentional experience in the transcendental ego, Husserl shows how what is other—fellow men, for example—is rooted in what is unique to subjectivity, to *own-*

8. Alfred Schutz points out: "It should be stressed that this transcendental intersubjectivity exists purely in me, the meditating ego. It is constituted purely from the sources of my intentionality, but in such a manner that it is the *same* transcendental intersubjectivity in every single human being . . . in his intentional experiences" (*Collected Papers*, I, 126). Also see Schutz's essay "The Problem of Transcendental Intersubjectivity in Husserl," in *Collected Papers*, Vol. III, and cf. José Ortega y Gasset, *Man and People*, p. 121 ff.

ness; and by searching for the source of the objective in transcendental subjectivity, he tries to lift the burden of history from the empirical ego and place it upon its initial bearer, that transcendental consciousness in whose life community is established. Husserl writes:

> Restricting ourselves to the ultimate transcendental ego and the universe of what is constituted in him, we can say that a division of his whole transcendental field of experience belongs to him immediately, namely the division into the sphere of his ownness—with the coherent stratum consisting in his experience of a world reduced to what is included in his ownness (an experience in which everything "other" is "screened off")—and the sphere of what is "other." Yet every *consciousness of* what is other, every mode of appearance *of* it, belongs in the former sphere. Whatever the transcendental ego constitutes in that *first* stratum, whatever he constitutes as non-other, as his "peculiarly own"—that indeed belongs to him as *a component of his own concrete essence* . . . ; it is inseparable from his concrete being. Within and by means of this ownness the transcendental ego constitutes, however, the "Objective" world, as a universe of being that is other than himself—and constitutes, at the first level, the other in the mode: alter ego.[9]

The most telling feature of the constitutive grounding of the communal world in transcendental subjectivity is the universality of the transcendental ego. Just as we found sameness to be the prime achievement of intentionality, so we now find an analogous identity to be operative at the transcendental level. It is possible, in reading Husserl, to speak of *the* transcendental ego or of transcendental egos.[10] Though a kind of monadology emerges, the meaning of "my" and "your" transcendental ego proves to be the meaning of *the* transcendental ego. Referred to in the singular or plural, "transcendental ego" signifies the primacy of consciousness. Despite Husserl's protestations, that primacy is sometimes attacked by philosophers who find in transcendental idealism a refusal of the independent power and causality of nature. Beyond the intending-of external force, so the criticism goes, there is that force itself; beyond consciousness-of nature, there is nature on its own, in command of its

9. Husserl, *Cartesian Meditations*, p. 100.
10. See Edmund Husserl *Formal and Transcendental Logic*, p. 239.

own powers. Whether or not consciousness may be traced back to constitutive sources in the transcendental ego, the world which consciousness inhabits transcends the phenomenological structure of intentionality. It would seem that some of our earlier formulations do not offer a satisfactory account of the world-consciousness relationship when viewed from the standpoint of man in nature. If so, we come to an impasse of sorts. In Husserlian terms, to recognize the force of nature is to affirm the existence of an empirical order which has its own scientific discipline proper to it and which has a crucial role to play in the development of consciousness in its neurophysiological aspect. But it would be a profound misunderstanding of phenomenology to assert that a change in nature means a change in intentionality. The point deserves closer examination.

A man struck on the head with a heavy object may lose consciousness. If the blow was completely unexpected, it would seem that there would be a loss of consciousness from a phenomenologically unintended source. There are two considerations which interest us here: first, the connection between the physical blow and the ensuing loss of consciousness; second, the relationship between receiving the blow and intending it. The first point requires little comment. It should be clear by now that phenomenology does not concern itself with matters of fact or with the content of physical science. The problem of loss of consciousness should be directed to neurologists and related scientists. When someone faints or is the victim of an accident, the person to call is a physician, not a phenomenologist. The only reason the question of the loss of consciousness arises at all in the present discussion is that in some quarters there is the mistaken belief that it presents a challenge of some sort for the doctrine of phenomenology. I am unable to see that. If a heavy chandelier suddenly falls on a mathematician lecturing to his colleagues and renders him unconscious, there is no effect on the content of his lecture; he is simply stopped from going on. As an empirical event in the real world, the accident does not touch mathematics as a pure structure: the a priori cannot be wounded. So it is with intentionality. The second point is more complicated. Although there is a sense in which something nonconsciously received is still passively experienced, it should be recognized that one moves toward a vanishing point in ideal cases. In principle, the phenomenologist does not need to deny the possibility of nonintentive reception. Certainly, the reflective dimension in the case of the blow is minimized to an ineffectual degree, if not ruled out altogether. But the more interesting problem is the hazy domain in which the loss of consciousness is not an absolute affair and in which the victim or patient does retain some marginal awareness of what struck him or of the sequence of events following the administering of an anesthetic. In these instances, I would suggest, consciousness continues to be aware of more than is often granted it by observers, including medical practitioners. In any event, we have moved to the outmost rim of intentional consciousness. Whatever ambiguity may be encountered there hardly affects the substance of Husserl's position.

The doctrine of intentionality is the axis of phenomenology. With the aid of reduction and the descriptive-analytic examination of the noetic-noematic aspects of consciousness, the inquirer comes to the central work Husserl inaugurated. It is at this point that a question familiar to phenomenologists is raised: How is phenomenology *done*? Those who may be impressed with Husserl's formulation of the tasks of philosophy and who may be intrigued by his methodology rightly insist on asking for a sample of the method actually applied. Unfortunately, what appears to be a quite reasonable request often leaves the questioner dissatisfied once he turns to examples of phenomenological work. I think that the source of the dissatisfaction is not so much the character of phenomenological performance as it is a confusion in the nature of the question itself. When one asks to see something applied, he assumes that the main issue at hand is whether that application is indeed possible. Also, he looks to the quality of work done, and he will not settle for an application which is technically performable but which yields worthless results. The issue, then, is whether a productive application can be made, not whether application itself is possible as a legitimate philosophical concept. In the course of ordinary inquiry, application is a presupposition within philosophical discourse. What is taken as problematic is its actualization and realization. In turning to phenomenology, the inquirer has unwittingly bracketed his doubts about application in his eagerness to assess results. As we shall see, there is no scarcity of phenomenological results, but there is a complex philosophical problem involved in trying to understand the meaning of application. In turning to the phenomenologist at work, we shall be concerned with a multiple task: trying to clarify the nature of application as a distinctively philosophical concept by examining an example of phenomenological performance. The discussion will, in turn, provide a bridge from intentionality to mundanity, from consciousness to what Husserl calls the "life-world."

6 / Phenomenology Applied

IN A SENSE, all of Husserl's writings are examples of phenomenology applied, for even when he discusses methodological problems and talks *about* phenomenology there is an effort to uncover meaning sedimented in the philosophy presupposed in the natural attitude and disguised in its taken-for-grantedness. But it is true that much of his work is of mixed character: sometimes Husserl writes as a pure phenomenologist; at other times he is preparing the reader for understanding pure phenomenology. Within the same book, he may be tracing out the constitution of logical structure and also explaining the problems involved in that very procedure. In *Cartesian Meditations*, the shift from application to explication is made within a larger framework, which may be interpreted as an exercise in the exploration of the history of the ego—what is sometimes referred to as "genetic phenomenology." But the reader who looks for a reasonably accessible specimen of applied phenomenology in Husserl's writings often retreats from the suggested texts with the complaint that between the language, the style, and the profound level of abstraction, it is difficult always to know where one is in one's grasp of the subject. In place of a direct appreciation of Husserl's descriptions and analyses, what frequently happens is that the reader asks for methodological assistance: "Has epoché been performed at this stage?"; "Is this statement made from the reduced sphere?"; "Are we dealing with phenomenological psychology or philosophy here?" Since the point of turning to an application of phenomenology was to get away from what some tend to think of as the aridity of pure method, it

[105]

is disconcerting to find that the questions raised bring us back to methodology. Perhaps in such instances the method was never thoroughly grasped to begin with. Still, there is something odd about a turn to application which results in a renewal of methodology. The relationship between them remains problematic.

It may be that a way out of the apparent impasse created by methodology in need of application and application in need of methodology lies in a new direction, one which will take us outside the province of Husserl's own philosophizing. If phenomenological method is a truly rigorous instrument, it should, according to Husserl, be utilizable by any properly trained investigator. How have others fared with applying phenomenology? And can we learn something about phenomenological results from an investigator who has mastered Husserl's ideas but who operates independently of the demands and restrictions self-imposed by the sage of Freiburg? Fortunately, there is a perfect choice available among those who had the advantage of direct contact with Husserl, whose work he approved as being faithful to the idea of phenomenology, and whose accessibility is manageable. In the work of Alfred Schutz we have, in my judgment, the finest example of phenomenology applied. Schutz was in personal touch with Husserl, who read his book with approval as revealing a thorough grasp of phenomenology.[1] At the same time, Schutz was concerned with the application of phenomenology to fundamental problems of the social sciences and social reality. From the outset, then, we have in Schutz's work a combination of concern with phenomenology and an effort to provide a philosophical foundation for the social world. But we have something more. Schutz was thoroughly trained in the social sciences as well as in philosophy. Rather than being an outsider to either domain, he was at home in both. The advantage was remarkable, for Schutz was able to concentrate three intellectual and disciplinary focuses in one career: he was philosopher, sociologist, and phenomenologist. The rarity of that unity in diversity is best appreciated when one reads the work of social scientists interested in the implications of phenomenology who pick up snatches of Husserl without grasping their philosophical

1. Alfred Schutz, *Der sinnhafte Aufbau der sozialen Welt: Eine Einleitung in die verstehende Soziologie* (Vienna: Springer, 1932); English version, *The Phenomenology of the Social World.*

foundation or philosophers bent on applying phenomenology to the social sciences but whose knowledge of the concrete problems of sociology or economics is that of a dilettante. From the one side we have, as Kant said, the blindness of percepts without concepts; on the other side, the emptiness of concepts without percepts. In Schutz, there is both vision and content.

In his own terms, Schutz conceived of his work as a "phenomenology of the natural attitude." The phrase needs some clarification. At first glance, it would seem that since phenomenology brackets the natural attitude, a phenomenology of the natural attitude would be a contradiction. On closer inspection, it should be evident that a phenomenology *of* the natural attitude may be understood as an effort to elucidate the structure of mundane reality in terms of the phenomenological attitude. In fact, Schutz's career was devoted to the systematic exploration of everyday life as the matrix of the natural attitude. In what he termed the "taken for granted" routines and "typifications" of daily life he found the materials from which social reality comes to be constructed as meaningful for ordinary men as well as for philosophers and social scientists. The "meaning-structure" of the social world is the central theme. For Schutz, the everyday world of man in the midst of his routine pursuits is meaning-laden and interpreted. He writes:

> Let us try to characterize the way in which the wide-awake grown-up man looks at the intersubjective world of daily life within which and upon which he acts as a man amidst his fellow-men. This world existed before our birth, experienced and interpreted by others, our predecessors, as an organized world. Now it is given to our experience and interpretation. All interpretation of this world is based on a stock of previous experiences of it, our own or those handed down to us by parents or teachers; these experiences in the form of "knowledge at hand" function as a scheme of reference.
>
> To this stock of knowledge at hand belongs our knowledge that the world we live in is a world of more or less well circumscribed objects with more or less definite qualities, objects among which we move, which resist us and upon which we may act. Yet none of these objects is perceived as insulated. From the outset it is an object within a horizon of familiarity and pre-acquaintanceship which is, as such, just taken for granted until further notice as the unquestioned, though at any time questionable stock of knowledge at hand. The unquestioned pre-experiences are, however, also

from the outset, at hand as *typical,* that is, as carrying open horizons of anticipated similar experiences.[2]

The world, on this account, is experienced "from the outset" as charged with meaning—an "outset" which refers to the logical rather than the chronological commencement of experience. "Meaning" is obviously the decisive term here and demands scrutiny. There is a larger and a narrower sense in which it is used by Schutz. As a general term, it refers to the interpretative act through which common sense locates its objects and events as pointing beyond their bare surface features to some intentional schema in which they find their grounding. Thus, something is seen as a mountain, not as a patchwork of related masses; the cry of "Fire!" in a crowded building is instantaneously understood by any normal English-speaking adult as an expression of danger and emergency rather than a monosyllabic utterance of Old English derivation; and a street scene is comprehended as a conflux of people purposefully going about their business, not a conglomeration of bodies occupying different and shifting segments of space. Furthermore, the larger sense of meaning carries an intersubjective reference: the mountain perceived, the emergency recognized, and the street scene apprehended are all grasped as being perceivable, recognizable, and apprehensible by fellow men. The intersubjective reference transcends the present, for interpretation goes back to earlier periods of the individual's (and Man's) past and points toward the world of those who will survive us and be the descendants of those survivors—our successors, in Schutz's terminology. As an interpreted reality, the world is meaningful in the first instance to those who intend it as *world.* As we shall see, it is the actor on the social scene rather than the observer who is the primary source and locus of meaning.

The narrower sense of meaning involves the phenomenological basis for what has been called the "subjective interpretation of meaning." Schutz distinguishes between spontaneity and reflection in experience and reserves the strict sense of meaning for interpretation involving a reflective moment. "Meaning . . . ," he writes,

is not a quality inherent in certain experiences emerging within our stream of consciousness but the result of an interpretation of

2. Alfred Schutz, *Collected Papers,* I, 7.

a past experience looked at from the present Now with a reflective attitude. As long as I live in my acts, directed toward the objects of these acts, the acts do not have any meaning. They become meaningful if I grasp them as well-circumscribed experiences of the past and, therefore, in retrospection. Only experiences which can be recollected beyond their actuality and which can be questioned about their constitution are, therefore, subjectively meaningful.[3]

Reflection, of course, can also apply to projected future action by imagining the action in the future perfect tense: "I look in my imagination at this anticipated action as the thing which *will have been* done, the act which *will have been* performed by me." [4] Altogether, the temporal structure at the root of meaning demands a caesura of consciousness in which reflection turns the lived-in experience into a project of action. The present tense makes itself heard in this way, for action, according to Schutz, "is always based upon a preconceived project, and it is this reference to the preceding project that makes both the acting and the act meaningful." [5] Although there are contexts and passages in which Schutz moves from the more embracing conception of meaning to the stricter employment, it should be understood that there is no contradiction between them. A phenomenological examination of the larger sense of meaning, for Schutz, comes by way of a transcendental reconstruction of the temporality out of which meaning is generated. Before we can see how Schutz carries out that examination, we must turn to his account of social reality.

As a mundane being, man finds himself in a world which existed before his birth, born of parents who are unique to him, the inheritor of a natural language, the scion of a history and a culture, and a participant in a life which includes fellow men, work, love, and the recognition of human finitude. The social world is not only an interpreted but a preinterpreted reality. Family, language, history, culture, intersubjectivity in all of its modes, and the comprehension of death are aspects of the frame of life within which the individual makes his choices. Unlike inert objects which are simply *in* the world, human beings *have* a world. That means, among other things, that what we find at

3. *Ibid.*, p. 210.
4. *Ibid.*, p. 215.
5. *Ibid.*, p. 214.

any moment of our social existence are the overt or hidden signs of the translations our predecessors have made of their experience. Language is a vast reservoir for preinterpretation, but social order as a whole reflects the historicity of things. When the individual finds meaning in his world, then, he is, tacitly at least, ascribing significance to a reality which already possesses significance. He is creating a construction of the second degree —a construction of an already existent construction.

The point of departure for the individual is always his "biographical situation." As Schutz expresses it:

> Man finds himself at any moment of his daily life in a biographically determined situation, that is, in a physical and sociocultural environment as defined by him, within which he has his position, not merely his position in terms of physical space and outer time or of his status and role within the social system but also his moral and ideological position. To say that this definition of the situation is biographically determined is to say that it has its history; it is the sedimentation of all man's previous experiences, organized in the habitual possessions of his stock of knowledge at hand, and as such his unique possession, given to him and to him alone.[6]

I recognize, of course, that although I share certain elements of my biographical situation with my neighbor he has, to some extent, different concerns, motivations, and goals. Just as he occupies a different spatial sector of the world, so our biographical situations vary. Yet, not only is there similarity between us, there is a shared world we hold in common—the everyday reality within which we have our mundane being. How is it possible for individuals who occupy different places and who have different biographical situations to hold a world in common? The answer, for Schutz, lies in the structure of common-sense experience, which proves to possess certain primordial consonances. There is a "reciprocity of perspectives" which permits individuals to enjoy the "same" world.

Two "idealizations" may be identified in the assumption of reciprocity: that in changing places with my fellow man I will see things in essentially the same way he does (and vice versa) and that in making that switch the differences in our biographical situations are no fundamental hindrance to our experiencing

6. *Ibid.*, p. 9.

essentially the same world.[7] The essentiality achieved in these assumptions is that of typicality, perhaps the most fundamental term in Schutz's philosophical vocabulary. In the reciprocity of perspectives, common sense takes for granted the possibility of the *same* object or event being perceived by individuals in different perspectives. Sameness has a referential orientation in this context: I expect that my fellow man will, under ordinary circumstances, see what I see when I ask him to help me lift a trunk, that when I urge him to shift his carrying position, he will understand that I want a more equitable or effective distribution of the weight, and that when I warn him to watch out for his fingers as we set it down, he will know what it is to get one's fingers caught by a heavy object. The idealizations which comprise the reciprocity of perspectives establish the beginnings of a widening network of typifications through which the social world as a whole is grasped by common-sense men. Schutz writes:

> By the operation of these constructs of common-sense thinking it is assumed that the sector of the world taken for granted by me is also taken for granted by you, my individual fellow-man, even more, that it is taken for granted by "Us." But this "We" does not merely include you and me but "everyone who is one of us," i.e., everyone whose system of relevances is substantially (sufficiently) in conformity with yours and mine. Thus, the general thesis of reciprocal perspectives leads to the apprehension of objects and their aspects actually known by me and potentially known by you as everyone's knowledge. Such knowledge is conceived to be objective and anonymous, i.e., detached from and independent of my and my fellow-man's definition of the situation, our unique biographical circumstances and the actual and potential purposes at hand involved therein.[8]

The shared world, then, is the typified world. But there is also an active translation of experience made by fellow men which brings to the social world the imputation of motives and attitudes. To speak of the typified world is to recognize that man is a typifying being: typified-typifying is the appropriate duality undergirding common sense. This means that the knowledge the individual has of his fellow man is already typified in its minimal form. Encountering a stranger presupposes typifying him as

7. *Ibid.*, pp. 11–12.
8. *Ibid.*, p. 12.

another sentient being, another adult male, another American, another soccer enthusiast. The circumstances in which we are strangers carry with them typified possibilities: it is not unusual to talk to a stranger in the stadium stands but less common to strike up a conversation with him in the public lavatory, despite the fact that the two places may be within fifty feet of each other. The typification of the loose but complex notion of "how to act with strangers" is rooted in the patterned knowledge the individual receives from his parents and teachers, but its organization presupposes an abstractive capacity: given *any* new situation involving strangers, some clue to appropriate behavior may be found in the construction "how to act with strangers." Nothing has been said about whether such a typification is always reliable. Indeed, on certain occasions it may prove to be detrimental. Still, the individual continues to believe in the utility of the recipe, for that belief is an emblem of a primordial commitment to the practicality of experience. It is the belief, as Schutz says, "that we will come to terms with this world for all good and practical purposes if we behave as others behave, if we take for granted what others believe beyond question." [9]

It is assumed by men in daily life that the actions of another person are meaningful and that they signify something to the one who performs them. Following Max Weber, Schutz develops this conception of social action into the postulate of the "subjective interpretation of meaning," the thesis that an act has primary meaning for the actor. In trying to understand man in movement in the everyday world, it is necessary to try to determine what the act means for the actor rather than the observer. The axis of inquiry is turned to the egological realm, where meaning is defined by how the individual interprets his own motives, plans, projects, and ultimately his own situation. The task of the observer is to reconstruct the actor's intentions in terms of what the actor means by his act. There are two large implications for Schutz in the conception of an actor-centered theory of social reality. First, meaning in social encounter is a function of what has been called "*Verstehen*," the interpretive understanding through which the individual comprehends his fellow man. In the simplest terms, *Verstehen* is the means through which men respond to each other's intentions. It is, as Schutz says, "the experiential form of common-sense knowledge

9. Alfred Schutz, *Collected Papers*, II, 157.

of human affairs." [10] Rather than being primarily a methodological tool of the social scientist, *Verstehen* is an achievement of the natural attitude, a naïve accomplishment of mundanity. Schutz maintains that in fact ordinary men respond to each other in typical situations as signifiers of meaning, not perceptual dummies: "The social world is experienced from the outset as a meaningful one. The Other's body is not experienced as an organism but as a fellow-man, its overt behavior not as an occurrence in the space-time of the outer world, but as our fellow-man's action. We normally 'know' what the Other does, for what reason he does it, why he does it at this particular time and in these particular circumstances. That means that we experience our fellow-man's action in terms of his motives and goals." [11] *Verstehen* in these terms is the method, par excellence, of common sense.

The second implication of an actor-centered theory concerns the status of action. In good measure, modern philosophy has taken perception as the paradigmatic problem for analysis in the theory of knowledge. That choice has often been followed by an emphasis on the logic of the natural sciences. Schutz argues for a reversal in philosophical direction: in the domain of the social world, not perception but *action* is the central issue. In trying to make sense of my fellow man's conduct, I ascribe to him a pattern of motivation and intent with regard both to his overt performance and to his covert activity. The last category is especially important. Refraining from action, failing to act, refusing to choose are all modes of action as long as they are purposive decisions, that is, as long as the individual bases his conduct "upon a preconceived project." [12] What appears to the alter ego as my indecision may prove to be a firm commitment to hold to a position for reasons I prefer to keep private for the time being. What I regard as his intemperate haste in demanding change may be an effort to overstate his case in the hope that his more extreme allies will be embarrassed into moderation. The traditional dichotomy of appearance and reality is transcended in this conception of action, for appearance is taken as reality and becomes reality to the extent that the individual interprets the meaning an action has for the actor. Error, miscalculation, misunderstanding, and grievous distortion undoubtedly occur.

10. Schutz, *Collected Papers,* I, 57.
11. *Ibid.*, pp. 55–56.
12. *Ibid.*, p. 19.

There is no categorical assurance that I will succeed in interpreting another's action as he intends it or that he will come to understand me. Much of daily life is built up out of such misconstruction, but the point is that whether or not people do understand each other properly, they live within the frame of their own interpretations. To be sure, common sense allows for the distance between translation and intention: "This is what I make of it" amounts to "*If* I understand him rightly." But the actor's intended meaning is only partially available to his fellow men. More profoundly, it is only partially available to the actor himself. In Simmel's words, which Schutz was fond of quoting, man is doubly fragmented, for he is at once part of general man and part of himself—a fragment of his own possibilities.

This highly condensed survey of Schutz's position brings us back to the problem of application in phenomenology. How has Schutz practiced what Husserl preached? Our answer will consist of displaying a sample of Schutz's analysis, presented in three distinct but overlapping stages: the primary articulation of a phenomenological attitude, the search for essential features of experience, and the exploration of their constitutive history. The theme will be the status of meaning in action, taken as the intentional structure of the social world. What we have already said about Schutz will, I hope, provide some background and support for what must necessarily be a concise account.

The reader of Schutz's works quickly finds a point of view undergirding all of his writings, an unexpressed but evident way of approaching both philosophy and the social world. That coherent standpoint might be called a phenomenological orientation to distinguish it from what we have earlier termed the phenomenological attitude. The latter is a formal aspect of Husserl's method; the former is a style of thought, a way of attending to phenomena as they are initially entertained by the mind. The stress is on subjectivity understood as consciousness intending a world which is alive with meaning for fellow men. It would be an error to translate the emphasis on subjectivity as an idealism which builds the social world out of mental acts, like some gigantic tinker toy put together out of conceptual pieces. For Schutz, man's initial impulse is the correct one: we find ourselves in a world whose primordial sociality is a brute given, something to be understood but not created. The comprehension of the structure of that sociality is the task of the social scientist who is willing to undertake philosophical labor. The way in which such a large effort is approached has everything to do with the way in which it is carried out. Specifically, Schutz maintains that the epistemological status of the reality investigated by most social scientists is ignored as a legitimate professional problem for sociology, social psychology, political science, or economics. The act of severance which in effect says, "Sociologists need not worry themselves about such questions as how knowledge of other selves is possible—that is the job of philosophers!" is a critical piece of academic legislation, one which has the most fundamental consequences for social science. By insisting on a recognition of the assumptions involved in turning away from the study of the reality basic to all experience in the social world, Schutz reintroduces philosophy into the purview of the scientist. The phenomenological orientation discloses itself here not so much by the ensuing analysis of social action as by the insistence on a return to what is basic to science, its grounding in a reality taken for granted both by the learned and the vulgar.

We find ourselves, then, in a world simply given as real to its denizens. Within that world we take for granted the "reality-status" of the objects and events with which we deal in day-to-day fashion. Put another way, the world of daily life is a meaningful one for common sense. How is such meaning constituted? We have already noted the broader and stricter senses of meaning which Schutz employs. Now it is important to turn to the narrower sense of meaning in a more cautious way. The essential point is this: meaning demands a reflective pause of consciousness in which action recollects or imagines its fulfillment as act. The world as flowingly lived in and enjoyed without such reflective realization is bereft of meaning. As Schutz writes, "By no means is the meaning of an experience a new, additional, and secondary experience which is somehow 'attached' to the first. By no means, either, is meaning a *predicate* of an individual experience—a conclusion suggested by such usages as 'having meaning,' 'meaning-bearing,' and 'meaningful.' . . . We will say that *meaning is a certain way of directing one's gaze at an item of one's own experience.* This item is thus 'selected out' and rendered discrete by a reflexive Act. Meaning indicates, therefore, a peculiar attitude on the part of the Ego toward the flow of its own duration." [13] During the ongoing course of my action, I am submerged in what Schutz calls "prephenomenal

13. Schutz, *Phenomenology of the Social World*, p. 42.

experience." [14] There is a "primordial intentionality of spontaneous Activity" [15] which gives to each experience its "my" character, but prephenomenal experience lacks meaning. To locate the
constitutive root of meaningful experience it is necessary to
explore the transcendental structure of time-consciousness.

Earlier, we referred to the reflective moment in which action
comes to be regarded as act, that is, as fulfilled action. In trying
to understand the intended meaning of my fellow man's action, I
impute some motive to his conduct. A jogger may be someone
taking exercise, an athlete in training, a cardiac patient following his doctor's orders, a prankster having fun, a publicist seeking attention, a model being photographed, or a prisoner in
disguise making a getaway. The meaning of his action turns on
what the jogger intends, on the project he is fulfilling. When
that project begins and ends is defined by the jogger's intentional
scheme of reference—something which can only be guessed at
by the observer. The "now" of the jogger refers back to his having
projected in the future perfect tense his accomplished mission,
just as that "now" anticipates the steps which must be accomplished in order for the act to be executed. What is ordinarily
termed "subjective" in the analysis of intention does not apply
here, for there is no distance between the intention and the
meaning of the action. Nothing is "added" to the action in the
intention of the actor. Schutz writes:

> The unity of the action is constituted by the fact that the act al-
> ready exists "in project," which will be realized step by step
> through the action. *The unity of the act is a function of the span
> or breadth of the project.* The unity of the action is, then, *sub-
> jective,* and the problem of inserting the subjective meaning into
> a piece of behavior which supposedly already has *objective* unity
> turns out to be a pseudo-problem. It must now be clear that an
> action is meaningless as action apart from the project which de-
> fines it.[16]

The "now" in which reflection takes place is an aperture
through which the constitutive history of the action or the unity
of the act may be viewed. As the project is being defined, it is
recognized that a series of steps must be taken and fulfilled in
certain ways if the envisioned result is to be gained. The novice

14. *Ibid.,* p. 56.
15. *Ibid.,* p. 57.
16. *Ibid.,* pp. 62–63.

must build up his wind over a period of months before he gets "in shape." He may imagine himself as being able to run five miles if he does a few miles a day for several months. He may also go into training in other ways, including diet and sleep. When he finally does run the five miles, he may, in effect, take that achievement as a unity without retracing the months of daily practice which enabled him to do it. The two sides of the performance are clear: the individual steps on the one hand and the completed result on the other. Taken as aspects of intentional consciousness, those sides may be considered in phenomenological terms as polythetic and monothetic accomplishments. As Schutz points out, "Our mind builds up a thought by single operational steps, but in hindsight it is able to look in a single glance at this whole process and its outcome. We can even go a step further: our knowledge of an object, at a certain given moment, is nothing else than the sediment of previous mental processes by which it has been constituted. It has its own history, and this history of its constitution can be found by questioning it. This is done by turning back from the seemingly ready-made object of our thought to the different activities of our mind in which and by which it has been constituted step by step." [17] The implications of this view are far-reaching not only for the theory of social action but for the entire phenomenology of the social world.

Taken as a monothetic result, the act may be separated from the polythetic steps which produced it. Indeed, in the social world the actor may at times grasp not only the Other but himself in unitary deeds stripped of their constitutive histories. In part, every person is reduced to this circumstance by the essential limitations of his biographical situation: we have precious little knowledge of vast domains of history and of the mundane world, yet we are able to organize our lives intelligently and efficaciously with regard to people we have never met and may never meet, events we never participated in and know only in vague and indirect ways, and laws, regulations, and protocols which we obey and follow without any real comprehension of their derivation, justification, or even their significance. What the individual is able to achieve in grasping a monothetic result unencumbered by its polythetic history is a typification of some aspect of experience. We come full circle to Schutz's theory of

17. Schutz, *Collected Papers,* I, 111.

abstraction. And now we are able to see that typification is possible because the time designations which are bound to the individual steps in the polythetic constitution of meaning may be set aside in attending to the monothetic result. While carrying out my project I have grown older and have encountered a variety of experiences which relate to my action, but in centering my attention on the act proper to that action, I may restrict myself to the typicality of the act, thus suppressing the particular circumstances surrounding the action. Finally, consciousness builds up networks of abstraction—"meaning-contexts," in Schutz's formulation—through which complexes of typification are developed. As he says, "Our whole experience . . . of the world as such is built up in polythetic Acts. We can synthesize these Acts and then think of the resultant synthesis as the experienced . . . , this becoming the unified object of monothetic attention." [18] Thus, typification proves to be the instrument through which social action is effected and the product of the abstractive capacity of inner time-consciousness.

For the greatest part, Schutz's phenomenological work is not carried out through reduction: He enters into transcendental investigations only when it is necessary to explore the nature of inner time-consciousness and promptly quits the reduced sphere as soon as it is possible for him to do so. When he is a guest in the home of transcendental phenomenology, his suitcase remains unpacked. Fully cognizant of his methodological whereabouts, Schutz writes:

The purpose of this work, which is to analyze the phenomenon of meaning in ordinary . . . social life, does not require the achievement of a transcendental knowledge that goes beyond that sphere or a further sojourn within the area of the transcendental-phenomenological reduction. In ordinary social life we are no longer concerned with the constituting phenomena as these are studied within the sphere of the phenomenological reduction. We are concerned only with the phenomena corresponding to them within the natural attitude. Once we have understood by eidetic description the "problem of the inner development . . . of the immanent time sphere," we can apply our conclusions without risk of error to the phenomena of the natural attitude. With one proviso, however: that we now as "phenomenological psychologists" remain "on the ground of inner appearance as the appearance of that which

18. Schutz, *Phenomenology of the Social World*, p. 76.

is peculiar to the psychic." Even then we do not set as our goal a science of the facts of this inner sphere of appearance, but a science of essence. . . . What we are thus seeking is the invariant, unique, a priori structure of the mind, in particular of a society composed of living minds. However, since all analyses carried out within the phenomenological reduction hold true essentially also in psychological introspection, and thus within the sphere of the natural attitude, we shall have to make no revisions whatsoever in our conclusions concerning the internal time-consciousness when we come to apply them to the realm of ordinary social life.[19]

There is, we suggest, an isomorphism which, according to Husserl, exists between findings in the transcendentally reduced domain and the world of the natural attitude. The root of that consonance is hidden in the phenomenological attitude, for when one is engaged in philosophical interrogation in Husserl's sense, he is at the same time attending to the world which men inhabit as mundane creatures. It is a matter of emphasis and level of attention: the same object may be regarded in its straightforward givenness as a real thing or in its reflective presentation as intended. The same object may be viewed as something intersubjectively valid or as something-for-me. And the same object may be perceived as simply *there* or as the sedimented result of an essentially historical process through which consciousness unfolds. For every item discovered in the transcendental domain, a parallel datum may be located in the realm of the natural attitude, provided that it is the essential structure of appearance which is portrayed and not psychological fact. Thus, the phenomenologist never really "leaves" the world of daily life; instead, he holds fast to it in the act of reflecting on it. For Schutz, the *irrealization* of the familiar is a recovery, not an abandonment, of the natural attitude. Following Husserl, he maintains that "in essence all analyses carried out in phenomenological reduction must retain their validation in the correlates of the phenomena investigated within the natural sphere." [20]

The character of Schutz's application of Husserl's method should now be clear. At least for the purposes of an understanding of the social world, the phenomenologist concerns himself with the constitution of the natural attitude. I must leave aside the question of whether Schutz's qualifications on the usefulness

19. *Ibid.*, p. 44. The sentences in quotes are from Husserl.
20. Schutz, *Collected Papers*, I, 139.

of transcendental reduction for his purposes are completely acceptable. The fundamental consideration underlying his arguments is that in its primordial character, sociality is an ineluctable datum of mundane existence and cannot be accounted for in transcendental terms. That does not mean that transcendental phenomenology has no role to play in the analysis of sociality; the point is that a constitutive analysis can reveal but can never establish intersubjectivity.[21] This leaves us with two thoughts. First, it would appear that Schutz's version of phenomenology applied is not only an analysis of the natural attitude but takes place within the natural attitude. If the examination of intentionality in its psychological aspect is equated with the work of empirical psychology, then Schutz is misread. However, a psychology of intentionality in Husserlian terms may be understood as a "constitutive phenomenology of the natural attitude." [22] At this level, being "in the natural attitude" means attending to phenomena as intersubjective unities, shared by men in the taken-for-grantedness of their mundane lives. Second, Schutz's placement of phenomenology at the heart of everyday life invites some reflection on the relationship between philosophy and mundanity. If phenomenology is at work at the epicenter of everydayness, in what sense can it be said to be "applied" at all? Is it not part of the fabric of consciousness, continuous with the reality it seeks to illuminate? In the end, what we are left with is a still larger question: In what sense can philosophy be said to be *applicable*? What *is* application anyway?

In conceptual terms, an application consists in bringing clarity to a particular sphere by the clarity won in a more general domain. The "face-to-face" encounter between individuals described by sociologists ought, in these terms, to be made clearer by the philosophical clarification of intersubjectivity. To "apply" Husserl's theory of the constitution of intersubjectivity ought to result in the illumination of the mundane world. But it should be evident that phenomenology does not deal with the empirics of experience. How, then, does the theoretical come into contact with the factic? What holds here for phenomenology holds equally true, I believe, for all philosophy. In a sense, philosophy cannot be applied at all. Either it is already in touch with the specific segment of the world it seeks to elucidate or it remains

21. See Schutz's *Collected Papers*, III, 82.
22. Schutz, *Collected Papers*, I, 132.

fugitive to experience in its concrete givenness. The clarification of the particular by the general—the notion of application I am advancing here—might serve as a description of the task of philosophy, provided that the "particular" at issue is understood as a restricted portion of experience rather than an actualization or instantiation of universal types. There is a difference in the relationship between a theory and some problem to which it may be applied and a philosophy and some aspect of experience which it seeks to clarify. In the former case, what counts as a problem is already specified by the terms of the theory; in the latter case, the field for inquiry is a qualitative continuum with no distance between what is to be accounted for and the intellectual region within which the accounting is attempted.

In the application of theory to social reality, the philosophic dimension of actuality shows itself. There, what counts as a problem may be predetermined by the nature of the theory, but the subject matter is already self-defined by the choices human beings have made in their interpretation of experience. Through his preinterpretation of mundane reality, the individual accomplishes what might be called a "protophilosophical" construction of experience. In the naïve constitution of everydayness, each of us builds a schema through which the elements of his world become meaningful. The task of a theory is to account for what common sense has already intended. This apportionment of work suggests a relationship between explanation and intention which can be stated outside of a phenomenological position. Von Wright says:

> A teleological explanation of action is normally preceded by an act of intentionalist *understanding* of some behavioral data.
> One can distinguish "layers" or "orders" of such acts of understanding. For example: I see crowds of people in the street moving in the same direction, shouting things in unison, some waving flags, *etc.* What *is* it that is going on? I have already understood the "elements" of what I see intentionalistically. The people are "themselves" moving and not being swept away by a wind or torrent. They are shouting—and this is to say more than that sounds emanate from their throats. But the "whole" which I observe is not yet clear to me. Is this a demonstration? Or is it perhaps a folk festival or a religious procession that I am witnessing? [23]

23. Georg Henrik von Wright, *Explanation and Understanding* (Ithaca: Cornell University Press, 1971), p. 132.

The organization of experience in mundane terms is a meaningful achievement whose sources and structure the philosopher tries to uncover. From a phenomenological standpoint, it might be said that what von Wright has pointed to, in stressing the intentionalist dimension of experience, is the philosophical material for analysis: the larger framework of analysis turns toward the more circumscribed elements and seeks their clarification. But this is to say that philosophy cannot be applied to anything outside itself because its universe of discourse is coextensive with its subject matter. Most bluntly: philosophy has no "outside." This view is consistent, I think, with a defense of more traditional assessments of the relationship between reflection and daily life. Philosophy is not divorced from the mundane world, nor does philosophy swallow up common sense. Rather, philosophy is disclosed as being immanent to the world it reflects on and as being an achievement of the very world it examines. Philosophy, one is tempted to suggest, is sedimented in experience: the clarity which philosophy brings is the hidden possibility of opaque reality, seized in its ongoing tumble as everydayness. The shock which wrenches man out of the natural attitude into philosophical awareness is an intramundane event. *Wonder*, phenomenologically interpreted, is the recognition that the restricted field of my own experience is continuous with the whole of reality, that my own immediacy is, in its infrastructure, amenable to universal analysis, and that my own reality has a rational order, a logos. The product of wonder in this sense is the realization that the ordinary assumption of the applicability of philosophy involves a misconstruction of its nature. That philosophy cannot move beyond itself, that it is confined to its own sphere, that it is caught in a "philosophocentric" predicament—these are imperfect formulations. It is because philosophy cannot transcend itself that it has universal "applicability" or, to say the same thing differently, it is because philosophy cannot be "applied" at all that it proves to be so effective an instrument for the clarification of experience.

If philosophy is thought of as in-the-world, then the natural attitude must reflect, in some way, the presence of man in a reality suffused with his own interpretations and responses. In fact, Husserl does go beyond his initial formulation of the natural attitude and comes to stress the texture of man's naïve orientation in the world in its distinctively social dimension: believing in the world means holding fast to the immediacy of fellow men, the constructions *they* place upon experience, the vital glance whose source is not an eye but an intelligence. It is necessary to distinguish between the natural and the "naturalistic" attitude.[24] The individual is not only in a physical world of bodies but in a personalistic world of selves. The body is always in a position which can be described by others in purely formal terms (standing, sitting, kneeling, etc.), but I encounter the body of the Other in terms of his action: standing in a vigil, sitting at a conference, kneeling in genuflection. Here, there are no prearranged rules for description, in contrast to the pathologist who is able to fix his descriptions in an autopsy report by virtue of the acceptance of the "anatomical position."[25] I find the Other's body in the course of his action, as a feature of the person, not the organism. As Husserl remarks, the Other is encountered as someone who knows something of his surroundings, who is aware of his fellow men and of the common reality they share. Moreover, the surrounding world is comprised of the reality of objects which have distinctive use, utensils which are inherently functional, and a great array of social, cultural, legal, and religious structures and values which transcend mere "things" and constitute the vital surroundings of a person. Finally, others are perceived not only as persons but as persons who are members of a social order, of communities, and associations which retain their status even though the individual members change.[26]

To the extent that the "naturalistic" attitude is followed, the world of everyday life is viewed in what is often called "objective" terms: descriptions are made from the standpoint of "the observer." In actual life, however, descriptions and reports are *mine* or *yours*, are the outcome of involvement in committed contexts of action in which positions are taken, emotional responses elicited, and directions are signaled by desire, refusal, and ambivalence. The position of observer is only one among many stances in mundane experience. As a participator, the

24. See Edmund Husserl, *Ideen*, Vol. II: *Phänomenologische Untersuchungen zur Konstitution*, p. 180 ff.

25. "The traditional anatomical position, which has long been agreed upon, places the body in the erect posture with the feet together, the arms hanging at the side, and the thumbs pointing away from the body" (Henry Gray, *Anatomy of the Human Body*, ed. Charles Mayo Goss [Philadelphia: Lea and Febiger, 1966], p. 2).

26. See Husserl, *Ideen*, II, 182 ff.

individual apprehends his fellow men as with him or against him, as supports or obstacles. The question is whether the natural attitude is able to reflect the urgency of human action and complicity as the stage on which persons act. The point of introducing the distinction between the naturalistic and natural attitudes is to report Husserl's recognition that his initial discussion of the natural attitude had opened up a deeper theme for analysis than was apparent. Followed to its innermost resources, the natural attitude proves to be the guide to the realm of man's immediate experience as a being in the midst of everydayness. There remains the truth of the naturalistic attitude, of man as a being in nature, but the point of access to that truth is man's interpretation of nature within the limits of his own life. So too with the social world: the individual grasps the meaning of the social scientist's reports within an essentially naïve schematism. There is no question here of choice between the two realms. Rather, Husserl's thesis is that the truth of the observer is grounded in the truth of the participant. To avoid any misunderstanding, let it be said at once that "grounding" in this context refers to the history of interpretation rather than to the logic of inquiry. The truth of science is not contingent on common sense, but in the course of daily life that truth is interpreted through mundane categories.

The recovery of the full meaning of the natural attitude leads back to the world which the philosopher seeks to understand. Our discussion of application ends with the mundane sphere first approached in the presentation of the phenomenological attitude and explored in the theory of intentional consciousness. The simplest way to see the relationship between consciousness and mundanity is to grasp them as a unity which may be examined in diverse ways. That unity of consciousness and world means that anything discernible in phenomenological reduction is "already" sedimented in naïve experience. We have been struggling with the explanation of phenomenological origin; once again we come up against its opaque belligerence. What does "already" mean when we speak of sedimentation? Perhaps our account of application offers a new way of restating the issue.

What the individual *as person* apprehends in the natural attitude is the surface aspect of the intentional activity of his fellow men. That surface is seized as leading back to the persons who are livingly aware of *their* surroundings, including *their* fellow men grasped as persons. Intending others in the naïveté of everydayness, I intend them as cointending me. The procedure of phenomenological reduction renders that intending and cointending thematic to reflection. At the same time, reduction reveals the progression in consciousness through which experience comes to attain its perceptual form at a given moment for ego and alter ego. With the enactment of reduction the "object" of application and the "subject" undertaking analysis are brought to an integral focus: the discipline of intentional consciousness in its noetic aspect is philosophy; in its noematic aspect, intentionality is the "object matter" of philosophy. Taken together, the integral meaning of intentionality is a "transcendental clue" [27] to the history of the mundane world as a reality lived by men in unreflective simplicity. The realm of experiential immediacy from which all interpretation derives is what Husserl calls the "life-world." And with the recognition of the life-world as a fundamental theme for phenomenological philosophy there comes the reengagement of the philosopher with the everydayness he seeks to reconstruct. Returned to his situation as a person together with other persons, he finds himself in a world made luminous by an interior urgency: the philosopher becomes the bridge between the solitude of radical reflection and the communality of human action.

27. See Edmund Husserl, *Cartesian Meditations,* p. 50 ff.

7 / The Life-World

THE PRISONERS in Plato's Cave were chained to illusion and deceit; only by being led out into the openness of truth could they recognize as false the shadows which passed as reality. It would seem that the world of everyday life is charged with error and distortion. From what vantage point in phenomenological terms can the truth of mundane existence be grasped? Is it necessary to transcend the life-world in order to comprehend it? Plato's prisoners were dazzled by the sunlight when they emerged from captivity. When they returned to take their seats in the Cave, their eyes were filled with darkness. On this account, it would seem that the ascent to truth demands overcoming, ridding oneself of one's prior condition of epistemic servitude, just as the descent suggests a break between two worlds in which the knower relinquishes his right to return to the world of shadows and rejoin his fellow prisoners. I think that the interesting part of the story involves the interval between being unchained and leaving the Cave. Did the prisoner have a chance to rub his neck and legs? Rather than being joyfully liberated, he is forced to stand up and move toward the light—painful commands. The account reads a bit like a military occupation in which an innocent jailed by one regime is placed under house arrest by another. Ultimately, instead of liberation, the prisoner is granted freedom, something quite different and, in its own way, devastating. But what does he take with him from his experience in the Cave? What are his memories and associations? Even if what he perceived there was deceptive, could not his recollection of what he saw and heard be veridical? And even if the community of prisoners were sharing a communal lie, would not their imaginings be authentic? What Plato discounts, Husserl redeems.

In the simplest terms, the life-world comprises the sum of man's involvement in everyday affairs: his knowledge, interpretation, response, and organization of his experience. The unsophisticated nature of much of common sense is a strong characteristic—a positive one—of daily life, but it would be a serious mistake to assume that what is naïve is necessarily empty or stupid. A number of different meanings of the naïve must be distinguished. First, the naïve is set over and against the technical. Ordinary men can make good use of what they do not understand: we all operate machines or use conveyances whose mechanics we don't fully understand; we depend on services and professional personnel whose procedures are most often strange and even incomprehensible to us; we receive and spend money with only a fragmentary grasp of the principles of finance. Second, the naïve may be thought of as the partial in contrast with the total: not only does the individual have a limited understanding of most segments of the world, but his view of the world is itself fragmentary. Within his own enclave of existence, each person has a more or less rough idea of what "the world" is like. Much of it remains not only distant but obscure. Third, the naïve is personal rather than public: within the round of the individual's daily routine, he finds and defines what is "normal" for him, what is "familiar," and also what is "strange." There is no point in time when an elder takes a child aside to tell him the facts of daily life, nor is there a manual for the exposition of the taken for granted. So fundamental is the realm of the naïve that it is not even assumed in any self-conscious fashion that each person will recognize the familiar when he sees it. Presupposed in the psychology of learning is the root assumption that what makes common sense common is its primordial privacy.

Taking-for-granted, naïveté, unsophistication are complex and rich modes of mundanity. This may be taken in two ways: there is a detailed logic of the realm of the naïve and there is an experiential density in everydayness which commands philosophical respect. The former, it would seem, does not differ in kind from the traditional fields of inquiry pursued by natural science; the latter, apparently, is an obdurateness which will dissolve as greater clarity is achieved in the special disciplines—

psychology, anthropology, sociology. Husserl takes a distinctively different approach to these matters, one which emphasizes the grounding of objective science in the very life-world to be analyzed. For him, there is a prescientific realm of experience from which and through which everyday activity arises. Although prescientific experience must be elucidated in rigorous terms, the only "science" which can qualify for that task is one which has clarified its own roots. Husserl writes: "There has never been a scientific inquiry into the way in which the life-world constantly functions as subsoil, into how its manifold prelogical validities act as grounds for the logical ones, for theoretical truths. And perhaps the scientific discipline which this life-world as such, in its universality, requires is a peculiar one, one which is precisely not objective and logical but which, as the ultimately grounding one, is not inferior but superior in value."[1]

The way into an examination of the structure of the life-world comes for Husserl by way of phenomenological reduction. Although somewhat different terminology is used in his *Crisis*, Husserl is concerned with what we have already discussed as epochē and reduction. In the earlier discussion the emphasis was on the prejudicial impact of the natural attitude; in the treatment of the life-world, the focus is on the bracketing of the operation and results of the objective sciences. The first step toward a phenomenology of the life-world requires an epochē of objective science. Husserl writes:

Clearly required before everything else is the epochē in respect to all objective sciences. This means not merely an abstraction from them, such as an imaginary transformation, in thought, of present human existence, such that no science appeared in the picture. What is meant is rather an epochē of all participation in the cognitions of the objective sciences, an epochē of any critical position-taking which is interested in their truth or falsity, even any position on their guiding idea of an objective knowledge of the world. In short, we carry out an epochē in regard to all objective theoretical interests, all aims and activities belonging to us as objective scientists or even simply as ordinary people desirous of this kind of knowledge.[2]

1. Edmund Husserl, *The Crisis of European Sciences and Transcendental Phenomenology*, p. 124.
2. *Ibid.*, p. 135.

The goal is to free the phenomenologist from a perspective which is implicitly and historically dominated by the results of the objective sciences. The question is, What was the world like prior to being interpreted by the scientific outlook? How is it possible to regain the *originary* constitution of the world by a consciousness viewed in its own habitat? The step beyond the epochē of objective science leads to a viewing of the pregivenness of the life-world: its intentional meaning for man in his becoming in the mundane world. The primacy of interpretation is placed on the relationship between the object viewed objectively and the constitution of that viewing in the subjectivity of man in the life-world. What sense does the individual make of objectivity? That question, pursued to its transcendental sources, is thematic to the life-world. In order to establish himself on the proper terrain for appreciating that kind of question, the inquirer must, according to Husserl, attempt a "universal epochē" through which the grounding of the life-world will become manifest and available for elucidation. Speaking of the transcendental epochē, the key to phenomenological reduction, Husserl writes:

> Through the epochē a new way of experiencing, of thinking, of theorizing, is opened to the philosopher; here, situated *above* his own natural being and *above* the natural world, he loses nothing of their being and their objective truths and likewise nothing at all of the spiritual acquisitions of his world-life or those of the whole historical communal life; he simply forbids himself—as a philosopher, in the uniqueness of his direction of interest—to continue the whole natural performance of his world-life; that is, he forbids himself to ask questions which rest upon the ground of the world at hand, questions of being, questions of value, practical questions, questions about being or not-being, about being valuable, being useful, being beautiful, being good, etc. All natural interests are put out of play. But the world, exactly as it was for me earlier and still is, as my world, our world, humanity's world, having validity in its various subjective ways, has not disappeared; it is just that, during the consistently carried-out epochē, it is under our gaze purely as the correlate of the subjectivity which gives it ontic meaning, through whose validities the world "is" at all.[3]

Illustrating Husserl's application of reduction to the life-world is not an easy task. But rather than paraphrase him, I will try to provide a fairly lengthy discussion of my own. I hope that

3. *Ibid.*, p. 152.

what may be gained in clarity will not be lost through inexactitude. The truth is that Husserl's own formulations are especially thick and call for sympathetic but, perhaps, independent reformulation. From time to time, I shall quote from the *Crisis*, but for the most part I shall follow my own path in trying to explain and exemplify what I think Husserl means by the phenomenological reconstruction of the life-world.

Familiarity is the primary characteristic of everyday life. Let us accept that statement for the moment as a pledge to be redeemed. Rather than "proving" that the claim is true or defending its general warranty, it is more suggestive for our present purposes to see what familiarity might mean in the context of phenomenology. Of course, we understand what the word means in ordinary terms: the familiar is what is intimately known. More basically, however, there is an experiential dimension to familiarity which brings the theme closer to the region of the life-world. In our everydayness we find ourselves again and again in familiar surroundings, in relationship to people we know intimately or well, engaged in pursuits which are typical to our lives, and going through the patterned routines of waking life and of sleep. In being aware of the familiar world about us, we recognize each new experience as both similar to what we have perceived in the past and continuous with the quality of past experience. At this level, the natural attitude functions as a conduit for the familiar: as far back as we can remember, events have been witnessed as stemming from and as being continuous with "ordinary" life. Now in epochē I turn toward that traditional "ordinariness" and, in egological terms, look to its organization.

I begin with the experiencing of a familiar object: a box of matches. In my perceiving the box, I attend to its presentative aspect. Now I see it from this perspective, its label showing, its blue side manifest. It is obvious that only a portion of the total box is seen from this angle, but if I restrict myself to my seeing of the box now, that knowledge of its partial givenness does not arise. Yet my perceptual glance falls on this *side* of the box, not on a blue surface alone. Moreover, each renewal of my glance goes toward the same side, toward *the* surface. Changing my location or that of the box, I continue to see *it* as the selfsame entity and I continue to perceive it throughout my many glances. In the multitude of seeings a dominant theme recurs: *the* surface is intended in each glance. Thus, "the pure thing seen, what is visible 'of' the thing, is first of all a surface, and in the changing course of seeing I see it now from this 'side,' now from that, continuously perceiving it from ever differing sides. But in them *the* surface exhibits itself to me in a continuous synthesis; each side is for consciousness a manner of exhibition *of* it." [4] But surely there is something amiss in perception in regarding "side-perception" as representing an adequate account of my initial seeing of the box. After all, it is the box I see, not some side. In terms of a philosophical theory of knowledge it would be possible to speak of the box as a construction out of sense data, but from the standpoint of the life-world a different situation exists. What is involved in the naïve perception of the object? The answer, phenomenologically speaking, is that, in perceiving the box, I intend it as an integral object, a sided something whose unity transcends my actual or virtual glance: "In seeing I always 'mean' it with all the sides which are in no way given to me, not even in the form of intuitive, anticipatory presentifications." [5]

From the vantage point of the "reality" of the box of matches, individual perceptions may or may not reveal what is "there": a light wood rectangle about two inches by one and one-half inches by one-half inch, containing an inner cardboard drawer of only slightly smaller dimensions designed to hold about thirty-five wooden matches. If perception is measured and judged by the criterion of the box as it "really is," then seeing the "same" surface can only mean seeing "the surface of the box." From the vantage point of the life-world, the surface-as-meant refers to a distinctively subjective process in which the box as naïvely perceived is constituted as a "something-there-for-anyone." The difference between the objective and subjective standpoints at issue here is the clue to the phenomenologist's interest in the life-world. In straightforward perception I grasp the object as simply "itself-there," but in a reflective moment I turn toward that "itself-there" perception as a performance or achievement of naïve consciousness. I attend to *"how* an object . . . exhibits itself as being and being-such." [6] A central factor in the unraveling of the "how" is the temporal continuity it presupposes. In attending to the box, I continue to perceive it over the span of a few minutes. The glances of a few seconds ago merge with

4. *Ibid.*, pp. 157–58.
5. *Ibid.*, p. 158.
6. *Ibid.*, p. 159.

my immediate perception and shade toward the expectancy of the box as expected to be there and to be the same a few seconds from now. I do not, strictly speaking, perceive the box as it was earlier or as it will be in the future, yet my perceiving is built upon earlier perceptions and looks toward imagined possibilities. Traditional theories of association might account for the psychological connections between present perception and its past and future connections. Such an analysis would be tied to what in fact the mind remembers and imagines and to its ways of remembering and imagining. In phenomenological terms, the problem is a different one: How can we account for the history of an intending, part of whose formative character consists in accepting and bearing the weight of its sedimented past and projected future in the temporal condensation of the present? Husserl writes:

> Perception is related only to the *present*. But this present is always meant as having an endless *past* behind it and an open *future* before it. We soon see that we need the intentional analysis of recollection as the original manner of being conscious of the past; but we also see that such an analysis presupposes in principle that of perception, since memory, curiously enough, implies having-perceived. If we consider perception abstractly, by itself, we find its intentional accomplishment to be presentation, making something present: the object gives itself as "there," originally there, present. But in this presence, as that of an extended and enduring object, lies a continuity of what I am still conscious of, what has flowed away and is no longer intuited at all, a continuity of "retentions"—and, in the other direction, a continuity of "protentions." [7]

Some of the elements of familiarity now begin to come into focus. The box is, within the life-world, a meant unity whose roots go back to the ground of temporality. Perceiving the box in subjective terms means bringing together in a continual intentive process the past intendings of objects in general and, more especially, objects of that kind. The bringing together at issue is not a cumulative act but a regenerative procedure in which, having intended objects and objects "like this one" in the past (as well as having projected their likely continuation), I find reflected the continuity of consciousness. Moreover, intending the box as a unity means intending it as a unity for my fellow

7. *Ibid.*, p. 160.

men as well as for me. For *them,* it will be perceived as a familiar object; for *them,* it will be available again and again as the same object. In the language we have appealed to earlier, it is through polythetic acts that the intentive process is built up, but it is through monothetic acts that meant unities may be grasped. The familiarity of sameness in the experience of objects consists in the capacity of consciousness to set aside the history of polythetic acts in perception in favor of attending to monothetic results.

The experience of objects is not the whole of reality, and in the domain of the life-world it is especially important to recognize that the paradigms of classical epistemology meet their limits. Husserl, like many philosophers before him, centers much of his discussion about the perception of objects; unlike his predecessors, however, he also turns to issues which concern the fundamental historical and cultural horizons in which the everyday life is lived. The world in which the matchbox is perceived is no less familiar than the box itself. Although that familiarity is most often unnoticed, there are times when experience undergoes an implosion of some order: a new way of regarding the familiar object leads to a singular angle of perception with regard to an experiential backdrop. The matchbox is one of the pitiful possessions found in the investigation of the death of a twelve-year-old heroin addict. The matches were used in the preparation of his heroin injections. A matchbox may be discovered in the possession of a spy. In place of one layer of matches there is a tiny transmitting set hidden in the bottom. An ordinary box may turn up in a museum exhibition as part of a historical collection, as an item representing an artifact of daily life in our time. Or it may appear as part of a still life. To the extent that we come to reflect on the object, see it in a new way, we *may* also come to reflect on the world within which the object is manifest in its sudden disclosure: the world of addicts leads back to the "ordinary" world; the world of spies to "normal" routine; the museum show to mundanity as "exhibitable"; the still life to the aesthetically bracketable world. If the transformation in attitude occurs, the taken-for-granted world becomes, momentarily at least, viewable *as* world. But it is clear that what has occasioned the change in attitude is not so much the matchbox as an object as its placement in some unusual horizon of the historical and cultural world. To explore the altered horizon it is necessary to move beyond the model of the perceptual object.

We have spoken of the shift from object naïvely perceived to world-horizon as occasioning at certain times an implosion of experience: the world becomes strange, familiarity is eclipsed. It might be helpful to examine this alteration more closely. A field for illustration which lends itself readily to discussion in this context is psychiatry. It often happens that in mental illness the "world" of the disturbed person undergoes an epistemological upheaval in which what has previously been accepted as real now assumes a bizarre character. But before anything further is said about mental illness, it should be pointed out that any discussion of the subject will have to acknowledge at least three spheres of experience: the disturbed person's world, the psychiatrist's model of that world, and the world of ordinary daily life in which both the disturbed and the undisturbed encounter each other. The life-world, then, is inhabited by all parties to the discussion of pathology. Three individuals need to be studied: the disturbed person, the analyst of disturbance, and the fellow man who shares responsibility for the ill and the well. Most often, the signs of illness are recognized not by psychiatrists but by fellow men—relatives, friends, associates. Without expert knowledge or even any practical experience in such matters, an individual may see that someone he is in touch with is acting in a fundamentally strange way. This is not to say that all mental illness displays itself in overt form, nor is it to say that pathological behavior is always recognized by fellow men. The sole point is that most people who go to or are taken to psychiatrists are interviewed by them after signs of illness or disturbance are perceived in the ordinary world by ordinary men, including the mentally ill. This calls for some further comment.

There are few of us whose actions and style of being are absolutely uniform at all times. To be human is to act in unusual ways, at least at certain times. A hysterical person is not deemed insane: there are many circumstances which could explain hysteria in a normal individual. So, too, we acknowledge the variance in types of human beings. A sharp, acid, biting, contentious, quarrelsome curmudgeon may be unpleasant to have around and to have to deal with, but he is hardly certifiable as insane. For a stranger, such behavior may seem incredible; for an intimate, it is normal for him or for "people like that." It may indeed be the case that a change takes place in the man: he goes from being ordinarily impossible to everyone to being persistently and unforgivably cruel to one person, an individual who is himself damaged and defenseless. The difference in behavior may completely escape a casual observer, but for those within the microcosm of the home or the office the change may be qualitative and profound. Without the context of the normal as defined by the members of the microcosm, the "change" cannot be comprehended at all—nor, for that matter, can the actors on the scene be understood in the course of their daily lives. Without context, understanding becomes distanced into anonymity.

Those who notice the change in the individual continue to share his world as a life-world. Arrangements for work, eating, and other routine activities must be allowed for. And, even in extreme cases of psychosis, the mentally ill person may also become physically ill. Whatever adjustments are made in the life of the ill man, he must continue to function as a member of the life-world, however aberrant and abortive that functioning may be. To get him to a psychiatrist or to a clinic, it is necessary to accompany him by foot, by car, or by ambulance. It is necessary to arrive at an appointed hour, to complete forms, and to be seated in some waiting area or to be taken to an office, a hospital room, or a ward. In short, whatever routine of ordinary existence has been abandoned in illness, other mundane procedures are introduced. Patient, psychiatrist, and fellow man all share in the regularities of the life-world, though these may be distorted or destroyed in part (and in different ways) for all of them. To the patient's interpretation of his own situation and circumstances must be added the constructions placed upon him by others, including his doctor and family. What has happened in illness is that, in some deep and fugitive way, the psychotic has become strange in the everydayness of the world. That strangeness may throw the "normal" structure of experience into relief. At least, it may cast some oblique reflection on a surface of reality otherwise unnoticed and conceptually neglected. Erwin W. Straus writes:

> We encounter the mental patient as a stranger in our everyday-life world (*Lebenswelt*, in Husserl's terminology). Whatever theories we may offer to explain psychotic behavior—whether we accept the thesis that mental diseases are brain diseases or search for a conflict between ego and id, ego and reality, and ego and superego—the frame of reference from which we start and to which we return is the structure of the everyday-life world. When Freud speaks about a break with reality, he refers to the reality

familiar and common to all of us—the reality of so-called naïve realism. This is the same for the learned and the illiterate, for the rich and the poor, for Lumumba and Hammarskjöld. Its characteristics are not taught in school. We live it, enact it, and respond to it, but we do not know it. Indeed, the failure of the mental patient to conform may cause us to stop and think about the *Lebenswelt*. Psychoses are, so to speak, basic experiments arranged by nature; the clinical wards are the natural laboratories where we begin to wonder about the structure of the *Lebenswelt*. We realize that, in order to account for its breakdown, we have to study its norm first. We suddenly notice that we are beginners in a field where we deemed ourselves masters.[8]

In the strangeness of mental illness, the familiarity of ordinary experience comes, fleetingly at least, into relief. It is somewhat like passing a grisly accident on the highway. For a little time afterward, one may drive more cautiously and appreciate not being the one wrecked and slaughtered. And, for at least a few seconds, a chill may penetrate the flow of normality—an ague of the life-world. Usually, the mood is soon thrown off, the bloody scene forgotten, and the tempo of everydayness picked up again. Apart from such dramatic incidents, however, strangeness penetrates familiarity as the potential debilitation of the structure of the life-world. If familiarity is the primary characteristic of everyday life, strangeness is the immanent threat of the loss of the familiar—an estrangement of man from taken-for-grantedness of any kind.[9] Moving back to our earlier discussion of the perception of the object, we may say that the intentional assumption that it is always possible, under ordinary circumstances, to return to the *same* thing again and again is fraught with an unspoken cognitive peril: suppose such a return is denied by consciousness. Suppose the ego is stripped of its capacity to grasp in a single act the plurality of its piecemeal perceptions. We would be left with a polythetic miscellany of consciousness. In effect, the primordial abstractive power of consciousness would be lost or at least flawed. What Husserl spoke of as the constitutive sources of continuity and repetition (the idealizations of "and so on" and "I can again") would be negated or partially paralyzed. In sum, the dynamic of mundane experience would be immobilized and the life-world shattered

8. Erwin W. Straus, *Phenomenological Psychology*, pp. 256–57.
9. See Maurice Natanson, "Philosophy and Psychiatry," in *Psychiatry and Philosophy*, ed. Maurice Natanson.

into incoherence. The threat, of course, is purely internal to consciousness. It is generated by the same forces that assure the stability of the world. There is in the intimacy of the strange the assurance that familiarity is recoverable. Only in death is that intimacy challenged. Paradoxically, perhaps, death might be considered the irrevocable loss of familiarity through the final negation of the strange.

Within the egological aspect of the familiar there is a communal reference. The individual living naïvely in the life-world "accepts" that world as *ours*. Without reflection or examination, he tacitly knows that his is a shared reality. As Husserl says,

> Each individual "knows" himself to be living within the horizon of his fellow human beings, with whom he can enter into sometimes actual, sometimes potential contact, as they also can do (as he likewise knows) in actual and potential living together. He knows that he and his fellows, in their actual contact, are related to the same experienced things in such a way that each individual has different aspects, different sides, perspectives, etc., of them but that in each case these are taken from the same total system of multiplicities of which each individual is constantly conscious (in the actual experience of the same thing) as the horizon of possible experience of this thing.[10]

In terms of prepredicative experience, the individual "knows" that what is naïvely there for him is also naïvely there for his fellow men. In communal gatherings of any kind—political rallies, concerts, receptions, picnics, fire drills—the same time structure is accepted as binding: the concert is scheduled to begin at eight o'clock. And it is assumed, *known,* that the quartet is the same quartet whether one is seated in one part of the room or another. In order to leave the concert hall, it is necessary to merge with the crowd, make way for some, step alongside others, and so find one's way out. The habitualities of past experience have *their* constitutive history, and so it won't do to speak of conditioning here. Within the routine of the life-world, the familiarity of situation and movement is known without mediation. It is not the proof of that immediacy which is at issue here but its phenomenological foundations. As we shall see, in the career of the familiar a certain dimension of history comes into view.

10. Husserl, *Crisis,* p. 164.

The life-world familiar to any individual exists at some time in history, and that means that any discussion of perception of objects or situational relevances implicitly carries with it some contextual reference to the age, the times, or the public circumstances of events. To begin with, the content of a life-world varies from period to period in history as well as from culture to culture at any time. What is taken as the normal current of everyday life may be qualitatively different, depending on war, depression, civil strife, or such religious beliefs as chiliasm. The variation in content is a function of a specific people in a given historical moment. But underlying content is a formal network of a priori conditions which are invariant for any actualized or possible life-world; they include space and time elements as defined by the subjectivity of human beings within daily life rather than the determinations of mathematicians, and they include the interpretation of causation as grasped by participants in the everyday world rather than by scientific observers. In a way, the phenomenologist is less interested in the examination of any actual life-world than he is in the possible structure of imaginable life-worlds. The "irrealization" of the particular in the eidetic attitude is mirrored in the irrealization of the life-world. As Aron Gurwitsch points out, "Starting from any actual *Lebenswelt*, we may freely vary it in imagination and thus contrive varieties of possible *Lebenswelten* merely as possible, with regard to which the question of their historical actuality is immaterial. The objective of this procedure is to disclose what essentially and necessarily pertains to a *Lebenswelt* as such, considered merely as to its possibility." [11] Not the history of the life-world but the constitution of history for the invariant structure of the life-world is the phenomenologist's theme. The historical circumstances in which particular events emerge at any time are taken as occasions for inquiring back into their developmental sources—into their origins.

The historical horizon of the life-world is of decisive importance. Here we come to a parallel of sorts between the history of the ego and the history of society. The phenomenological genesis of the ego, which Husserl has traced out through his analysis of intentionality, is characterized by a movement toward sociality. From the resources of the transcendental ego, the world

11. Aron Gurwitsch, *Studies in Phenomenology and Psychology*, p. 426.

of man with fellow men comes to be constituted. At the same time, however, there is the mundane history of societies in which concrete, actualized life-worlds have existed and continue to exist. From the specificity of men in action in daily life, it is possible to move back to the conditions which make possible their experience-of their surrounding world as they perceive it and interpret it. Such a regression is the province of a phenomenology of the life-world and may be considered the complement to constitutive phenomenology. In one direction we move from the ego to its world; in the other direction we travel from the world to the ego. The subjective aspect of history—the experiential dimension—is sometimes referred to as "historicity." If we adopt that language, it is possible to restate matters in this way: A phenomenology of the life-world is an effort to account for the historicity sedimented in the career of consciousness. At any time that we attend to man in the midst of his everyday routine, we take for granted the historical background of his institutions, associations, and even his language. All of his involvements presuppose historical placement and context. A very brief excursus into the contextual character of language may illustrate our point.

The phrase "in the life" may signify little on its own. "In the life of what?" the listener or reader may ask. It would be possible, of course, to suggest dozens of possible continuations. But suppose the phrase is taken on its own. At least two interpretations are possible if we supply an appropriate historical and social context. They turn out to be rather different. A woman who is said to be "in the life" is a prostitute. A meeting which is said to be "in the life" is a successful Quaker religious gathering for worship. The words of the phrase on their own would seem to be neutral; the context decides everything. In some instances, it is nearly impossible to understand what is being said without contextual guidance. What could one make of the following language taken by itself: "the courage of self-denial shown by a bishop." The natural tendency would be to suppose we were being referred to a martyr of the church. In fact, this bishop at the time of his martyrdom was posted at QKt2.[12] Words on their own are fragments of their possibilities. Or to put the case differently, words

12. A. Niemzowitsch, *The Praxis of My System: A Text-Book on Practical Chess,* trans. J. Du Mont (London: Printing-Craft, 1936), p. 310.

are never on their own. They carry with them the legends and intimations of their historical circumstances and development. The perceptual world and the historical world interpenetrate and suffuse each other: language becomes a parsing of the familiar. For all of the contemporary interest in language, something of its historical power has been missed, a power more nearly caught in the rhetoric of an earlier generation. Francis March writes: "The definition is an idea, a solid intellectual center; the emblems which have been felt with it rise in memory with it, and give it an aureole, a halo, a nimbus, a glory, spheres of radiance. A word is thus a living power, with an individuality embodied in its root and affixes. It has a history; it has a character derived from its history." [13]

Husserl's thesis that the individual "knows" himself to be living within the horizon of his fellow men now takes on an added character: that "knowing" is historically inflected. Within the life-world, I expect my contemporaries to share an awareness of a more or less common past, to recognize the social world as an achievement rather than a spontaneous irruption, and to assume that I too regard social reality as a historical product. Such expectations are tacitly present in the individual's performance on the social scene; they are nonetheless consequential and efficacious in the ordering of experience. In their typified expression they comprise the force of the familiar. In this way, we come at last to a question which has trailed the discussion: What is the relationship between typification and familiarity? For the most part, we might say that typification is the generic term for an abstractive process one of whose central accomplishments is the experience of the familiar. I take typification to be the broader term, then, and I understand familiarity as one of its species. In this case, however, the species is widely distributed, for in the results of typification I am able to recognize the boundaries of my world: even the strange is typically constituted and appropriated as a limit of the familiar. In practice, the terms "typification" and "familiarity" may be more loosely applied, so that the life-world is taken both as typical and as familiar. There is some point to holding to a stricter utilization of the language of typification and familiarity, at least at certain

13. Francis A. March, Foreword to *A Thesaurus Dictionary of the English Language,* ed. Francis Andrew March and Francis Andrew March, Jr. (Philadelphia: Historical Publishing Co., 1902).

times in analysis, especially when distinctions are called for between the horizon of world as such and the typified objects which appear within that horizon.[14] In any case, the difference between the two should not be overemphasized; their relationship is certainly an intimate one.

The discovery of familiarity as a primordial feature of the life-world carries with it some implications for philosophy itself. The recognition of the familiar *as* a structure of experience creates a paradox: As soon as the familiar manifests itself *as* familiar, it is rendered strange. It is a bit like repeating a word over and over again—pencil, pencil, pencil, pencil, pencil—until it begins to sound peculiar and a noise replaces the word. So, in some circumstances, a circumscribed experience may be seized on its own, divorced from its surroundings, and made strange: the greeter is perceptually caught at mid-mouth; what was a smile has congealed into the rictus of a large bird, like one of those hawk-men drawn by Leonardo. But these examples do not touch the core of our problem. They are restricted to piecemeal inversions of the familiar: the repeated word leaves unchanged the familiarity of language and the beakish smile hovers over a still recognizable face.

The full transformation of the familiar demands a radical alteration in the horizon of world as such. We have already encountered such a change in the movement from the natural to the phenomenological attitude. Yet it would seem that Husserl emphasizes everything which is retained in the transposition from naïveté to philosophy whereas I have stressed the element of strangeness. It must be acknowledged that such stress opens up phenomenology to a line of criticism for which Husserl is not responsible. The criticism is this: the phenomenologist harps on the strangeness of experience, announces its remarkable character when viewed under the aspect of epochē, and finally succeeds in putting reality in italics. But there he stops, as though calling the world strange were equivalent to analyzing it. I am not unwilling to assume responsibility for interpreting Husserl in this way, though I do not accept the formulation or the implications of the criticism. First, it is not phenomenology in particular but philosophy in general which disorders experience and gives us, in Hegel's phrase, the inverted world. Phenomenology, as I understand it, is an intensification and purifi-

14. Edmund Husserl, *Experience and Judgment*, 124 ff.

cation of a radicality already present in nascent form in all genuine philosophical reflection. Second, the inversion of the ordinary world is a reflective act which already involves analysis: exhibiting the root strangeness of experience is not a preparatory step toward analysis but in fact a substantive part of philosophical work. Third, even if my first two claims are not warranted, phenomenology does more than point its finger at strangeness. The examination of the constitutive history of intentional experience displays the formative character of the life-world within which familiarity and strangeness present themselves. It is quite possible, then, to follow Husserl's discussion of the life-world without emphasizing, as I have, the primacy of the familiar and the irruption of the strange. What might be lost, however, is the appreciation of precisely that radicality which demarcates Husserl's venture from that of his philosophical contemporaries and predecessors.

It is not difficult to see why Husserl's critique of the separation of objective science from its roots in the life-world applies with special urgency to the thematic problem of familiarity. Apart from a psychology of habituality, it is hard to find an objective-scientific approach to the familiar. Indeed, the tendency is in the opposite direction: objective science practices its own methodological suspension in which the realm of immediately experienced reality and everydayness is bracketed. The ideal of such science is to remove itself as far as possible from the contingencies of everyday life. In place of man as an actor on the social scene, the scientific observer is introduced. His allegiances are restricted by definition to the history and methodology of his discipline. His audience is his fellow scientists. His own status as a man among men in the life-world is set aside to the extent that he operates ideally as a scientist. Even his language undergoes alteration, changing from the idiom of family life or the vernacular of the street to the formalized vocabulary of the professional. Beyond any change in words, there arises a qualitative shift in language itself, a movement from natural to formal language. That science is furthest along in its development which can use the language of mathematics. It is easy to misinterpret Husserl's position at this point. He is not attacking objective science because it makes use of mathematics. He is not criticizing the natural sciences for excluding the stratum of daily life from their purview. He is not suggesting that science is inadequate because it is removed from the current of mundane existence. Husserl is saying that the nexus between objective science and the life-world must be explored by philosophy because the phenomenological grounding of all knowledge is to be found there; that for science—including objective science—to be secure in its superstructure it must trace out its epistemic foundations in the immediacy of mundane experience; that all mathematical constructions must ultimately find their translation into natural language, so that their grounding in consciousness is the origin of all definition, postulation, and derivation.

Among the dangers in divorcing objective science from the life-world is the creation and fostering of a particular attitude which, if rightly understood, is deeply antiscientific but which is a profound danger to both science and the life-world if it is misinterpreted. That is the view that objective-scientific knowledge is the absolute paradigm for all knowledge. Built into that claim is, to borrow a phrase from Hume, a hideous hypothesis: the assumption that usefulness (or ultimately power) is the final criterion of truth. The acceptance of that criterion overtly or covertly may be termed "scientism." There is an inevitable connection between scientism and the repudiation of the life-world. When scientism accelerates into a program for objective science, the philosophic rift with the human world becomes apparent. According to Eric Voegelin, "The scientistic creed . . . is characterized by three principal dogmas: (1) the assumption that the mathematized science of natural phenomena is a model to which all other sciences ought to conform; (2) that all realms of being are accessible to the methods of the sciences of phenomena; and (3) that all reality which is not accessible to the sciences of phenomena is either irrelevant or, in the more radical form of the dogma, illusionary." [15] If opposition to scientism in this sense is equated with opposition to objective science, then phenomenology is indeed antiscientific. Enough has been said, I believe, to show that no such equation has been made by Husserl. As a thinker well trained in mathematics and the physical sciences, he remains an ally of the scientific tradition. It is as a friend of science that he insists on the repudiation of scientism.

The distance between science and the life-world is an ironic consequence, for Husserl, of the failure of science to secure its own foundations or, looked at from a different angle, the failure

15. Eric Voegelin, "The Origins of Scientism," *Social Research*, XV, no. 4 (December, 1948), 462.

of philosophy to provide an absolute grounding for science. For such grounding to be accomplished, it is necessary to trace out the concepts of science to their origin in the world of immediate experience, to display the intentional constitution of all fundamental terms of discourse, to intuit *in person* the formative elements of the life-world. The demand for the clarification of experiential roots is one which is to be found throughout Husserl's career. In his essay "Philosophy as Rigorous Science" Husserl insisted on going beyond linguistic analysis in searching for the grounds for conceptual knowledge. The danger of such analysis is that it derives "analytical judgments from word meanings, in the belief that it has thereby gained knowledge of facts." [16] The phenomenological analyst, to the contrary, "derives no judgments at all from word concepts but rather looks into the phenomena that language occasions by means of the words in question" and "penetrates to the phenomena constituted by the fully intuitional realization of experimental concepts." [17] The search for an absolute foundation for science is integral to the development of a presuppositionless philosophy and continuous with the attempt to build knowledge on the bedrock of intuitive certainty. The theme sounded in "Philosophy as Rigorous Science" is repeated in a new variation in the *Crisis*, where Husserl's concern with science is transposed into historical form. And just as he sought to oppose psychologism in the earlier essay, so in his later effort he tried to rally the forces of philosophy against reductionism. The arguments against historical relativism presented in "Philosophy as Rigorous Science" reappear in transposed form in the *Crisis*. Again, there is the struggle toward the genuinely invariant but against the abstractive as a surface procedure. Phenomenological analysis remains rooted in the becoming of the life-world.

It is sometimes said that Husserl's philosophy of the life-world marks a break with his earlier thought, that it is, if not a turning in his intellectual life, at least a decisively new development. But it has also been argued that, apart from the particular language of the life-world, the concern with the structure of everyday life and its constitutive sources is a long-standing interest of Husserl. I tend to agree with the latter judgment, for it

16. Edmund Husserl, "Philosophy as Rigorous Science," in *Phenomenology and the Crisis of Philosophy*, p. 95.
17. *Ibid.*, pp. 95–96.

seems clear to me that Husserl's work, throughout his career, is marked by an unwillingness to accept already-formed positions, attitudes, methods, and conceptions. In all cases, he tries to trace out the philosophical origin of experience and to illuminate its history in consciousness. The repudiation of philosophical naturalism is an early and lasting factor in the development of phenomenology. In a way, the truth of the life-world is vindicated through a refusal to translate its character in terms of naturalistic categories. And the emphasis on epochē and the characterization of the natural attitude are attempts to display the texture and scope of naïve experience. In these terms, it might be said that the historical weight of the later thought of Husserl is introduced through his effort to view science and human reality from the vantage point of sociality, of man within the web of intersubjectivity. Looking toward the theme of the life-world from the time of "Philosophy as Rigorous Science," one sees it as a possibility for analysis to be approached on the basis of a prior clarification of subjectivity. At the time of the *Crisis*, however, the history of the life-world is viewed through the prism of history—not only the development of science but the fate of European man in our century. There is always the most intense seriousness in all of Husserl's writing, but a studied optimism which can be detected in "Philosophy as a Rigorous Science" becomes darkened in the *Crisis*. In 1910 Husserl was able to say: "Our age is called an age of decadence. I cannot consider this complaint justified. You will scarcely find in history an age in which such a sum of working forces was set in motion and performed with such success."[18] Twenty-five years later, he warned against "the downfall of Europe in its estrangement from its own rational sense of life, its fall into hostility toward the spirit and into barbarity."[19]

The distance between the ego and the world, between philosophy and science, and between the life-world and history may be the same whether measured from one terminus or the other, but there are further considerations. As Péguy put it, the road from Paris to Chartres is not the same as the road from Chartres to Paris. The continuity I find in Husserl's work does not preclude

18. *Ibid.*, p. 145. I have changed the translation slightly. For a useful edition of the original, see Edmund Husserl, *Philosophie als strenge Wissenschaft*.

19. Husserl, *Crisis*, p. 299.

critical differentiations in emphasis. Whatever his despairs—
and they were very real—the early Husserl and the middle Husserl persisted in working at the foundations of knowledge. For
the late Husserl the undeniable signs of a new decadence had
appeared: the sickness of Europe was a prelude to the destruction of reason, the lapsing of man as a being capable of philosophy. It was not that the events of the times overwhelmed Husserl; it was rather that he recognized in them a suicidal impulse,
a lust for the void. In the solitude of a philosophy of the ego,
Husserl calls on men to rediscover and reaffirm the sovereignty
of reason and spirit. That means returning to the radical reflection that defines philosophy, which is sedimented in its own
history and which provides the ultimate moorings for man's
accountability. The life-world becomes the meeting place for the
discordant voices of the specialists, the clearing house for language, and the locus of philosophical disputation. In continuity
with an older tradition, philosophy returns to the market place
as a concern of daily life. Whether one cave has been exchanged
for another is a question we shall leave moot for the present, but
it is clear that Husserl's rejection of scientism and his critique of
objective science—and ultimately his defense of science—demand a new allegory.

Imagine the condition of men living in an open, sun-drenched
city. The dark passageway from which they came has long been
sealed off and forgotten. Since childhood, they have lived in the
city, free to move at will and stroll along the lucid avenues and
cloudless thoroughfares. Every street is clearly labeled, its geo-
graphic placement given in degrees of longitude and latitude.
The entire city rests on a mathematical grid. There are no words
for "here" or "there"—instead graph points from the grid are
instantaneously available by transistorized signals. The city is
pronounless: in place of "me" and "you," code terms are designated to avoid any possible confusion. A central vault houses the
details of each life. No shadow falls on this city of eternal day.
Error and deception have been eliminated. Nor is the healing of
unwisdom any longer practiced. "Philosophy" has become an
archaic term of uncertain origin and dubious linguistic legitimacy.

8 / Phenomenology and Existence

THE RECOVERY OF THE LIFE-WORLD as an authentic theme for philosophical analysis leads to existential considerations. It would seem that an examination of the structure of everyday life would entail an inquiry into the life of the individual, not his biography but his career as an *existent*, a being whose specificity demands philosophical comprehension. For present purposes, the history and disputes concerning existentialism shall be left aside. After a generation of debate and analysis, it is obvious that "existentialism" is an orphaned word: where there is concurrence about the meaning of existentialism, there are no existentialists around, and where existentialists are to be found, there is no agreement on doctrine. Any history of twentieth-century existentialism would have to include such thinkers as Heidegger, Jaspers, Marcel, and Sartre, yet all of them in different ways have repudiated the label "existentialist" as a misnomer, or as an inexact and misleading term. However, the term persists because it possesses a certain systematic as well as historical legitimacy. Despite the sometimes profound differences between various existential thinkers, what binds them together proves to be stronger than what keeps them apart. Heidegger may be a thinker or poet of being, yet existential themes pervade his thought. Marcel may be a Neo-Socratic, but no reader of his works can avoid their existential import. Sartre has passed on to Neo-Marxian dialectics without abandoning the roots of his earlier thought. Jaspers, perhaps, is the most consistent and existentially persistent figure in the group, though he prefers to speak of *Existenzphilosophie*. The truth, I suspect, is not so much that we are stuck with a word as that we are recipients of a development through which each of the existentialists has passed. The later thought of a Heidegger or a Sartre is prepared for in his earlier work; it is impossible to strip the earlier thought away from the later work. In a sense, in order to see why the existentialists are so sensitive about the names they are called, it is necessary to appreciate their own evolution. Such a task must remain presupposed; it cannot be undertaken here. My immediate concern is with the convergence of existentialism and phenomenology.

Let us approach the matter of existence in systematic terms. Existentialism is an effort to confront and elucidate the reality of the concrete individual. The Cartesian "I" is the subject of the statement, "I think." It is an "I" without depth, equally evident and available to anyone who wishes to assume the posture of the *cogito*. One slips into the "I" as one tries on a shoe. There is no indication that the "I" can be ravaged, that the course of experience may be dark, that mood and desire are central to the ego. The "I" whose existence is affirmed by Descartes is apparently sexless—an epistemic neuter. Whatever the philosophical inadequacies of the natural attitude, at least it has passion. Thrust into the world of daily life, the individual finds himself on the scene, in the midst of activities, involved in work, enticed by real and illusory goals. The movement from "I" to *I* is the measure of existential history. What relationship is there between the abstract career of the self and the concrete reality of the individual who is already me or you? How can philosophy arrive at last at the person in his uniqueness? A major clue to a response to these questions was given by Kierkegaard, whose claim to priority in the history of existentialism is more than nineteenth-century status assures: he unites, I think, almost all of the existential thinkers. In his writings you find a resonance with everything which follows in existentialism, even when it contradicts Kierkegaard's views. The essence of his method might be expressed as the refusal to accept philosophical conclusions without direct knowledge of their human premises. If the choice is between the grandeur of metaphysics and the truth of a single person, there is no contest: metaphysics falls before the presence of an individual like a house of cards at the touch of a child. Yet the choice between a philosophy of the whole and the reality of the person—the solitary individual, in Kierkegaard's words—does not imply a refusal of philosophy in favor of naïve existence.

To the contrary, Kierkegaard's own philosophizing is infinitely sophisticated and charged with dialectical difficulty. What he offers is not naïveté in place of abstraction but indirection in place of intellection.

If one focuses on Kierkegaard's method for the sake of understanding existentialism rather than Kierkegaard, then philosophical indirection may be interpreted as a kind of Socratic ignorance in which the master is as troubled as the disciple—in which the ignorance is, in a way, genuine: what starts as a maieutic device ends by giving us, in the case of Kierkegaard, a self-cutting anguish, a desolation. The individual is taunted into movement inward by a guide who insists on keeping him away from security, somewhat like a perverse sheep dog who nips at the feet of his charges whenever they try to flock together. For Kierkegaard, it is the relationship which the individual has to what he knows that establishes the problem of knowledge. The individual is in movement, in process. His world must conform not to the prescriptions it inherits but to the demands of the solitary creature who finds himself in a reality which he did not create yet for which he is responsible. A frontal assault on the world is always just about to begin in the world Kierkegaard describes, but the general has misplaced a crucial medal for his uniform. The grandeur of a coronation is embarrassed by the intrusion of the palace cleaning woman who always comes on Tuesdays. Kierkegaard's philosopher has a room in the same building occupied by Dostoevski's paradoxalist. In such quarters the rent is paid sporadically, an evil smell lingers in the stairwell, shrieks are frequently heard, and liver trouble is a common complaint. Philosophy moves from the heaven of Plato's Ideas to the ranker and remoter reaches of his Cave—to places where the light of the fire does not carry, where there are not even shadows, but only darkness.

What emerges from the philosophy of indirection is Kierkegaard's insistence on the truth of what he calls "the subjective thinker," the one who forces his way toward the truth of his own life. A strong case might be built up to show that Kierkegaard is an antiphilosopher, a denier not only of philosophical systems but of philosophy itself. Indeed, Kierkegaard provides us with plenty of data for his entry in the register of antiphilosophers. But if we take him at his word we sacrifice too much: what he is against is not philosophy, but philosophy without the philosopher. His point is that the moment of concrete existence, the actuality of the person at the most trivial point in his routine, cannot be caught in the circle of abstraction. And, if the trivial cannot be snared by categories, there is something primordially elusive about human existence: the truth of the individual is not to be found in the sweep of public pronouncements but in the way the person stands in relationship to the immediacy of daily life. As with Dostoevski, the trivial is a talisman for the transcendental. We may be pulled to heaven by clutching the root of an onion. But then we are thrust back on ourselves in a new way, for the individual must decide what events in his career are significant, wherein that significance lies, how it is to be taken, how it may be communicated, and what, finally, the tokens of earth mean in relation to God. It is in the reduction of the person to essentials that the method of Kierkegaard demonstrates or enacts its universal existential persuasiveness. From the security of the taken-for-granted world, the individual is forced back to a situation of minimal possession. Not only must he make do with what is ultimately his own but he is compelled to rebuild his world from the minima of uprooted experience. To one who has suffered and comprehended spiritual fragmentation, the hope of the Gospel torments Kierkegaard's pages, but, even in the religious domain, *becoming* and not being is the decisive category. For the individual who does not seek salvation but who does demand clarity, the barrenness of Kierkegaard's landscape is an appropriate setting for self-examination.

Of the existential heirs to Kierkegaard's legacy, Sartre in particular has appreciated the paradoxical relationship between the denial of abstraction in the name of the concrete and the power of dialectic to illuminate the particular. There are sins on both sides: the distraction of Hegel is matched by the artificiality of Kierkegaard—at their worst both thinkers mimic each other. Sartre accuses each of them and defends both of them: "Hegel is right: unlike the Danish ideologist, who obstinately fixed his stand on poor, frozen paradoxes ultimately referring to an empty subjectivity, the philosopher of Jena aims through his concepts at the veritable concrete; for him, mediation is always presented as an enrichment. Kierkegaard is right: grief, need, passion, the pain of men, are brute realities which can be neither surpassed nor changed by knowledge." [1] What emerges from the Kierke-

1. Jean-Paul Sartre, *Search for a Method*, trans. Hazel E. Barnes (New York: Knopf, 1963), p. 12.

gaardian critique of abstraction is the relocation of the habitat of philosophical work. Now it is within the inwardness of the life of the individual that change occurs. The pure intellectual career of the person gives way to the indirection of suffering, despair, and humiliation. Sartre writes:

> Kierkegaard was perhaps the first to point out, against Hegel and thanks to him, the incommensurability of the real and knowledge. This incommensurability may be the origin of a conservative irrationalism; it is even one of the ways in which we may understand this ideologist's writings. But it can be seen also as the death of absolute idealism; ideas do not change men. Knowing the cause of a passion is not enough to overcome it; one must live it, one must oppose other passions to it, one must combat it tenaciously, in short one must "work oneself over." [2]

The compression of experience to the bare limits of selfhood and the ensuing struggle with what one has in the immediacy of his life are nuclear to existential questioning. In the Sartrean context (on which I shall concentrate) that compression comes to the recognition that human freedom is a function of the incessant flux of consciousness, a need to build again and again the elements which constitute the ordered world. *What there is does not have to be.* The experiential appropriation of that insight, for Sartre, yields the image of the self as a perpetual overcomer of negation who nevertheless remains rooted in nihilation. The overcoming is a momentary victory, destined to the reprisals of consciousness. In turn, we may say that consciousness is a mobile force, whose essence consists in its intentional character.[3] The nothingness which Sartre finds at the center of consciousness must be understood as a deliverance from the stagnation of an introspective psychology. The self which finds itself compressed to its own severe truth is not turned into a guardian of morbid thoughts and bizarre illuminations. Existential awareness becomes a recovery of the naïve perception of mundanity. What Sartre opposes is the philosophical engorgement of experience: knowledge which seizes chunks of reality in perception, chews them up in some Kantian machinery of cognition, swallows them,

2. *Ibid.*, pp. 12–13.
3. We are speaking of the early Sartre as well as the author of *Being and Nothingness*.

and holds them captive. "O philosophie alimentaire!" [4] Knowledge, Sartre holds, is directional, not absorptive. In knowing, one is in the immediate presence of the known. He writes:

> To know is to "burst toward," to tear oneself out of the moist gastric intimacy, veering out there beyond oneself, out there near the tree and yet beyond it, for the tree escapes me and repulses me, and I can no more lose myself in the tree than it can dissolve itself in me. I'm beyond it: it's beyond me. Do you recognize in this description your own circumstances and your own impressions? You certainly knew that the tree was not you, that you could not make it enter your dark stomach and that knowledge could not, without dishonesty, be compared to possession. All at once consciousness is purified, it is clear as a strong wind. There is nothing in it but a movement of fleeing itself, a sliding beyond itself. If, impossible though it be, you could enter "into" a consciousness you would be seized by a whirlwind and thrown back outside, in the thick of the dust, near the tree, for consciousness has no "inside." It is just this being beyond itself, this absolute flight, this refusal to be a substance which makes it a consciousness. [5]

What Sartre has done is to translate Husserl's doctrine of the intentionality of consciousness into an existential conception of the nihilating impulse of the ego. If there is no "inside" to consciousness, then man is present to the world without protection or cover of any kind. The world is disclosed to consciousness because consciousness is in the world. And just as Sartre has repudiated the "digestive" theory of knowledge, so he rejects philosophical realism. Being in the world is not like the being of things, a stolid identity, the dumb plenum of stones and cabbages. In fact, Sartre adopts the language of "being-in-the-world." With that shower of hyphens, Heidegger's presence announces itself. In following the path of *Being and Time,* Sartre propels Husserl in the same direction. Heidegger's "being-in-the-world" is a movement in which the "being-in" is an interior denial of self-identity. Now we can appreciate the way in which intentionality has been appropriated by Sartre in his attempt to Heideggerize Husserl:

4. Jean-Paul Sartre, "Une Idée fondamentale de la phénoménologie de Husserl: L'Intentionalité," in Sartre, *Situations* (Paris, 1947), I, p. 31.
5. Jean-Paul Sartre, "Intentionality: A Fundamental Idea of Husserl's Phenomenology," pp. 4–5.

To be is to fly out into the world, to spring from the nothingness of the world and of consciousness in order suddenly to burst out as consciousness-in-the-world. When consciousness tries to recoup itself, to coincide with itself once and for all, closeted off all warm and cosy, it destroys itself. This necessity for consciousness to exist as consciousness of something other than itself Husserl calls "intentionality." [6]

It is reasonable to ask whether this is so much a Heideggerization of Husserl as it is locating an undeveloped theme in Husserl's conception of intentionality. I think that there is indeed an existential dimension secreted in Husserl's theory, though Sartre has interpreted it for his own purposes and has, I believe, failed to appreciate the radical implications of phenomenological reduction—which he repudiates—for the existential consequences of intentionality.[7] The Husserl whom Sartre praises is the author of the *Logical Investigations,* not the *Cartesian Meditations.* In his *Transcendence of the Ego,* Sartre has endeavored to defend Husserl against Husserl, to bring the phenomenologist back to the "nonegological" theory of consciousness bypassed in the *Ideas.* But not all of those who accept Sartre's argument in *The Transcendence of the Ego* follow his reconstruction of consciousness in *Being and Nothingness.*[8] With the existentialization of intentionality comes a host of consequences, some of which are incompatible with much of phenomenology. It is as if Sartre were dazzled by the power of Husserl's fundamental idea and wanted it for his own, to do with as he pleased. The attraction is that of immediacy: the world in phenomenological terms is cogiven with consciousness, self and reality are unitary, the "subjective" is finally transcended into the world:

So it is that all at once hatred, love, fear, sympathy—all these famous "subjective" reactions which were floating in the malodorous brine of the mind—are pulled out. They are merely ways of discovering the world. . . . Husserl has restored to things their horror and their charm. He has restored to us the world of artists and prophets: frightening, hostile, dangerous, with its havens of mercy and love.[9]

6. *Ibid.,* p. 5.
7. See Maurice Natanson, *Literature, Philosophy, and the Social Sciences,* chap. 2.
8. See Aron Gurwitsch, *Studies in Phenomenology and Psychology,* chap. 11.
9. Sartre, "Intentionality: A Fundamental Idea of Husserl's Phenomenology," p. 5.

What Sartre relinquishes by refusing to follow Husserl in the employment of transcendental reduction is the historical progression of the ego. Consciousness is a spontaneity, an irruption, a blazing Roman candle. But what of its sources, its constitutive roots, its origin? Where Husserl opens up a vast field for inquiry under the name of constitutive phenomenology, Sartre moves along a different horizon: the ontology of a consciousness whose essence it is to be essenceless. In denying the reduction in favor of the earlier Husserl, Sartre falls into the following difficulties: first, he comes to a theory of intentionality which can only be understood within the natural attitude; second, the history of the ego and the world as well are lost in the restriction of intentionality to the bursts of its own intensity; third, the existential implications of the regress of consciousness to its minimal resources—the return of the ego to its stripped and exposed roots —are obscured if not denied by failing to take Husserl's entire transcendental turn with full seriousness. Of course, it is easy to defend Sartre. He wants to avoid the excesses of Neo-Kantianism: the transcendental machinery of passive and active syntheses, the unifying agency of a primordial ego, the very constitutive function of consciousness—all tend to "produce" the object of experience. Sartre wants reality, not representations, images, or constructions. The danger, for him, of the transcendental Husserl is that the world is created by consciousness instead of disclosed by an intentionality which is already in-the-world. In fear of losing the unity of the real, Sartre has, I think, fallen into a different kind of error. He has denied the historicity of consciousness at the level of intentionality within the context of *Being and Nothingness* (in some ways, an effort to recoup the historical is presented in the *Critique of Dialectical Reason*). Most simply, I am saying that Sartre has missed the existential force of reduction.

Within the natural attitude, the individual at times comes to transmundane experiences at critical junctures in his life. The traditional existential categories of fear, suffering, anguish, and death are indicators of the kinds of crises at issue. Existential fear may be appropriated—or at least kept at bay—by masking it as worldly fear, focalized fear, psychologized fear. The anguish of being may be hauled into court, accused of neurotic crimes, and assigned to a docket of causal improprieties. Death may be buried in a pauper's grave. But the transmundane has a way of exacting its own revenge: anguish may be reduced to extreme anxiety, but it haunts the scene of its dismissal. The individual who experiences anguish can only report his encounter with the *nihil;* the individual who is inclined to translate such experience into mundane or scientific categories may himself experience anguish and may come to see that the principle of subsumption —that we have *cases* of anguish—no longer holds when the concrete person strives to understand his own experience. When the reports of others have been received and filed, the assessor himself must contend with his own existence. What we referred to earlier as the movement to roots may now be seen at the existential level. Without being able to appeal to tradition and practice, the existent confronted with his own immediacy is nevertheless burdened with the whole of the world, for in returning to absolute solitude he finds himself as the source of all beliefs, attitudes, associations, and commitments related to his experience with fellow men. There is no external pressure which can compel the person to confront such roots; the motive force must be internal. What does in fact occur in experience, however, is a rupture of routine in which the transcendental emerges.

The portraits which have been drawn in existential literature of the "reduced man"—the person *in extremis*—reveal a movement downward in which status, acclaim, possessions, and even simple recognition have all lapsed or been qualitatively diminished. The alone individual has no resources other than his primal possessions: the capacity to intend and sustain a microcosm; the ability to suffer the cunning of others; and the cunning to penetrate the disguises of each man's countervailing forces, the refusal of allies, the resentment of friends, and the loyalty of fools. What existential man is left with is the need for getting on with being, and this means that inevitably he is thrown outward toward the social reality out of which he was hounded. The destruction of experience—its sundered façade—opens up the way for a reverse movement toward reconstruction. Left with the fragments of a world, the individual is given the intrinsic possibility of doing again what he has immanently already accomplished: building a world. Two movements reveal themselves. First, the deformation of the world into its elements is the victory, however devastating, of the individual. Second, the potential for recreating a microcosm is the triumph of consciousness, its surge toward resolution. Split apart, these movements lead to the foundering of the self. Man reduced to rubble and denied the sustenance of any continuation of his being is locked into a world bereft not only of transcendence but even of immanence. The movement toward reconstruction may be solitary and wretched but it is at least *work*, the employment of the ego in recovering its own history.

Sartre's interpretation of intentionality ultimately robs man of both movements. On the one side, the present loses its sedimented history; on the other, the present reveals a diremption of consciousness in which the future is without purpose. To be sure, man chooses himself, but that choice is translated into abandonment: drained of historicity, the chooser bursts into the world; severed from any *telos* of the spirit, he spins, like a gyroscope, on his own axis. All of Sartre's efforts to right the imbalance of consciousness divested of its constitution seem to fall short of what is needed. His emphasis on "situation" proves to be a back door through which history can enter the ontological scene, for, in the end, the situated self is responsible for his situation. It is no wonder, then, that Sartre was sensitive to Merleau-Ponty's criticism of *Being and Nothingness*—that Sartre had failed to take into account the *weight* of history. How seriously that judgment was taken can be seen in the changes in Sartre's thought represented by the *Critique of Dialectical Reason.* In phenomenological terms, however, the shift to a Neo-Marxian view of man as a historical being hardly compensates for the inadequacies of Sartre's interpretation of intentionality. What was lacking in Sartre's initial critique of Husserl is only more glaringly absent in the *Critique of Dialectical Reason:* the becoming of subjectivity in the transcendental constitution of consciousness. For a sense of the existential aspect of Husserl's thought it is necessary to return to the meaning of transcendental reduction. Paradoxically, there, where Sartre refuses to follow Husserl, lies the clue to an authentic existential reality.

The historical motif which transcendental reduction opens up is existential to the extent that the tracing of constitution returns the individual to his being in the life-world. The formation of perceptual experience is analogous with the becoming of a person's life: at any moment in the process of reflection the individual finds himself in the world, tacitly aware of his involvement in events which are products of antecedent circumstances. The practice of constitutive phenomenology contributes an elucidation of the meaning of antecedence which presents the source of man's activity in life—his complicity in mundane existence. As long as the natural attitude holds sway over the individual, his sense of being in reality cannot be expressed, let alone comprehended. The winning of a radical egological standpoint which reduction secures is essential to posing the existential problem because the individual's involvement in the world demands some reflective liberation. As long as one simply *is*, no grasp of the significance of that "is" will ever arise. Artists who capture the existential quality of experience are artificers, not somnambulists of the underground. In fine, the expression of existential concern presupposes a critical point of access to the reality in question. Kierkegaard astonishes the reader into discovering that point of access for himself. As soon as one tries to formulate it, however, one comes to phenomenological problems. The historical theme I have emphasized must be understood in connection with the display of concrete existence as a reflective problem. The uncovering of the historicity of the ego is inevitably the enlargement of the reflective process.

It might be argued that transcendental phenomenology is in principle a movement away from the problem of existence and from all concrete existents. The turn to the disinterested observer within the transcendentally reduced sphere would seem to deny the very possibility of confronting existential questions. But the "disinterested" observer is not the "uninterested" observer.[10] Everything experienced within the natural attitude and within the lifeworld has its transcendental analogue. From a different side, we may say that every transcendental insight has its implications for man as a being in the mundane world. Husserl holds that "every new piece of transcendental knowledge is transformed, by essential necessity, into an enrichment of the content of the human soul. As transcendental ego, after all, I am the same ego that in the worldly sphere is a human ego. What was concealed from me in the human sphere I reveal through transcendental inquiry. Transcendental inquiry is itself a world-historical process insofar as it enlarges the history of the constitution of the world, not only by adding a new science to it but also by enlarging the content of the world in every respect."[11] The emphasis on the return to the world in phenomenological reduction is quite power-

10. Stephan Strasser, in *The Idea of Dialogal Phenomenology,* mistakenly assumes that "disinterested" and "uninterested" are synonymous (pp. 9 ff.).
11. Edmund Husserl, *The Crisis of European Sciences and Transcendental Phenomenology,* p. 264.

ful and certainly evident in Husserl's thought. "When I turn away from the naïve exploration of the world to the exploration of the self and its transcendental egological consciousness," he writes, "I do not turn my back on the world to retreat into an unworldly and, therefore, uninteresting special field of theoretical study. On the contrary, this alone enables me to explore the world radically and even to undertake a radically scientific exploration of what exists absolutely and in an ultimate sense." [12]

What is most disturbing to man in the natural attitude is the suggestion that his assured reality has presuppositions, that naïve experience is not as securely grounded as it appears to be, that *becoming* in the world is not identical with chronological continuity, and that age is more than a function of time. The upset which existential crises announce is a distinctive characteristic of philosophy, for such crises return the person to where he has been, to the course of his activity as a being in the world. I am suggesting that the individual stands to his biographical career as the phenomenological observer stands to the constituted world. The tracing back of human achievements in the life-world finds its transcendental explication in the work of the phenomenologist. In that work, the existential quality of man's historicity shows itself in the insistence on revealing sources, in getting to absolute foundations, and in working one's way back to egological rigor. Here reduction is not only the method of Husserl, it is the meaning of phenomenology. Fritz Kaufmann writes:

> Phenomenology as the analysis of the original constitution of consciousness tries to penetrate into the very depths from which the various formations of consciousness originate. The search for these original springs, modes and structures of life presupposes and sharpens a *sense* of the original, a capacity of retracing familiar appearances to their sources, of renewing and intensifying insights of the past and piercing through conventional interpretations so as to understand where and why they veil rather than unveil the essential truths of life.[13]

My interpretation of transcendental reduction as revealing an existential dimension to Husserl's thought is not likely to make many friends. The arguments against this kind of interpretation

12. Edmund Husserl, "Phenomenology and Anthropology," p. 141.
13. Fritz Kaufmann, "Cassirer, Neo-Kantianism, and Phenomenology," p. 820.

are impressive. First, I doubt that Husserl would have been very open to such a view. His rejection of Heidegger's movement beyond phenomenology hardly gives encouragement to the position which I have advanced. Furthermore, Husserl was always quick to resist any tampering with phenomenology which would lead it toward "anthropologism," which he sought to avoid as much as psychologism. By the time of the *Crisis*, in any case, Husserl was on guard against any philosophy which could be interpreted as antirationalistic. Certainly, I have not tried to prove that Husserl's texts support my views. Rather, I am suggesting that if I am correct in placing the emphasis I have on the concept of origin, then Husserl can be read as providing a philosophical grounding for an essential aspect of existential thought. This is not an attempt to existentialize Husserl; it is, on the contrary, an effort to show that phenomenology never loses touch with the concrete reality of the life-world, that phenomenological constitution is at work in the crises of human life no less than in the logical ordering of experience.

Second, there is a substantial segment of opinion among phenomenologists that the entire question of reduction is a purely methodological matter, that the device of epochē and the effecting of transcendental reduction have nothing whatever to do with the experience of the "strange" or with "astonishment before the world." Husserl, so they think, was exclusively interested in refining logical and epistemological procedures for technical purposes alone. In these terms, what I have made of the radicality of reduction has little to do with phenomenology as rigorous science. No doubt reduction is a problem of methodology, but that leaves open the question of what philosophical implications there are to a method which clearly carries with it startling transformations. The development of the theory of reduction is a tangled one in which Husserl sought again and again to generate and purify a philosophical instrument capable of securing absolute knowledge. The word "methodology" tends to slight the philosophical side of Husserl's quest in favor of technique. I find it difficult to make sense of his thirty years' war over reduction if the distinctively philosophical issues were not, all along, the primary ones. In turning to the darker side of reduction, I am saying that phenomenology is centered in intentionality, that intentionality is opened up by reduction, that reduction involves origin, and that origin is the transcendental clue to existence.

Third, I can expect little support for my views from existential quarters. As we have seen, Sartre wants nothing to do with reduction. Everything he needs in phenomenology he finds available in the *Logical Investigations* (and in a reading of *Ideas* grounded in pretranscendental phenomenology). Jaspers, too, was attracted to the early Husserl. With the publication of "Philosophy as Rigorous Science," however, his relationship to phenomenology changed dramatically. Jaspers writes:

> Husserl impressed me most, comparatively speaking, although his phenomenological method did not strike me as a philosophical procedure. I took it—as he himself did at first—for descriptive psychology. As such I used it to make psychopathological descriptions and formulated it in principle for the purposes of psychopathology. Husserl approved vigorously. In 1913, when I told him I still failed to understand what phenomenology really was and asked about its philosophical implications, he replied, "You are using the method perfectly. Just keep it up. You don't need to know what it is; that's indeed a difficult matter." Long before this I had read his essay on philosophy as a science . . . with distaste —for there, acutely and consistently reasoned, was what seemed to me another denial of the philosophy I deemed essential. The essay became my illumination. To my mind it clearly reached the point where the claim of strict science put an end to everything that could be called philosophy in the great sense of the word. As a philosophy professor, Husserl seemed to me to have committed the most naïve and pretentious betrayal of philosophy.[14]

It is curious that Jaspers misses the existential implications of the two most decisive elements in "Philosophy as Rigorous Science": its insistence on beginnings which the philosopher must trace out for himself with radical courage and its emphasis on knowledge—true science—which has been built up out of experience apprehended directly, experience intuited with utter immediacy and clarity. Of course, these themes are not ignored; they are interpreted as scientific in the narrower sense of the word, that is, Jaspers thinks Husserl is denying the speculative and existential concerns of philosophy in favor of a systematic account of knowledge. Husserl's stress on rigor and on absolutivity, certainty, and apodicticity can, of course, be treated as calls to a quite positivistic philosophy. Yet it should be clear

14. Karl Jaspers, *Philosophy*, Vol. I, trans. E. B. Ashton (Chicago: University of Chicago Press, 1969), pp. 6–7.

from a study of his thought that Husserl's concern is with what is given in experience rather than with what may be formally constructed. Husserl's a priori is not that of the mathematicians or logicians who find certainty because they have stipulated that it be there. It is not in conventions and definitions that phenomenology locates the apodictic but in the cast of intuition as an unmediated seeing of experiential givenness. Husserl is not a philosopher of system but a returner to egological certitude. Most of all, he insists on the inquirer's doing things for himself, not accepting the work of others. In a sense, phenomenology must be begun all over again by each phenomenologist, for he must start from his own resources in validating the research of his colleagues. He can take nothing for granted.

The way into a philosophy of system is the same in principle for any investigator; the way into phenomenology must be found by the phenomenologist himself. Husserl urged his students to find *their* way into phenomenology, the way proper to the concrete individual.[15] Progress in phenomenology presupposes a movement forward in extending work but also a continual return to the starting point to assure the adequacy of results and also to make it possible for the phenomenologist to see for himself. It is not a matter of one step forward and one step back. Husserl's own career shows what genuine advances are possible for phenomenology. But the demand for returning to beginnings helps to explain at least part of the paradox involved in phenomenological work: Whatever the results of the phenomenologist, he must always be on his methodological guard. That means that Husserl's dissatisfaction with his formulation of epochē and reduction was, in part, a function of his own demand for apodicticity arrived at egologically. The marriage of certainty and subjectivity is the crux of the matter. Husserl's position amounts to this: certainty is rooted in subjectivity and subjectivity is the locus of absolute knowledge. The concrete person who strives for certitude must come to phenomenology in his particular—we might say existential—way, but he finds in reduction the entrance to a transindividual realm. The empirical ego gives way to the phenomenological observer. Yet nothing is lost in that transition. If Husserl is correct in maintaining that everything disclosed in the transcendental sphere has its analogue in the natural attitude, then

15. See Husserl's letter to Dorion Cairns in *Edmund Husserl: 1859–1959*, p. 285.

the concrete orientation of the person to phenomenology—*his* way—is retained in its transcendental aspect. In essence, the existential reality of the concrete individual, the truth of his inwardness, is illuminated and not destroyed or discounted in phenomenological reduction. In an oblique way we come back to the problem of application in phenomenology, this time to the application of phenomenology to existence.

If phenomenology begins with the irrealization of the particular, is it ever possible to gain access to the particularity of a concrete life? Will there not always be a shift from specificity to some intentional correlate? And even if Husserl assures us that transcendental reduction retains the *sense* of the mundane, what about the concatenated particularity of my own or your own existence? Can the richness of that web of detail be honored in phenomenological terms? From the side of existential philosophy it would seem that the multiplicity of personal life has been given its due. Although it is misleading to lift a segment of a philosopher's work from its conceptual matrix, I think that there is something to be gained from turning briefly to what Sartre calls "existential psychoanalysis." [16] After having constructed an ontology of human reality, Sartre suggests that it is possible to reconstruct the specificity of an individual life on the basis of the theory presented in *Being and Nothingness*. The general projects of human freedom may be seen in their applicative uniqueness in the actual career of Flaubert, Baudelaire, Genet, or Sartre himself. Almost thirty years before he published the first volumes of his incredible study of Flaubert, *L'Idiot de la famille*, Sartre pointed to Flaubert as a prime candidate for existential psychoanalysis. The psychological categories of literary criticism are in principle incapable of establishing the relationship between general laws and concrete human facts. The "why" of psychological explanation—indeed, the very notion of "explanation" itself—reduces to correlations between antecedent states of affairs and consequential results when the meaning of there being "antecedent states of affairs" is the fundamental problem to be understood. Why should a given result be interpreted in terms of an earlier state of affairs? On the side of the general, there is an incapacity to show in principle how any concrete result comes about; on the side of the particular, there is an accretion of detail, a superfluity of fact added to fact. In the hiatus between

16. See Jean-Paul Sartre, *Being and Nothingness*, pp. 557 ff.

these equally unsatisfactory positions, Flaubert slips away from us. Sartre asks:

> Why did ambition and the feeling of his power produce in Flaubert *exaltation* rather than tranquil waiting or gloomy impatience? Why did this exaltation express itself specifically in the need to act violently and feel intensely? Or rather why does this need make a sudden appearance by spontaneous generation at the end of the paragraph? And why does this need instead of seeking to appease itself in acts of violence, by amorous adventures, or in debauch, choose precisely to satisfy itself symbolically? And why does Flaubert turn to writing rather than to painting or music for this symbolic satisfaction; he could just as well not resort to the artistic field at all (there is also mysticism, for example). "I could have been a great actor," wrote Flaubert somewhere. Why did he not try to be one? In a word, we have understood nothing; we have seen a succession of accidental happenings, of desire springing forth fully armed, one from the other, with no possibility for us to grasp their genesis. The *transitions*, the becomings, the transformations, have been carefully veiled from us, and we have been limited to putting order into the succession by invoking empirically established but literally unintelligible sequences.[17]

The practice of existential psychoanalysis assures the most thorough scrutiny of everything associated with the origin of a project. The history of the individual's interests and associations and the development of his talents and involvements are all examined for originary motives. Nothing is superfluous; everything has its interpretative role. Like its Freudian counterpart, existential psychoanalysis brings an intensive seriousness and hermeneutic brilliance to the fragmentary, the slight, the seemingly uninteresting, and the apparently meaningless. Unlike Freud, Sartre looks to being as the scene of human choice. For our purposes, however, the question is not whether Sartre's criticism of Freud is convincing but whether the method of existential psychoanalysis serves to ally Sartre with Husserl. I suggest that it is possible to interpret the search for the meaning of an original project as a form of phenomenological uncovering or displaying of the sedimentation of meaning. Clearly, allowances must be made for the shift from an ontological to an eidetic standpoint. The point is that *were* the phenomenologist interested in tracing out the stages in the development of the career of a particular

17. *Ibid.,* p. 559.

person and trying to account for the choices that were made in that career, he would confront the problem Sartre is concerned with at this point. Like Husserl, Sartre is not interested in an empirical examination of the life of his heroes. Unlike Husserl, Sartre seeks to penetrate the tangle of concrete action by rebuilding the ontology of human existence. Yet it is possible to take the case histories of the existential psychoanalyst as exemplars of phenomenological possibilities. Tracing out the sedimentation of meaning in the biography of Flaubert is then seeing a mundane counterpart to transcendental history.

The phenomenological motive in existential psychoanalysis consists in its recognition of unified meaning or totality in the presentation of the part or the fragment. Each element has its own intentional reference: the given points to the unity of which it is a part. In a sense, we are given a new physiognomy of experience in which every gesture signifies a totalization. The new physiognomy is thus a new hermeneutics through which the unity of a concrete life may find expression. In Sartre's world, everything done, said, imagined, and avoided points back to the fundamental project through which the individual chooses his history. But the analysis of these performances of consciousness requires the services of the alter ego: it is *the other,* as psychoanalytic observer, who is in a privileged position to appreciate and elucidate the concrete life of the ego. Of course, self-analysis is possible, but then, Sartre holds, the subject "must renounce at the outset all benefit stemming from his peculiar position and must question himself exactly as if he were someone else." [18] Sartre trying to comprehend his apparent decapodaphobia must become an observer of himself. He must, in fact, move from being the one whose consciousness *is* his past to a formal observer, someone who interrogates his past in essentially the same way that a psychoanalyst responds to his patient. But if existential psychoanalysis presupposes the existence of a formal observer, then it should acknowledge some resonance with Husserl's turn from the ego to the disinterested observer. In both instances, the need is for a kind of distancing in which the object of analysis is not compromised but preserved in the perspective of a higher and more powerful evidence.

It may be argued that whatever the success of existential psychoanalysis, it can do nothing more than present us with an

18. *Ibid.,* p. 570.

interpretation of the life of a subject. Like an extraordinary novelist, the psychoanalyst may vivify the history he seeks to reconstruct, but in the end access to that life is from the outside. That, of course, is Sartre's point: the core of consciousness is nihilation, the ground of the ego is a void, relationship with other human beings is ultimately abortive, the foundation of human reality is ontological instability. That the Other should know me better than I know myself is hardly cause for comment in Sartrean terms. On the contrary, if the reverse were true, the Sartrean universe would be confounded. But if the Other occupies a privileged position, then either he is responsible for understanding the concrete life of the person or else each one of us must become his own existential psychoanalyst. What would Kierkegaard make of this kind of analysis? [19] It would seem that the search for the concrete turns out to demand an exchange of standpoints through which subjectivity is scrutinized by a formal observer. Even if the individual serves as his own analyst, the choice of entering into existential psychoanalysis is distinctively un-Kierkegaardian. In place of the solitary individual we have the observed (even if self-observed) patient; instead of indirection we have instructive analysis. Alone before God and in the presence of my own terror, I search out my proper way. In response to my analyst and from the distance of inspection by the Other, I explicate my predicament. Kierkegaard and Sartre. Yet their goals and even their methods are not that far apart. For both, concreteness is the challenge; for both, method is put in the service of the self. The itinerary of the individual is a theme com-

19. Flaubert mediates, in a way, between Kierkegaard and Sartre. Had he lived to read it, Kierkegaard might well have recognized in *Madame Bovary* an author not unlike himself. Adi Schmuëli writes: "Flaubert . . . is worthy of being considered a master of indirect communication because he does not intrude himself into the development of the novel nor take any part in it. He himself is simply an objective witness, and his own inwardness remains incognito. It required a trial to determine the real intentions of Flaubert, just as it required one to judge the proposals of Socrates. But the inwardness of Flaubert, or Socrates, or any master of indirect communication will always be a secret, a secret object that one tries to take possession of, to no avail. And like the inwardness of Flaubert or Socrates, that of Kierkegaard is also a secret, for the philosophy of Kierkegaard is an indirect communication which hides his inwardness from us" (*Kierkegaard and Consciousness*, trans. Naomi Handelman [Princeton, N.J.: Princeton University Press, 1971], p. 129).

mon to their different enterprises. In the end, the bond between them may be understood phenomenologically. It is too easy to say that route becomes root, but it is not facile to translate biography into history. In these terms, existential psychoanalysis may be understood as the factic counterpart to a phenomenology of origin.

The points of convergence between phenomenology and existentialism that have been emphasized should not prevent us from recognizing the substantial differences and distance between the two approaches to the nature of philosophy as well as human existence. A catalogue of distinctions is unnecessary. It should be clear to any reader of Kierkegaard and Husserl that their views of reason involve divergent conceptions of the nature of man.[20] So too in different ways with Sartre and the other existentialists. From an existential standpoint, it might seem as if Husserl represents the last great inhabitant of the Crystal Palace: he still believes in man's capacity for good, his capacity for rational action, his advancement through genuine science, his brotherhood with men of good will. In a sense, Husserl is the last European *Professor*. It is hard to picture him carrying on epistolary duels or engaging in aesthetic sabotage in the style of Kierkegaard, and it is equally difficult to think of *Geheimrat* Husserl reveling in existential rebellion against the Establishment. But Husserl's place was never in the cavalcade of skirmishers; it was in the company of those who labor at foundations in awkward places at a discouraging pace. In fact the image of the Crystal Palace is misplaced with regard to Husserl. Far from being a simple-minded advocate of progress, he was a conceptual revolutionary. Far from being the last inhabitant of the Crystal Palace, he was born scorched with its ashes. Queen Victoria is reported to have said of the opening of the exhibition: "the greatest day in our history." The infinite miscalculation of that sentiment is the mark of the twentieth century. The reader of the *Crisis* will find

20. That such divergence did not keep Husserl from appreciating Kierkegaard is attested to by Lev Shestov, who writes: "Learning that I had never read Kierkegaard, Husserl began not to *ask* but to *demand* —with enigmatic insistence—that I acquaint myself with the works of the Danish thinker. How was it that a man whose whole life had been a celebration of reason should have led me to Kierkegaard's hymn to the absurd?" ("In Memory of a Great Philosopher: Edmund Husserl," in *Russian Philosophy*, ed. James M. Edie, James P. Scanlon, Mary-Barbara Zeldin, III, 254).

it impossible to avoid Husserl's bitter commentary on the contemporary scene. It would be unforgivable to mistake Husserl's defense of reason with naïve rationalism.

By the time Husserl was writing his last pages, the Europe he sought to warn was least able to listen. Forbidden entrance to his own university, old in a time of spiritual decomposition, confronted with the likelihood of the loss of his manuscripts, powerless in the rampancy of the Third Reich, Husserl is no herald of meliorism. He is in the midst of a living ruin, calling Europe back to its civilized possibilities. Here the existential theme of his career comes to the fore. Europe is sick. It suffers from an insufficiency and congestion of the spirit. Looking backward, we find European Man disinherited from and disinheriting his beginnings in Greece. Looking forward, we find him cut off from his *telos*, from his fulfillment in either knowledge, reason, or science. A cultural torso, European Man—contemporary man— has become historical debris, purposeless and inflamed with self-doubt. What has been lost is philosophy itself. On the surface, the sickness Husserl describes is the failure of reason to recognize and resolve the problems of man as a being in the life-world. That failure would mean the irrelevance of philosophy for the concrete problems of human existence. More basically, what Husserl is pointing to is the ground of reason itself, not a particular expression of philosophical rationalism. It is philosophy which is at issue in the crisis which Husserl proclaims. The failure of surface rationalism—"enlightenment rationalism"—has led to a loss of confidence in philosophy. In turn, irrationalisms of various kinds, including the savage side of existential thought, have rushed in to fill the vacuum left by the capitulation of classical philosophy. In the thick of such disruption and disorientation, at the center of Europe's disorder, Husserl defines himself by continuing his own work, by demonstrating in his own philosophizing the incorruptibility of reason when it is rooted in truth. It is said that Hegel completed his *Phenomenology of Spirit* with the guns of Jena booming in the distance. Husserl composed the *Crisis* with a more ominous sound in the background: the shattering of twenty-five centuries of *Kultur*.

9 / The Crisis of Reason

DOSTOEVSKI TERMINATES *Notes from Underground* by having his antihero say:

As for what concerns me in particular, I have in my life only carried to an extreme what you have not dared to carry halfway, and what's more, you have taken your cowardice for good sense, and have found comfort in deceiving yourselves. So that perhaps, after all, there is more life in me than in you. Look into it more carefully! Why, we don't even know what living means now, what it is, and what it is called. Leave us alone without books and we'll be lost and in confusion at once. We'll not know what to join to, what to cling to, what to love and what to hate, and what to respect and what to despise. We are oppressed at being men—men with real individual flesh and blood, we are ashamed of it, we think it a disgrace and try to contrive to be some sort of impossible generalized man. We are stillborn, and for generations past have been begotten not by living fathers, and that suits us more and more. We are developing a taste for it. Soon we shall contrive to be born from an idea somehow. But enough; I don't want to write more from *underground*.[1]

Following this statement we are told, in brackets: "The notes of this paradoxalist do not end here, however. He could not refrain from going on with them, but it seems to us that we may stop

---

1. Fëdor Dostoevski, *Notes from Underground*, trans. Constance Garnett and revised by B. G. Guerney, in *A Treasury of Russian Literature*, ed. Bernard Guilbert Guerney (New York: Vanguard, 1943), p. 537.

here." [2] This ending invites comparison with another one. In the *Crisis* Husserl writes:

> Only blindness to the transcendental, as it is experienceable and knowable only through phenomenological reduction, makes the revival of physicalism in our time possible—in the modified form of a logicist mathematicism which abandons the task, put to us by history, of a philosophy based on ultimate insight and on an absolute universality within which there must be no unasked questions, nothing taken for granted that is not understood. To call physicalism philosophy is only to pass off an equivocation as a realization of the perplexities concerning our knowledge in which we have found ourselves since Hume. Nature can be thought as a definite manifold, and we can take this idea as a basis hypothetically. But insofar as the world is a world of knowledge, a world of consciousness, a world with human beings, such an idea is absurd for it to unsurpassable degree. [3]

And in a footnote the editor adds: "The text of the *Crisis* breaks off here." [4]

It might seem at first glance that Dostoevski's onslaught would find in phenomenology its paramount target, that the transcendental ego succeeds in sterilizing consciousness, and that, despite Husserl's protests, one logicism has replaced another, leaving man adrift in a sea of essences. Such a reading would be superficial. Quite apart from the return to the life-world and the implications of phenomenology for existentialism, the language of the *Crisis* is remarkably close to that of Dostoevski. Husserl is protesting against a false utopianism of science, against a logic divested of its experiential roots in consciousness, and against a conception of both Nature and philosophy blind to human history and unwilling to push questions to their ultimate source. We are, in fact, back to the wreckage of the Crystal Palace. What can be said to those witnesses who refuse to believe the fire ever happened? What reply is possible to those who call for "a new and better Palace?" The final response to these questions is given not by the paradoxalist but by Dostoevski: *Notes from Underground* is that answer—a coherent, shattering but unshattered work of art. Husserl's answer is quite different, not merely because he

2. *Ibid.*
3. Edmund Husserl, *The Crisis of European Sciences and Transcendental Phenomenology*, p. 265.
4. *Ibid.*

offers a philosophical treatise but because he has the audacity to proclaim the truth of a Reason beyond the failures of rationalism, the truth that philosophy is consequential. All of the severe differences that do exist between Dostoevski and Husserl should be approached from the perspective of their final sympathy and resonance, for both thinkers have diagnosed our contemporary sickness in trenchant terms. If, in the end, Husserl is convinced that the cure for deracinated man is a return to the true root of Reason and Dostoevski holds that reason of whatever quality and form is irreparably damaged, the process of analysis common to them both compels us to retrace our steps, answer to ourselves for the wilderness of spirit we have created in our time, and turn to history in a radically new way, if not for redemption at least for self-respect.

The sickness which Husserl reports is essentially a malaise of the spirit, though it has differing aspects. Western man— European man,[5] in Husserl's language—has lost or is losing the universal impetus of philosophy which came into being in ancient Greece. Philosophy (and all authentic science) in its original sense expresses the recognition of totality in the limited horizon of the mundane: the universal truth which transcends occasion and instance. The defining characteristic of man's search for the universal is the teleological nature of reason. To speak of teleology in this context is to emphasize the connectedness and directedness of consciousness with and toward its goals. Thought is not a reality given in self-contained bursts; it moves toward fulfillment, toward its proper *telos*. Taken in piecemeal fashion and fragmented into isolated excursions of consciousness, thought

5. "Europe" has an express significance for Husserl. He writes: ". . . we refer to Europe not as it is understood geographically, as on a map, as if thereby the group of people who live together in this territory would define European humanity. In the spiritual sense the English Dominions, the United States, etc., clearly belong to Europe, whereas the Eskimos or Indians presented as curiosities at fairs, or the Gypsies, who constantly wander about Europe, do not. Here the title 'Europe' clearly refers to the unity of a spiritual life, activity, creation, with all its ends, interests, cares, and endeavors, with its products of purposeful activity, institutions, organizations. Here individual men act in many societies of different levels: in families, in tribes, in nations, all being internally, spiritually bound together, and, as I said, in the unity of a spiritual shape. In this way a character is given to the persons, associations of persons, and all their cultural accomplishments which binds them all together" (*Crisis*, pp. 273–74).

becomes disjointed from its originary locus; it ceases to be part of reason and becomes instead a matter of happenstance. What started in Greece, for Husserl, was the recognition that philosophy is the breakthrough of consciousness toward universal understanding in which the philosopher moves toward reflective fulfillment. To deny the whole for the part is to destroy both. The first sign of spiritual decay, in Husserl's terms, is the willingness to turn away from universal truth. That is what has happened to philosophy—its comprehensive mission has been deemed quixotic and its own practitioners have suffered a loss of confidence. The result for philosophy has been a profound unsettlement and disorientation, but the effect for Western man has been the crisis which Husserl describes.

In the simplest terms, the argument is this: Husserl claims that the integrity of European man rests on the integrity of Reason, that Reason depends on the integrity of philosophy, and that philosophy demands a transcendental foundation. The healing of Europe's sickness will come when causal and not symptomatic elements are treated: phenomenology is the clue to the treatment of philosophy's ills, philosophy made whole can in turn restore Reason to its proper condition and station, and Reason restored means Spirit reanimated. This outline of pathology and therapy might appear to be abstractly grandiose. That it should seem that way to many nonphilosophers is hardly surprising, but that some philosophers would find Husserl's critique of civilization farfetched is a commentary on the state of present-day philosophy. Behind Husserl's abstractions are the grimness and corrosion of our own time in its most demonic form. The *Crisis* may be read as a philosophical response to the sundering of Reason in the name of "progress," in the name of "science," in the name of "will," in the name of "destiny," and in the name of "a thousand years of historical transfiguration." Where are the philosophers who have tried *as philosophers* to understand what has happened to us? The medical image persists: for the many who have tried to relieve the pressure, there are the very few who have sought to diagnose the disease. But it would be a mistake to appreciate the foreground of European history as the theme of the *Crisis* at the expense of the larger history of Western civilization. Our troubles began not with the tragedies of the twentieth century but with a much earlier turning away from the ideal of Reason through the beguilements of scientism and pseudoenlightenment. Husserl writes:

The "crisis of European existence," talked about so much today and documented in innumerable symptoms of the breakdown of life, is not an obscure fate, an impenetrable destiny; rather, it becomes understandable and transparent against the background of the *teleology of European history* that can be discovered philosophically. The condition for the understanding, however, is that the phenomenon "Europe" be grasped in its central, essential nucleus. In order to be able to comprehend the disarray of the present "crisis," we had to work out the *concept of Europe as the historical teleology of the infinite goals of reason;* we had to show how the European "world" was born out of ideas of reason, i.e., out of the spirit of philosophy. The "crisis" could then become distinguishable as the *apparent failure of rationalism.* The reason for the failure of a rational culture, however, as we said, lies not in the essence of rationalism itself but solely in its being rendered superficial, in its entanglement in "naturalism" and "objectivism." [6]

Husserl's position at this point is perfectly consistent as well as continuous with the ideas he presented in "Philosophy as Rigorous Science" almost twenty-five years earlier. In 1911 Husserl wrote that his "arguments are based on the conviction that the highest interests of human culture demand the development of a rigorously scientific philosophy." [7] The hopes of such a radicalized conception of philosophy had, by 1935, been subjected to a devastating war, the return of barbarism to Europe, and the prospect of renewed war. Yet the Husserl of the *Crisis* is undiminished in his insistence on the privileged role of Reason in the unfolding of the human Spirit. The irony is painful. It was in a newly launched journal *Logos* that "Philosophy as Rigorous Science" appeared. The full title is significant: *Logos: Internationale Zeitschrift für Philosophie der Kultur.* Concerned with the implications of the inauguration of such an enterprise, Husserl writes:

It may well be that the proposals presented in the world-renowned scientific works of philosophy in ancient and modern times are based on serious, even colossal intellectual activity. More than that, it may in large measure be work done in advance for the future establishment of scientifically strict doctrinal systems; but for the moment, nothing in them is recognizable as a basis for philosophical science, nor is there any prospect of cutting out, as

6. *Ibid.*, p. 299.
7. Edmund Husserl, "Philosophy as Rigorous Science," in *Phenomenology and the Crisis of Philosophy*, p. 78.

it were, with critical scissors here and there a fragment of philosophical doctrine. This conviction must once more be expressed
boldly and honestly, and precisely in this place, in the first issue
of *Logos*, whose aim is to testify to a significant revolution in
philosophy and to prepare the ground for the future philosophical
"system." [8]

By the time of the *Crisis*, both *Logos* and logos were in eclipse:
"In 1934, when the journal was completely Nazified, Richard
Kroner was replaced as editor in chief (a post which he had held
since 1910) and Ernst Cassirer, Edmund Husserl, Friedrich
Meinecke, and Rudolf Otto were summarily removed from the
roll of collaborating editors." [9]

For Husserl, the historical and political disasters of the first
third of the twentieth century presuppose a philosophical basis,
a debilitation of reason. The sickness of Western man amounts
to the loss of the idea of philosophy. Of the various types of alie-
nation which have been ascribed to modern man, none of them
suggests that the loss of philosophy is the clue to our sickness.
The phenomenological thesis is that the primordial estrangement is historical and consists in the denial of the teleological
impetus of Reason. Philosophy is lost when its underlying idea
—the tendency toward the universal—is denied. It must be
understood that the commitment to the universal does not imply
a metaphysics in which a unitary philosophical system is the goal
of knowledge. It should be clear by now that Husserl was not a
protagonist of a monolithic "System"; to the contrary, he was in
some respects a proponent of diversification. In any case, the
universal transcends any conception of formal unity. What is at
issue is, on the one hand, a conception of absolute truth and, on
the other hand, the principle of historical continuity. The avoid-
ance of either one implies the denial of the other. An illustration
of sorts may help to advance the discussion at this stage.

In place of "a conception of absolute truth" let us speak of a
common-sense view which holds that the only reality is that of
here-and-now fact and power, and in place of "the principle of
historical continuity" let us speak of immediacy and improvisation. In one direction the bond between the present and any

8. *Ibid.*, p. 75.
9. William Gerber, "Philosophical Journals," in *The Encyclopedia
of Philosophy*, ed. Paul Edwards (New York: Macmillan and Free
Press, 1967), VI, 205.

transcendent meaning possible to it is severed; in the other direction, the present is not only isolated from the past which generated it but celebrated as finally liberated from history. Together, the denial of the continuities of past and future creates *present*-dominated man, a creature for whom philosophy can have no meaning but for whom antiphilosophy is alluring. Imagine, then, a person thrust into the present without history or transcendence. This does not mean, of course, that we are suggesting an individual who knows nothing of traditional history or who is unacquainted with the claims of classical philosophy or religion. Rather, we are speaking of the negation of what is known: the constriction of interest to immediacy or at least to the confines of a roughly hewn here and now. The example is by no means obscure or remarkable. Present-domination represents a counterpart to earlier hedonism. Instead of pleasure's being the operative principle, the pulsation of the immediate is the decisive consideration: not what is produced as much as what is kept out. The merger of present-domination with hedonism yields decadence, but, kept separated from the intoxication of pleasure, present-domination creates its own lightness of spirit by accepting the gifts of the moment. Our hero of immediacy moves in a freedom which denies the possibility of continuity between what he has been and what he may become. It would appear that his life consists of one long perceptual volley. How is the person to be heard in the midst of such din?

In truth, the individual hides in our example. The present-dominated man seems faceless. But it would be wrong to restrict his movements on the contemporary scene. There may be claims to the discovery of communal transcendence, a primal religiosity, or an aesthetic of the transitory. That we live in a time of the rhapsody of the group is enough to be on guard against such claims. But the man without history, however he defines his interests, falls into isolation and ends in aloneness, for the thesis on which he bases his life is that of his self-sufficiency. In Christian terms, present-dominated man is guilty of the sin of pride. His secret was found out by Kierkegaard:

> Every human existence which is not conscious of itself as spirit, or conscious of itself before God as spirit, every human existence which is not thus grounded transparently in God but obscurely reposes or terminates in some abstract universality (state, nation, etc.), or which, in obscurity about itself, takes its faculties merely

as active powers, without in a deeper sense being conscious whence it has them, which regards itself as an inexplicable something which is to be understood *per se*—every such existence is after all despair.[10]

The other side of the euphoria of immediacy, whether decadent or "religious," is its own insufficiency, its incapacity to make sense of itself, its propulsion toward nothingness. The despair of the person caught in this directionless acceleration lies outside the limits of what he is willing to acknowledge as a legitimate concern for humanity. When history breaks through the implicit brackets of immediacy, it appears in distinctively individual terms—i.e., it is the person who is challenged to make sense of himself before others or before God. The sickness we have been examining consists, in strong measure, in accepting man per se and, in consequence, taking his origin for granted. The recovery of philosophy begins with reversing that acceptance. In turn, historical consciousness is reborn in philosophical reflection.

Phenomenology, for Husserl, is the ultimate clue to historical reconstruction. The sense he gives to this thesis can be stated simply enough. Philosophy gives coherence to experience; phenomenology elucidates the idea of philosophy; transcendental phenomenology traces out the constitution of the world; the becoming of the world is the theme of history; history is rooted in the life-world. Brought together, these strands establish the focus of Husserl's concern with history as an intentional product. The task of phenomenology is to illuminate the total process through which the intentional world is constituted in transcendental consciousness and to do so in a manner which grounds all description and analysis in originary intuition. The task, as Husserl himself emphasizes, is an infinite one.[11] It involves not only the clarification of the roots of the sciences but the comprehension of the life-world in its essential entirety. But the scope of the venture should not be confused with its inner dynamic: the logic of the phenomenologist's enterprise involves a meditation on Reason carried out by reason—a meditation whose task is also infinite and whose name is philosophy. The history of the philosopher's reflection on Reason becomes part of the subject mat-

10. Sören Kierkegaard, *The Sickness Unto Death,* in *Fear and Trembling and the Sickness Unto Death,* trans. Walter Lowrie (Garden City, N.Y.: Doubleday, Anchor Books, 1953), p. 179.
11. Husserl, *Crisis,* p. 279.

ter of his inquiry. Philosophy's history is the container as well as
the chronicle of Reason. Perhaps now it is possible to appreciate
the ultimacy which Husserl attributes to phenomenology. As the
method of Reason, phenomenology is devoted to fulfilling the
mission of philosophy: the achievement of universal knowledge.
"Achievement," it must be said, is hardly an easy word here. By it
Husserl understands the struggle for secure ground, for what he
terms "apodictic" knowledge. Rather than presupposing a
Heaven of Ideas, Husserl envisions human life as a critical becoming in which the truth of Reason may be attained. Not fixity
but development is the sign of Reason; it is no less the mark of
history. Husserl writes:

> Reason is the specific characteristic of man, as a being living in
> personal activities and habitualities. This life, as personal life, is
> a constant becoming through a constant intentionality of develop-
> ment. What becomes, in this life, is the person himself. His being
> is forever becoming; and in the correlation of individual-personal
> and communal-personal being this is true of both, i.e., of the
> individual man and of unified human civilizations.[12]

It is Reason, then, which is at the center of human history,
whether one approaches Reason from the standpoint of theory
or from the clamor of the life-world. In the end, Reason is the
source and *telos* of Man. Yet it is exactly that centrality which
may be subjected to serious criticism. Shestov in particular has
taken up the critique of rationalism. The conclusion he comes
to is that Husserl abandons his phenomenological rigor in accepting reason as the crux of philosophy. "Husserl," he writes,
"*believes* that reason needs no justification; that, on the contrary,
everything has to justify itself before reason. And the moment he
loses this faith, . . . then what is left of the theory of knowledge founded on self-evidences?"[13] The advantages of so condensed a statement for purposes of critical clarity are compromised by their simplistic polarization: belief and faith on the
one side, rigor and self-evidence on the other. The situation, as
Shestov understood, is by no means so easy. To be sure, Husserl
equates Reason with philosophy, but he regards them both as
products of Greek civilization, as gifts of history through which
Western man has won his way to self-reflection. The critical

12. *Ibid.*, p. 338.
13. Lev Shestov, *Potestas Clavium*, p. 402.

tools of dialectic and analysis are sharpened in that self-reflective process. One does not have "faith" in philosophy; one justifies his philosophical career by practicing philosophy. Arrogance and disparagement with regard to philosophy are as much to be expected as attack and recrimination, yet philosophical certitude undergirds the reflective life for those who are willing to entertain criticism. Now it is possible to say that such certitude is established and sustained by a primordial choice of the individual, the choice of Reason, and that an alternative choice is also possible—that of a world accepted as beyond critique, a world given in Faith. But the announcement of a theological equivalent of a "separate but equal" doctrine is not the same as the renunciation of the autonomy of philosophy. The matter needs closer scrutiny.

For Husserl, the genius of phenomenological reduction carried out to its full transcendental possibilities consists in its final lucidity; i.e., nothing perceivable, thinkable, or imaginable is excluded from the purview of intentional consciousness. To the contrary, the phenomenologist has a mandate to confront everything in its essential givenness. That means, for Husserl, a methodological commitment to be responsive to opposing no less than supporting views. The claim to self-evidence is not a retreat from criticism but an acceptance of the principle of philosophical responsibility. That principle can be formulated in straightforward terms: the philosopher places the requirements of his discipline ahead of his personal proclivities. The psychology of the philosopher involves qualitatively different considerations. The individual may have more or less intense devotion to his calling, but the meaning of philosophical work transcends the psychology of its representatives. At least one benefit of Husserl's refutation of psychologism should be the freeing of the philosopher from the charge of personal idiosyncrasy. There *are* genuine problems concerning the relationship between philosophy and the philosopher, problems for both philosophy and psychology, but the exploration of such problems cannot be carried out convincingly if, from the outset, we assume that all analysis is relativized by psychological reference, such an assumption would invalidate any warranty which psychology itself might have. We cannot avoid returning to the province of philosophy if we wish to assess philosophical claims.

"Belief" or "faith" in philosophy is nothing more than the acceptance of Reason; that acceptance entails the persistent will-

ingness of the philosopher to pursue inquiry. Shestov is correct
when he says that Husserl "believes that reason needs no justification"; his error consists in italicizing "believes." Reason needs
no justification because it is the matrix of justification. Nor is
it a matter of axioms. Husserl does not "believe" in his a prioris.
He accepts them in their intentional givenness. Of course, no
one can be compelled to accept anything if he abandons logic
and requiredness. "Two plus two equals four" means nothing to
a mind which has negated or relinquished all claims to universality. Shestov is right to quote Dostoevski's paradoxalist:
" 'Twice two is four' is in my opinion simply an impertinence!
'Twice two is four' is a lout; he plants himself across our path,
arms akimbo, and spits on the ground." [14] Nothing can keep man
from vomiting up reason if he chooses to nauseate himself or if
he is tortured into conceptual frenzy. Then one breaks off from
history, disclaims continuity with Man, and turns not to, but
upon, oneself. The alternative is faith. The Underground Man is
caught between two worlds: he howls down reason and cannot
pledge himself to faith. Yet faith remains the great alternative.
It can, of course, be argued that any analysis of faith must
eventually come before the court of philosophy, though it can
equally well be claimed that philosophy and theology have no
jurisdiction over each other.[15] What is important here is the recognition that choosing to accept the logic of the heart leads to
the discipline of love and the search for grace, but not to a foundation for philosophical commitment. In fine, it may be true that
reason and faith must remain perpetual antagonists, but it is
false to assume that their intimate enmity leaves them both un-
affected.[16] Reason does not need faith to "believe" in its mission.
The power of faith is that it *cannot* serve as a ground for reason;
its talent lies elsewhere.

If there is an ultimate standoff between reason and faith,
then on what basis is it possible to defend one's choice of either?
Perhaps no defense is possible at the level of fundamental value
orientation without presupposing the question we are trying to

14. *Ibid.*, p. 400.
15. For example, Paul Tillich holds that "there is no possible conflict between theology and philosophy because there is no common
basis for such a conflict" (*Systematic Theology* [Chicago: University
of Chicago Press, 1951], I, 27).
16. See Leo Strauss, *Natural Right and History* (Chicago: University of Chicago Press, 1953), p. 75.

answer: Can reason generate its own legitimacy? The value of reason would seem to lie outside the scope of reason. If it does, what criterion is there to judge value? Questions of this order are part of the traditional discussion of what, following Max Weber, has come to be called "value-free science." To the extent that fundamental questions of value impinge on the meaning of vocation, we are concerned as well with matters of professional choice and decision. It is unnecessary to rehearse Weber's position on the nature of value and the meaning of science. It is enough to say that for him science and value have qualitatively different roots. In the terms we have employed, reason and value can never justify each other. How then does the individual make his choice in committing himself to scientific work or in refusing to? For the most part, the individual drifts into decision. Within the natural attitude, he finds himself "interested" in this or that, directed toward goals whose nature is often obscure and whose axiological grounding is hidden. The very taken-for-grantedness of the life-world supports naïve man in his choices, buoys him up in the eddies of theoretical conflict. In these terms, the "value" of scientific work is hardly a problem. Similarly, reason is accepted as a kind of backdrop for the action of daily life. The point at which the taken for granted comes to be thematized into self-reflective clarity is in the education of the person. Coming to see—being brought to see—how one's position relates to ultimate values is the key, for Weber, to self-comprehension and the life of reason. He writes:

> In terms of its meaning, such and such a practical stand can be derived with inner consistency, and hence integrity, from this or that ultimate *weltanschauliche* position. Perhaps it can only be derived from one such fundamental position, or maybe from several, but it cannot be derived from these or those other positions. Figuratively speaking, you serve this god and you offend the other god when you decide to adhere to this position. And if you remain faithful to yourself, you will necessarily come to certain final conclusions that subjectively make sense. This much, in principle at least, can be accomplished. Philosophy, as a special discipline, and the essentially philosophical discussions of principles in the other sciences attempt to achieve this. Thus, if we are competent in our pursuit . . . we can force the individual, or at least we can help him, to give himself an *account of the ultimate meaning of his own conduct.* This appears to me as not so trifling a thing to do, even for one's own personal life. Again, I am

tempted to say of a teacher who succeeds in this: he stands in the service of "moral" forces; he fulfils the duty of bringing about self-clarification and a sense of responsibility.[17]

Coming to see the design and origin of conduct in Weber's sense involves a *willingness* of the person to reflect on himself in the life-world. That willingness cannot be legislated; it can only be assumed in education. But what it signifies most deeply is revealed in the voluntative root of the word: what we are appealing to, as well as relying on, in teaching is the *will* of the individual to be educated, the will to see connections and implications once intelligence presents them. The relation of will to value is of paramount interest here, for what Weber is pointing to is the nexus between reason and value. It is through will that the predication of value is made of reason. We come to this: By itself, value can attract the allegiance of the person but can never demonstrate that one value-orientation is superior to another; by itself, reason can demonstrate the truth but cannot persuade the individual that truth is desirable; by an act of will, man can choose to bring together value and truth. To will reason without value or value without reason leads, in Weber's penetrating formulation, to the "mechanized petrification . . . of specialists without spirit or vision and voluptuaries without heart." [18] Weber's pronouncement is close to Husserl's diagnosis of the crisis of Western man.[19] But if the solution of the crisis lies in a unifying will which insists on the integrity of reason and value, then it is necessary to examine the notion of will more closely in the context of its performance in phenomenology.

Throughout the account of phenomenological method, we have tacitly relied on a certain placement of will, disguised by such words as "decision" or "resolve." The abstention which is characteristic of epochē involves a decision to restrict inquiry in a certain radical manner. It is assumed by Husserl that the phenomenologist is not only capable of making such a decision but

17. Max Weber, "Science as a Vocation," in *From Max Weber: Essays in Sociology*, trans. H. H. Gerth and C. Wright Mills (New York: Oxford University Press, 1946), pp. 151–52.

18. Max Weber, *The Protestant Ethic and the Spirit of Capitalism*, trans. Talcott Parsons (New York: Scribner's, 1958), p. 182. I have followed the translation of Leo Strauss, *Natural Right and History*, p. 42.

19. See Aron Gurwitsch, *Studies in Phenomenology and Psychology*, p. 401.

that it is clear what the meaning of decision is here. Husserl devotes his efforts to explaining the results of epochē: *"We put out of action the general thesis which belongs to the essence of the natural standpoint,* we place in brackets whatever it includes respecting the nature of Being: *this entire natural world therefore* which is continually 'there for us', 'present to our hand', and will ever remain there, is a 'fact-world' of which we continue to be conscious, even though it pleases us to put it in brackets." [20] But the explanation does not face the question of the nature of the decision which permits these results. In the narrower methodological sense, the decision to perform the epochē seems to be modeled after the procedures of the mathematician, who is free to specify his definitions, postulates, and rules. But that model will not do when we move to the transcendental epochē and the domain of phenomenological reduction. There the decision of the phenomenologist carries with it a transformation not only of method but of fundamental philosophical orientation toward the world. To "resolve" to perform the reduction would seem to presuppose a kind of freedom which is akin to the acceptance of intellectual responsibility. That freedom, implicit in man's being in the life-world, is identified by Husserl with reason. He writes:

Human personal life proceeds in stages of self-reflection and self-responsibility from isolated occasional acts . . . to the stage of universal self-reflection and self-responsibility, up to the point of seizing in consciousness the idea of autonomy, the idea of a resolve of the will to shape one's whole personal life into the synthetic unity of a life of universal self-responsibility and, correlatively, to shape oneself into the true "I," the free, autonomous "I" which seeks to realize his innate reason, the striving to be true to himself, to be able to remain identical with himself as a reasonable "I." [21]

What Husserl calls "a resolve of the will," Weber speaks of as "following one's demon." Both are necessary for man's integral life as a rational as well as value-bearing being, yet both are presupposed by the realms of reason and value. We are reminded of Shestov's criticism of Husserl. But Shestov missed the decisive point: Husserl does not accept reason through faith but through will. "Be rational!" "Fulfill thy entelechy!"—these are the hidden imperatives addressed to the person deemed intrinsically capable

20. Edmund Husserl, *Ideas,* p. 110.
21. Husserl, *Crisis,* p. 338.

of choosing to honor them. And they presuppose a voluntative resolve: "I *will* assume the responsibility of freedom!" There can be no compulsion in the exercise of will, for all of the persuasive strategies which might be employed are based on the assumption that at the final point of choice the individual must accept them, i.e., must will to act. Yet what appears to be a choice made in solitude is, for Husserl, a resolve sedimented in history. The individual may be the source of willful determination, but he is himself rooted in the past and bears its imprint. The fact is that the exercise of will is the heritage of the person, for in choosing he may come to recognize that others have chosen before him, that the *telos* of Reason is reflected in the history of philosophy no less than in egological purity. In affirming rational action the individual uncovers the past of Man as a being committed to self-reflection. Moving back into history, retracing one's formative path, uncovering the sedimentation of meaning in the history of our becoming—all of these efforts are varying facets of the search for origin which is the essence of philosophy. The will to pursue origin is the clue to the philosopher's autonomy. Husserl writes:

> This manner of clarifying history by inquiring back into the primal establishment of the goals which bind together the chain of future generations, insofar as these goals live on in sedimented forms yet can be reawakened again and again and, in their new vitality, be criticized; this manner of inquiring back into the ways in which surviving goals repeatedly bring with them ever new attempts to reach new goals, whose unsatisfactory character again and again necessitates their clarification, their improvement, their more or less radical reshaping—this, I say, is nothing other than the philosopher's genuine self-reflection on what he is *truly seeking,* on what is in him as a will coming *from* the will and *as* the will of his spiritual forefathers. It is to make vital again, in its concealed historical meaning, the sedimented conceptual system which, as taken for granted, serves as the ground of his private and nonhistorical work. It is to carry forward, through his own self-reflection, the self-reflection of his forebears and thus not only to reawaken the chain of thinkers, the social interrelation of their thinking, the community of their thought, and transform it into a living present for us but, on the basis of the *total unity* thus made present, to carry out a *responsible critique.*[22]

22. *Ibid.,* pp. 71–72.

The affirmation of reason, then, has a communal dimension: it is at once the expression of will in the individual and the location of the history of autonomous choice in Western civilization. This brings us to a fresh aspect of the traditional duality of reason and value. If will cannot be generated from any source other than itself, it is still the case that history reveals the expression of will: men in the past *have* chosen. Either those choices were oriented toward Reason or not, i.e., either the expression of will was concerned with autonomy or was merely a psychological accretion. But the recognition that will *can* be directed toward self-autonomy in Reason alters the conditions under which the individual operates. He may be free to deny the historical possibility of will, but his denial cannot be ahistorical. The history of past choices is sedimented in the career of the person charged with decision. He may deny that history, but he cannot eradicate it. In phenomenological terms, the recognition of will directed toward autonomy is the appreciation of the intentional stratum of decision as bound to teleological fulfillment. In willing something I am tacitly continuing an earlier historical activity. It is the potential of such willing that it become self-conscious and articulate in the life of the subject. More is involved than nostalgia. Husserl maintains that the will to fulfill Reason's entelechy is itself an expression of Reason. If we abandon or compromise our willingness to continue and extend what others have attempted in the history of philosophy, then we are negating at least one central feature of the self: its capacity to persist in searching out and maintaining the directedness of the past. That a negation of will is possible is not denied. To the contrary, Husserl's point is that the sickness of European man is the result in good measure of such negation. And by the greatest of ironies, the most hateful and damaging attack on Reason in recent times came in the name of "Will"—a butchered version of self-determination. The philosophical consequence of the ultimate negation of will as the bridge between reason and value is nihilism.

If the final reality of will is freedom, then the choice of a coherent life instead of nullity rests with the individual. But just as Weber points out that the object of philosophy is to help the individual "to give himself an account of the ultimate meaning of his own conduct," so it is possible in reflection to bring the person to historical awareness. *Seeing* that the sources of reason are constitutive of reason becomes a historical act, for that see-

ing demands the rehearsal in consciousness of man's development. In a way, the path of will leads full circle back to the
meaning of self-evidence. The Underground Man mocked the
Socratic claim that to know the Good is to act in accordance with
it, yet the force of that precept persists if we assume that knowledge and action remain tied to the demands of reason. As long as
the individual will honor the truth of intuition, he opens himself
up to the requirements of reason: that fundamental assumptions,
prejudices, and dogmas be scrutinized, that their sources and
implications be acknowledged, and that the history of their becoming be studied and appropriated. With Weber, Husserl might
well have agreed that there is a therapeutic quality to such a
procedure, one which should not be underestimated in evaluating the life of the person. To refuse to abide by reason, however,
is to choose to deny the very concept of evidence. For the man
who claims independence from reason there can be no science
of beginnings, no discipline of origin, no idea of philosophy. The
refusal of reason is tantamount to the celebration of a nihilism
more fundamental than any of its political manifestations.[23] Philosophy cannot assure that Western man will heed his demon,
but it can preserve and extend itself by assuming the responsibility on behalf of mankind of reflecting in the most radical
fashion. Phenomenology thus becomes the privileged instrument through which Reason sustains its historical momentum
toward lasting autonomy.

On the surface it would seem to be the case that Husserl's
assessment of the crisis of reason amounts to an appeal for the
importance of philosophy in guiding Western man out of his
confusions. Philosophy, in turn, is called upon to make itself
thoroughly rigorous. But can it really be said that if philosophy
today had the methodological exactitude of mathematical physics
the sickness of man in the twentieth century would be qualitatively alleviated, let alone cured? Can it honestly be maintained
that if phenomenology had been all worked out the history of
Europe in our time would have been decisively different? We are
asking the wrong questions in the wrong way. Husserl's conception of history is not based on or concerned with a recitation of
events. In any case, philosophy of history is not a particular

23. A theme developed in my essay "On Conceptual Nihilism,"
in *Life-World and Consciousness: Essays for Aron Gurwitsch*, ed.
Lester E. Embree (Evanston, Ill.: Northwestern University Press,
1972), pp. 287–305.

version of historiography. The questions which phenomenology poses are concerned with meaning, not facticity. If our presentation of Husserl's thought has been effective, at least one thing should be clear: the world of intentional consciousness is a *meant* world, world as phenomenon, world as the correlate of transcendental subjectivity. At the same time, it should be no less evident that, for Husserl, what is comprehended at the transcendental level has its isomorphic counterpart in the natural attitude. Thus, a crisis in meaning in the intentional sphere is reflected in the course of empirical history as it is grasped in the orientation of man in everyday life. The isomorphism in question is understood by Husserl as founded on an a priori principle; it is implied in the very meaning of the phenomenological reduction, for to regard the world as phenomenon is to regard mundane experience from a certain interpretative angle which does not deny or relinquish the empirical but instead fastens on it as intentional object. Everything given to experience in the natural attitude is essentially retained in the phenomenological attitude. The full significance of that retention is to be found in the life-world.

If the prime characteristic of mundane life is taken to be its intersubjective impulse—that this world is *ours*—then sedimented in the taken-for-grantedness of the natural attitude is the historical character of that communality. Not only is the world shared by fellow men but our common past is itself intersubjective in nature. It is assumed that when the individual comes to learn something about world history he will understand that those who lived in the past were like us because, whatever their language, customs, and attitudes, they too conceived of *their* past in the same way—as an intersubjective reality. The assumption lies dormant in the attitude one brings to the study of history, just as the natural attitude implicitly contains the naïve conviction that the world is real. But if the thesis of intersubjective history is a presupposition of daily life, it is no less the case that the naïve acceptance of mundane existence as shared is grounded in a transcendental source. Ultimately, it is the individual who accepts the world, whatever forces impinge upon him. That acceptance in its essential aspect is the theme of phenomenological reconstruction. But coming to accept mundane existence as intersubjective is something tacitly expected of every one of us. Two assumptions then are in operation: that the individual will find his way into the natural attitude and that we expect him to expect the same of others. In both assumptions there is a kind of natural maturation presupposed. The person is not regarded as a creature who may normally develop in any way he pleases; he is assumed to be bound to a historical continuity and development through which his identity as a being in the world of daily life will be nurtured and fulfilled. In brief, the life-world has its own conception of teleology, its own implicit historicity, and its own directive for vindication.

In bringing what is implicit in the life-world to reflective expression, phenomenology is validating its own tendency toward clarification. The entelechy of reason, viewed from the standpoint of the life-world, demands the perpetuation of philosophy. A short account of the idea can be offered. Along with what is prepredicatively grasped in everyday life as "the world," there is also intended the comprehension of that world as a potential of consciousness. This means that what is tacitly apprehended bears within itself the possibility of being brought to clarity. To see something is to be able to grasp that seeing in a reflective act. In sum, philosophy is sedimented in the life-world as the inherent possibility of self-understanding. Although the phenomenological dimension of that possibility may remain opaque in mundane existence, there is in everydayness the appreciation of the finality of seeing that something is the case. If we ask as common-sense men whether meeting someone in the flesh fulfilled the expectation we had of that person, there is no need to explain the epistemological structure of direct perception in relation to imagination: we *know* what meeting and imagining are even though, in reality, we are ignorant of epistemology. But to "know" in this context is nevertheless to recognize that epistemological questions lie outside the sphere of common sense. The distance between mundanity and philosophy is appreciated in protophilosophical terms. If that is true, then man in everyday life is in touch with philosophical reflection, if only to hold it in abeyance. We are reminded of Schutz's "epochē of the natural attitude." The acceptance of routine existence as philosophically "problemless" hides within itself in provisional form the idea of philosophy. The task of phenomenology is then to uncover what common sense has accomplished despite itself. Embedded in the history of everydayness is the genesis of philosophy as the clue to a philosophy of origin.

The crisis of Reason, then, finds its counterpart as well as its source in the crisis of the life-world. Men in daily life have given up philosophy; the idea of reflective knowledge leading to universal truth seems remote from the exigencies of everydayness. But if common sense never put much stock in philosophy it at least had some respect for history. Today, history, too, is something of a casualty of mundane existence. However, it can be argued that if giving up philosophy and history are the signs of the crisis of the life-world then such "crisis" is a normal state of affairs, for the life-world in every epoch is characterized by a deficiency of philosophical and historical interests. Such pursuits are delegated or at least left to particular and sometimes peculiar individuals: philosophers and historians. The representative function of the philosopher is recognized, however obscurely, by men in daily life. It is his task to present to the rest of us an image of our own restlessness and impatience with transcendental investigation and meditation. It is no longer possible to restrict that function to traditional religion—it too has suffered its own crisis. Indeed, the twentieth century is rich in its conceptual and affective afflictions: Reason and God seem to be casualties of hidden warfare. From the side of the Academy, the outlook does not seem too promising. Not infrequently, some professors seem to have lost their way, confess to be just as confused as their students, and even claim that their own disciplines are bankrupt and in need of revitalization by the very students who came for instruction. The public, for a welter of reasons, is frequently disaffected with both professors and their students. The result is that those charged with being representatives no longer believe in what they are supposed to represent; those to be represented are called on to lead the representatives; and those who watch the strange procession conclude that there is no longer anything worthy of being represented.

Yet representation remains rooted in the life-world as its interior *telos*. It may not be necessary to reflect on the crisis of reason, but it is *possible* to do so. That possibility is of decisive significance for the meaning of will. To refuse to be represented by those committed to the reflective life is a different decision than to refuse to engage in the reflective life oneself. I may not choose to read Proust; indeed, I may not choose to do any serious reading at all. But I may nevertheless recognize that Proust deserves to be read by others or that serious authors should continue to be studied. Those engaged in such study stand, in some sense, in my place; they are subjunctive agents who carry forth the impetus of my acknowledgment. However, to deny the need for such representation is to choose a mode of self-sufficiency for human beings which not only repudiates reason but which rejoices in the cleavage between man and what can represent him. Ultimately, we may choose not to read Proust, but the recognition that something vital is relinquished in dispensing with those who represent us in relation to Proust is essential to the life of reason. If that recognition falters we are thrust back upon ourselves without the hope of philosophy. It is curious that so many students today look to their professors not for their learning, not as representatives of their disciplines, but for some sign of how they live, of what they have made of their lives. It is as if a professor's representative function had less to do with reason than with feeling. The argument would seem to be: If you are a meaningful representative of reason, then your personal life will be harmonious; I find your life to be chaotic, therefore you are not a hero of reason. That it should be the student's prerogative to judge the matter at all is the first disgrace of the situation. The second disgrace is even worse, for if the determination had been that the personal life in question was harmonious and the conclusion drawn that the person was therefore a legitimate representative of reason, the student would find himself a stranger not only to reason but to logic as well.

For Husserl, the philosopher is humanity's representative, its delegate of reason, and its advocate of Spirit. To deny the role of the representative is to reduce the philosopher to himself as a mundane being among his fellow men. But he has never sought to deny his situation as a human being. The task he assumes lies in a different region. It is the definitive point of phenomenology's critique of reason that man has three choices: either he can settle for a rationalism defined by objective science, accept the idea of progress, and redraft the old blueprints for a new age of discovery; or he can repudiate both history and objective science in favor of an age of improvisation, a time of affective ingathering to be accompanied in the distance by the drums of the nihilists—a Crystal Night of the spirit; or, finally, he can assume in full seriousness the obligations of a will to Reason in its absolute form: the infinite task of searching out the constitution of our capacity to represent to ourselves what we may yet become—"servants of humanity." Husserl's vision of the goal of phenomenology has been criticized as having a "messianic" undertone.[24] There is some truth to that, but it is a messianism of reflection whose herald is the philosopher; it is the messianism of a philosophy which is aware of the problem of evil; and it is the messianism of expectation rather than deliverance. Within its redemptive limits, Husserl emerges as the philosopher of infinite tasks.

24. Efraim Shmueli, "Critical Reflections on Husserl's Philosophy of History."

10 / Conclusion

IT IS INAPPROPRIATE to bring a discussion of phenomenology to an end by artificially trying to tie together stray bits
of critical thread. Neither expository recapitulation nor interpretative summation will heighten what we have written or bring
into balance the assortment of analysis which has been presented. If phenomenology is a search for beginnings, so should
this conclusion continue that search. In place of "results," I
prefer to speak of continuing difficulties. But a few "metacritical"
points deserve to be made. Underlying this study has been the
conviction that Husserl's thought constitutes a unity which has
unfolded in a complex but essentially continuous fashion. For all
its inadequacies, the psychological position of *Philosophie der
Arithmetik* contained the seed of the position advanced in the
Logical Investigations, whose critique of psychologism prepared
the way for the phenomenology of the *Ideas.* In turn, the methodology developed there went far beyond the propounding of
technique and evolved instead into a transcendental logic on
the one hand, as developed in *Formal and Transcendental Logic,*
and a transcendental monadology on the other hand, as portrayed in *Cartesian Meditations.* And with the full expression of
transcendental phenomenology, Husserl turned to his most profound theme, the search for a philosophy of the life-world which
could revitalize the meaning of history through a new critique
of reason. Throughout his career, Husserl sought to expose the
roots of his problems, to account for the constitution of the perceptual and social world, and, perhaps most decisive of all, to
accept nothing which did not show itself in originary presence by

way of a philosophy which itself had to pass the same phenomenological test. What I find in Husserl's development is the expression of a dominant, enlarging, and deepening idea: the establishment of philosophy by transcendental phenomenology. I cannot claim much company in taking this view.

Many followers of Husserl as well as most of his critics fall into three groups: first, those who find in the "early" Husserl—the author of the *Logical Investigations*—the truly important thinker, the philosopher whose contributions to logic and epistemology are unencumbered by transcendental baggage; second, those who see in the "middle" Husserl—the author of *Ideas* and even, perhaps, the later *Formal and Transcendental Logic*—the expounder of a potentially significant methodology as well as the investigator of the meaning-structure of certain levels of perceptual experience which have not received their due from traditional epistemology; and third, those—a much smaller band—who take the transcendental turn of the *Ideas* and accept its extension and radicalization in the final period of Husserl's work through the *Cartesian Meditations* and into the *Crisis*. Although Husserl inspired his students and aroused their philosophical loyalty, there are very few, if any, of his followers who can be called orthodox Husserlians in all respects. To the contrary, phenomenology has proved so powerful a doctrine and Husserl so magisterial a figure that inevitable reactions set in. Although the situation of phenomenology was not analogous with that of psychoanalysis, it would not be difficult to create a scenario replacing Freud by Husserl (Heidegger would be the Jung of phenomenology). But rather than dramatic breaks, defections from Husserl's teachings were more a matter of his disciples' being unable to continue along the path their master followed. They remained phenomenologists of the earlier Husserl rather than striking out on their own and creating new systems. Although Husserl was disappointed that some of his students having come this far could not go further with him, he insisted on the individual's seeing for himself and finding his own proper way. He sought to encourage, not to dictate.

The trichotomy just presented does not, of course, include a considerable range of interest in and interpretation of Husserl. I shall not attempt a typology of the many kinds of followers and critics of Husserl's thought. There are some who think he deserves considerable credit for the *Logical Investigations* (while also asserting that a good deal of that work is now of chiefly historical importance—its critical content having been outmoded) but place him in the history of logic rather than phenomenology; others regard his later thought as containing interesting elements which need to be disentangled from their transcendental framework so that they can be shown to be basically similar in nature to the contributions of Anglo-American linguistic philosophy and, presumably, absorbed into the dominant tendency of contemporary thought; still others regard the discovery of the life-world as the most promising development in phenomenology, one which will enrich and in turn be enriched by existential and hermeneutical thought. Finally, there are fringe elements to be noted—those whose acquaintance with Husserl's writings is slight or indirect but who are attracted to phenomenology as an invigorating force in the social or humanistic disciplines. Not infrequently, technical phenomenology seems to stand in their way. The total result of all of these varying responses by followers, critics, and enthusiasts appears to yield a sense of dispersion and fragmentation. How integral is phenomenology today?

As I have said, few phenomenologists can be called orthodox Husserlians in all respects, but it would be misleading to interpret this to mean that occasionally some trivial family quarrel has arisen to separate Husserl from his followers. The sore points are substantive and, in many instances, go to the vitals of phenomenology. So, for example, there has been profound disagreement about Husserl's theory of "hylē" or sensation,[1] the egological conception of consciousness,[2] the theory of intersubjectivity,[3] and the philosophical neutrality of phenomenological method.[4] Even those sympathetic to his enterprise have questioned the status of his most fundamental concepts and have asked whether such axial terms as "phenomenon," "constitution," and "epochē" are not ultimately unclarified problems which function in an ancillary fashion in phenomenological research.[5] Lists of points on which all phenomenologists may

1. See Harmon M. Chapman, *Sensations and Phenomenology*.
2. See Aron Gurwitsch, "A Non-Egological Conception of Consciousness," in *Studies in Phenomenology and Psychology*.
3. See Alfred Schutz, "The Problem of Transcendental Intersubjectivity in Husserl," in *Collected Papers*, Vol. III.
4. See Marvin Farber, *The Foundation of Phenomenology*, 3d ed., and *Phenomenology and Existence*.
5. See Eugen Fink, "Les Concepts opératoires dans la phénoménologie de Husserl."

agree,[6] helpful as they are in other respects, do not face the underlying issue of the generation of internal conflict in Husserl's thought. The fact is that phenomenology today is not a univocal philosophy represented by thinkers in perfect doctrinal harmony with each other. It is the kind of sympathy and agreement they do have which is the interesting consideration. If there is as much disagreement over fundamental issues as I have suggested, then why is not phenomenology a theoretical shambles? Why is it, to the contrary, a movement in the ascendancy? And why, with all its internal unrest, has it succeeded in arousing the profound concern of so many thinkers in the social and humanistic sciences?

The essential answer is that disagreement in philosophy need not be destructive. Indeed, it is through conflict that the strength of a position comes to be understood. In the case of phenomenology, conflict is especially easy to comprehend. Husserl did not establish a system, he did not write out all of his books in the style of a typical German professor, he did not move like philosophical clockwork from one set problem to another. As I have tried to suggest, we are considering a philosopher of gigantic but tormenting fragments, a perpetually dissatisfied searcher of foundations, an archaeologist convinced that the bedrock of civilization must be reached once and for all. In such a quest, the instruments of the search must be forged and reforged if they prove wanting. And since philosophical tools demand their own conceptual analysis, the circle of inquiry widens. If ever there was a philosopher destined to produce friction, it was Husserl. Yet the startling fact is that despite internal criticism, phenomenology has not only survived intact but has emerged as a coherent philosophy. Why? I think that the answer lies in a number of interrelated factors. First, there is an attraction to the radicality and freshness of phenomenological method—an attraction which goes beyond any narrow interpretation of epochē or reduction. Second, there is an immediacy about the theory of intentionality, for it offers a new way of interpreting the nature of consciousness and of man's involvement in mundane existence. And third, the historical impetus of phenomenology is penetrating and challenging because, in demanding a return to beginnings, it presents man with an image of himself trying to make sense of himself—the image of Reason. Whether

6. See Herbert Spiegelberg, *The Phenomenological Movement*, II, 658 ff.

or not an individual phenomenologist accepts all of these points, I believe that they are sedimented in the meaning of phenomenology. Like the "sparks" of the cabalistic tradition, they come to life in unexpected ways. In any event, those who depart from Husserl's doctrine claim, for the most part, to remain true in their own way to his teaching. Although such a claim is almost a commonplace in the history of philosophy (which is also a history of aberrant discipleship), it deserves some attention on its own.

René Le Senne has observed that one remains faithful to a philosophy by going beyond it. That truth needs to be taken cautiously. To be sure, no philosopher with a genuine calling wants *followers* in the literal sense of the word; eventually one must strike out on his own. But philosophy, unlike natural science, is not a discipline of replacement. Classical work carries with it in philosophy more than antiquary honor. The task of the disciple is not only to extend his master's work but to *do* that work, i.e., to inquire into the master's philosophical activity with the same critical rigor he uses in working at "new" problems. The act of extension in this instance is equivalent to an act of retrenchment. In a sense, one may go beyond a philosophy only by carrying it along, not out of sentimentality but of necessity. In the case of phenomenology, progression comes by way of retrogression, if we understand by the latter a moving back to origin. Certainly, it would be hard to understand, in phenomenological terms, what "going beyond" Husserl could mean. It is obvious that the unexplored terrain of problems whose outlines Husserl discovered is open for analysis and that phenomenology claims only to have touched the immensity of the work still to be done. But "going beyond" has nothing to do with that. Rather, we might say that if there is a "beyond" to Husserl, it lies in the generational dimension of his endeavor. It was Husserl's dream that phenomenological work would be carried on by colleagues of the future who would not only take up special provinces of common work but who would relive in their own careers the career of Reason. The "beyond" of phenomenology is then the teleological impetus of philosophy itself: its intentional resolve to fulfill its infinite responsibility. To go beyond Husserl in that sense is indeed to remain faithful to him.

Criticism of phenomenology has come not only from outsiders and followers, but also from Husserl himself. He was, in fact, his most unrelenting critic. Apart from various dissatisfactions with his own formulations, however, there were fundamental misgivings. So, for example, Husserl remained discontented with his results in a crucially important domain, that of the problem of intersubjectivity. Perhaps his most penetrating recognition of a problem internal to phenomenology came not from a specific substantive theme in epistemology or logic but in the appreciation of certain paradoxes at the center of his work. The clearest expression of these paradoxes appears in a formulation by Eugen Fink. The general claim is that phenomenology by its very transcendental nature generates fundamental paradoxes of communication, language, and logic. The first paradox is that of "the position from which statements are made." [7] It comes into being with the performance of the reduction. Fink writes:

> The "phenomenologist" addresses himself to the "dogmatist." Is such communication possible? Does not the phenomenologist withdraw from the transcendental attitude when he communicates? The phenomenologist's statements clearly presuppose a basis shared by both him and the dogmatist. Is such a basis given, or can one be produced? While all men, no matter how different their manner of thinking, share the common basis of the natural attitude, the phenomenologist has broken out of this basis in performing the reduction. Considered more closely, however, he must not step out of the transcendental attitude and return to the naïveté of the natural attitude in communicating with the dogmatist. Rather does he place himself within the natural attitude as within a transcendental situation which he has already grasped. His communication with the dogmatist is now burdened by the difficulty that, for the speaker, the position from which statements concerning phenomenological knowledge are made is transparent with respect to its transcendental meaning, whereas it is not so for the listener. Is it therefore possible for them to speak about the same things? [8]

In communication between the phenomenologist and the dogmatist it is presupposed by the former that discussion may serve as a transitional stage which prepares the way for the latter to enter into phenomenology himself. From the standpoint of the dogmatist, it may be that although the meaning of what the phenomenologist says is not comprehended, it does suggest a

7. Eugen Fink, "The Phenomenological Philosophy of Edmund Husserl and Contemporary Criticism," p. 142.
8. *Ibid.*, p. 143.

way or path which might lead to a different mode of experience and expression. The psychological variables here are great and, to some extent, interfere with the appreciation of the paradox. The linguistic difficulties in the problematic relationship between phenomenologist and dogmatist are relatively unimportant *at this point.* Defining and redefining one's terms will not set either party at ease. The trouble is that radically different spheres of reference are in question when, in principle, every attempt to communicate phenomenological knowledge meets with what might be termed an auditory dislocation—a reception which unwittingly assumes the translatability of transcendental into mundane experience. The dogmatist has little patience with paradox and so may assume that when translation falters or fails, somebody rather than something is at fault. Yet paradox permits rather than precludes an intimation of phenomenology. The barrier is severe but not, ultimately, intransigent.

The second paradox, grounded in the first, is that of "the phenomenological statement." [9] Fink writes:

The phenomenologist who desires to communicate has only worldly concepts at his disposal. He must express himself in the language of the natural attitude. The mundane meaning of the words available to him cannot be entirely removed, for their meaning can be limited only by the use of other mundane words. For this reason no phenomenological analysis, above all the analysis of the deeper constituting levels of transcendental subjectivity, is capable of being present adequately. The inadequacy of all phenomenological reports, caused by the use of a mundane expression for a nonworldly meaning, also cannot be eliminated by the invention of a technical language. Since phenomenological communication is chiefly a communication addressed to the dogmatist, such a language would be devoid of meaning. Phenomenological statements necessarily contain an internal conflict between a word's mundane meaning and the transcendental meaning which it serves to indicate. There is always the danger that the dogmatist will grasp only the mundane meaning of words and overlook their transcendental significance to such an extent that he will imagine his mistaken explication of phenomenology to be correct and capable of calling upon the text for its justification.[10]

9. *Ibid.*
10. *Ibid.*, pp. 143–44.

The second paradox goes beyond questions of misunderstanding or the distortion of language. It is language itself which is at issue in the phenomenologist's effort to transcend the formation as well as formulation of mundane experience. Within the natural attitude reflection on language arises in the horizon of language: one linguistic enterprise comes to question another. In transcendental terms the situation is quite different: the becoming of protolinguistic experience as well as natural language is explored in its intentional constitution through language which is, in a sense, borrowed in order to be reconstructed. The ensuing transformation of language is only partly grasped in appreciating the technical vocabulary of the phenomenologist. What that language *intends* is the essential consideration. Yet the paradox of language prohibits the establishment of any founding structure which might serve as a neutral basis for communication between phenomenologist and dogmatist—as a third language might serve two individuals who did not know each other's tongue. Again, paradox does not produce an absolute obstruction between potential communicants. Oddly enough, there is a resonance of meaning in the paradox of language which might be indicated by paraphrasing T. S. Eliot: phenomenology communicates before it is understood.

"The third and final paradox," Fink concludes,

> is closely connected with the first two. It is the *logical paradox of transcendental determinations*. This does not mean that the sphere of transcendental subjectivity is a sphere in which no logic whatsoever would be valid, but indicates solely those logical *aporias* which occasionally occur in the determination of basic transcendental relations, relations which cannot be mastered by logical means. . . .[11]

As an example of an aporia—[12] philosophical blockage—Fink mentions the problem of "how we are to determine the identity of

11. *Ibid.*, p. 144.
12. F. E. Peters presents a suggestive account of the term "aporia": "*Aporia* and its cognate forms are closely related to dialectic . . . and hence to the Socratic custom of interlocutory discourse. According to Aristotle's analysis . . . philosophy begins with a sense of wonder . . . growing from an initial difficulty (*aporia*), a difficulty experienced because of conflicting arguments. . . . Both the *aporia* and its attendant wonder can be paralleled in Socrates' fre-

the transcendental and human egos." [13] Are they the same or separate egos? The sense of identity at issue here cannot be construed in terms of the logic of the natural attitude but is a function of the relationship between a mundane and a transcendental being. Phenomenology requires its own transcendental logic in order to illuminate the foundations of mundane logic, which in turn is presupposed by the natural attitude in any attempt to interpret the meaning of transcendental logic. The latter kind of presupposition is inessential and can be overcome in the phenomenological reduction, but demonstrating that possibility in mundane terms leads one into paradox. The first two paradoxes can at least be stated with some ease and understood in their general import. The third paradox is the despair of the other two: it leaves one with the feeling that even if the problems of communication and language could be resolved, mundane man would still find the phenomenologist unfathomable.

The paradoxes taken together suggest the approximative character of any attempt to explain what phenomenology is, if not the failure in principle of trying to understand its problems and method without becoming a phenomenologist. [14] But they

---

quent protestations of his own ignorance. . . . But this initial state of ignorance, compared by Aristotle to a man in chains, . . . yields to a further sense where *aporia* . . . assumes the features of a dialectical process . . . and where the investigation of the opinions . . . of one's philosophical predecessors is a necessary preliminary to arriving at a proof. . . . Thus, the *aporia* are posed, previous opinions on these problems are canvassed, and a solution . . . is worked out. The solution may take a variety of forms. . . . But whatever the solution, the posing of the problem and the working from problem to solution, which is the heart of the philosophical method, is a difficult and onerous task" (*Greek Philosophical Terms* [New York: New York University Press, 1967], pp. 22–23).

13. Fink, "The Phenomenological Philosophy of Edmund Husserl and Contemporary Criticism," p. 144.

14. Marvin Farber writes: "The paradoxes are reminiscent of Gorgias, whom Husserl is inclined to take seriously, and to credit with the discovery of the problem of transcendence. Indeed, the first paradox states that the phenomenological realm cannot be 'known,' i.e., in natural terms; and the second informs us that it cannot be 'communicated,' i.e., in natural language, or in any language for that matter. The third paradox, in effect, removes the realm of phenomenology beyond proof or disproof in their customary sense, in that it declares for the inadequacy of 'mundane' logic. The formulation of the paradoxes, especially the third one, shows that one may not hope for a satisfactory answer, or in fact for any answer at all, on the

also point toward the radical character of philosophy itself, philosophy as a strange appraisal of taken-for-grantedness rather than a particular school or position. Part of the philosopher's problem is to communicate with those who are not philosophers, but an equally notable task is for the philosopher to live in the world he has conceptually upended. If the dogmatist finds the phenomenological sphere impenetrable, the phenomenologist has to adjust in his own way to the move from the reduced to the natural attitude. If Plato's prisoner had to rub his eyes to get accustomed to the light, so the one trying to set him free had to strain his eyes to compensate for the darkness. What connection is there, finally, between philosophy and the world? We have returned to our starting point: Who needs philosophy? If the best that comes from phenomenology, on Husserl's own admission, is paradox, then it would seem that whatever crises confront us today, the phenomenologist is too caught in philosophical quicksand to be of much help. Once again, it would seem that philosophy is marginal to history. As a last resort, one can always appeal to "wisdom," which is something like saying, "Yes, Grandfather is feeble, but look how old he is!" It would be a mistake, however, to dismiss phenomenology by giving it the consolation prize of wisdom. Here again Shestov admonishes the student of phenomenology by reminding him of the distinction which Husserl makes between wisdom and science.

Toward the end of his analysis of historical relativism in his *Logos* article, Husserl writes:

> Profundity is a mark of the chaos that genuine science wants to transform into a cosmos, into a simple, completely clear, lucid order. Genuine science, so far as its real doctrine extends, knows no profundity. Every bit of completed science is a whole composed of "thought steps" each of which is immediately understood, and so not at all profound. Profundity is an affair of wisdom; conceptual distinctness and clarity is an affair of rigorous theory. To recast the conjectures of profundity into unequivocal rational forms—that is the essential process in constituting anew the rigorous sciences.[15]

---

basis of the natural attitude concerning matters pertaining to the transcendental sphere. One can therefore never be convinced of phenomenology in natural terms, but must adopt the phenomenological attitude" (*The Foundation of Phenomenology*, pp. 559–60).

15. Edmund Husserl, "Philosophy as Rigorous Science," in *Phenomenology and the Crisis of Philosophy*, p. 144.

Shestov seizes on this and related statements with surgical dexterity. He writes:

This opposing of philosophy and science, on the one hand, and wisdom and profundity of thought, on the other hand, is extremely original and curious. As far as I know, it was first expressed in this formulation by Husserl. Before him it had always been admitted that wisdom and profundity of thought, which were everywhere driven out, could find asylum only in the bosom of philosophy, where also, as is known, virtue, which is forever hunted down, finds rest. But Husserl energetically refused to let philosophy be the refuge of wisdom and virtue. He is prepared to accord to the latter all marks of respect, . . . but wisdom and virtue must seek their means of existence elsewhere, even though they be reduced to applying to public or even private charity.[16]

Although Shestov makes some valuable points in his emphasis on Husserl's preference for science over wisdom, he construes the case too narrowly. It is in the context of a discussion of *Weltanschauung* philosophy that Husserl distinguishes between the two. It is in order to overcome the role of philosophical personality that profundity is set apart from rigorous knowledge and, to some extent, even caricatured. Wisdom as the fundament of a particular world outlook, no matter how impressive, is tangential to philosophy's ultimate mission: universal knowledge. But Husserl's own emphasis on the beginnings of rigorous science in "the Socratic-Platonic revolution of philosophy" should be enough to warn the reader that the duality portrayed with regard to relativistic philosophy breaks down when it is the total scope of knowledge which is at stake. The wisdom of Socrates is not synonymous with the wisdom of Dilthey; the profundity of Platonic thought is not to be identified with the profundity of *Weltanschauung* philosophy. A fascinating document would have been a commentary by Shestov on the philosophy of Husserl's *Crisis*. As he read the *Méditations Cartésiennes*, I wonder what Shestov made of Husserl's introductory warning: "Anyone who seriously intends to become a

16. Lev Shestov, *Potestas Clavium*, p. 293. An interesting controversy ensued on this point between Shestov and one of Husserl's students, Jean Hering. See Hering, "Sub specie aeterni: Réponse à une critique de la philosophie de Husserl," *Revue d'histoire et de philosophie religieuses*, VII, no. 4 (July–August, 1927), 351–64 and Shestov's reply, "What is Truth?," in *Potestas Clavium*. Also compare Benjamin Fondane, *La Conscience malheureuse*.

philosopher must 'once in his life' withdraw into himself and attempt, within himself, to overthrow and build anew all the sciences that, up to then, he has been accepting. Philosophy— wisdom (*sagesse*)—is the philosophizer's quite personal affair. It must arise as *his* wisdom, as his self-acquired knowledge tend- ing toward universality, a knowledge for which he can answer from the beginning, and at each step, by virtue of his own abso- lute insights." [17] Did Shestov have any second thoughts about Husserl on wisdom? Is it possible that Shestov recognized in the portion of the *Crisis* which was published in 1936 [18] a movement beyond the position he ascribes to Husserl? And, finally, would he have continued to maintain, in the face of the full phenome- nological critique of European man, that Husserl's conception of knowledge was divorced from a philosophy of wisdom? And how would Husserl have responded to a new critique by Shestov? I have no answers to these questions. Both men died in 1938, a time in which wisdom and science were in retreat.

The paradoxes of phenomenology and its conception of wisdom as autonomy are also the paradoxes of philosophy and its demand for representatives who assume the responsibility of thematizing man's capacity to reflect on his own origin. Philos- ophy presupposes at least the tacit acceptance on the part of men of having the possibility of critical self-reflection repre- sented by the activity of the philosophers. Philosophy is thus possible through the acceptance of the principle of representa- tion; in turn, representation itself is a necessary theme for philosophical analysis. [19] Two forces are at work: one, reflection as the possibility of men who act; the other, recognition that *someone* is responsible for comprehending the relationship be- tween reflection and action. A society which accepts itself with- out recognizing the need to continue to account for its own representative capacity alters its own image in a qualitative and, perhaps, irreversible way. Relinquishing the principle of rep- resentation is like draining the language of everything but the

17. Edmund Husserl, *Cartesian Meditations*, p. 2.
18. Edmund Husserl, "Die Krisis der europäischen Wissenschaf- ten und die transzendentale Phänomenologie: Eine Einleitung in die phänomenologische Philosophie," *Philosophia*, I, Fasc. 1–4 (1936), 77–176.
19. For a discussion of the larger problem of "representation," see Eric Voegelin, *The New Science of Politics* (Chicago: University of Chicago Press, 1952).

vocabulary of Basic English: communication at some level may be possible, but an inquiry into the meaning of the shift in language is no longer thinkable, let alone discussable, within the new linguistic establishment. Qualitative change in this sense signifies a cardinal but most subtle transformation: the choice of categorial matrices which ultimately render possible or preclude reflective analysis. Not whether one interpretation is to prevail or another, but whether there is to be interpretation at all is the problem.

The meaning of representation in the career of philosophy is reflected in the life of the individual. At the mundane level, I find myself engaged in action which I can accept as "real" without the need of philosophical justification. I know that there are questions of "reality," but they belong in someone else's bailiwick. It is a standard joke of everyday life to assign subjunctive questions to the realm of "philosophy." Opinions may differ on whether the professional philosopher's work is important, but common-sense men would at least hesitate to destroy the possibility of continuing that work, were it in their power to do so. Attacks against philosophers and even philosophy are not the same as the refusal of the possibility of any philosophical activity at all. At some point, it is recognized that as men of everyday life we stand in need of those who legitimate our station; in a way, they tell our story. But even those who would deny the function of philosophy must still face the fact that they are opposing something which is a part of historical order. It then becomes necessary to ask why others have accepted philosophy and to inquire into its traditional activities. As long as the individual who opposes philosophy is given pause in thinking about its historical grounding, there is a framework common to both sides: those who support and those who deny philosophy recognize that historical placement demands notice and respect. When that common framework trembles the quality of the social order is, in the most fundamental sense, endangered. Philosophy can withstand the strongest attacks from without and the most profound unsettledness from within, but it cannot survive the dissolution of representation. If the essence of philosophy is reflection, then the pursuit of a genuinely reflective life presupposes the articulation of its own activity: self-representation.

The reflective function of philosophy has been attacked by some philosophers who see in the stress on the interpretative life a pathetic or vicious quietism. The Marxist stress on the unity of theory and practice comes in part from a disgust with what are taken to be the excesses of pure philosophy. Oddly enough, the greater the political power of the Marxist, the less weight is attached to the question of the unity of theory and practice. The question is pursued most passionately by those out of power. But Marx's statement about the philosophers in his *Theses on Feuerbach* must be taken with the utmost seriousness—a seriousness beyond the notoriety the statement has attracted—because it reveals, in paradigmatic form, philosophy's potential mistrust of itself or loss of faith in its own mission. In what I believe to be the most profoundly antiphilosophical sentence ever written by a philosopher, Marx said: "The philosophers have only *interpreted* the world in various ways; the point however is to *change* it." [20] The splitting apart of interpretation and reality is itself the result of interpretative analysis. How is one to grasp the nature of change without an interpretative act, let alone an interpretative apparatus? In any case, how is change to be evaluated? And how is evaluation possible without interpretation? Such questions are not deliberate efforts to misconstrue the obvious point of thesis xi, that a world in need of historical transformation demands more than traditional philosophy has to offer, that only a truly revolutionary philosophy can hope to effect historical change. But it should be noted that the acceptance of Marx's conception of the role of philosophy carries with it a representational charge: the philosopher as revolutionary is to locate the meaning of his own activity in the midst of the world rather than at a reflective remove from reality. That interpretation of the locus of the philosopher cannot be absorbed into action or ingested by change without losing its own force as a principle of the critique of history. If that is true, then it would be more just to say with all candor that revolutionaries have only changed the world; the point is to interpret it.

Representation, in phenomenological terms, rests on but is by no means restricted to the philosopher. For Husserl, the resolution of the crisis inevitably involves a broad circle of thinkers, starting with philosophers concerned with the grounding of Reason and ending with fellow men who may be distant from philosophy but who are touched by its implications and drawn to it. The tremor of philosophy moving out to the world is felt

20. Karl Marx, "Theses on Feuerbach," in Frederick Engels, *Ludwig Feuerbach* (New York: International Publishers, 1935), p. 75.

first in ancient thought, where the force of individuals of genius is recognized by nonphilosophers as well as theoreticians and absorbed into the cultural life of the society. Husserl writes:

Through isolated personalities like Thales . . . there arises . . . a new humanity: men who live the philosophical life, who create philosophy in the manner of a vocation as a new sort of cultural configuration. Understandably a correspondingly new sort of communalization arises. These ideal structures of *theōria* are concurrently lived through and taken over without any difficulty by others who reproduce the process of understanding and production. Without any difficulty they lead to cooperative work, mutual help through mutual critique. Even the outsiders, the nonphilosophers, became aware of this peculiar sort of activity. Through sympathetic understanding they either become philosophers themselves, or, if they are otherwise vocationally too occupied, they learn from philosophers. Thus philosophy spreads in a twofold manner, as the broadening vocational community of philosophers and as a concurrently broadening community movement of education.[21]

It would be unfair to charge Husserl with naïveté. He has not given us an idyll in which bands of enthusiasts dance after philosopher-heroes. To the contrary, Husserl points out that the spread of interest in philosophy does not lead to a homogeneous result but instead involves conflict and persecution. However, what is possible to the history of interest in philosophy is the recognition by at least some individuals that the recovery of Reason undergirds all other values. If the nonphilosopher gets the idea, then what he becomes attracted to in philosophy is the search for a universality which goes much deeper than traditional rationalism has allowed. In the end, it is the revolutionary character of phenomenology that distinguishes the radical search for absolutivity from pedestrian rationalism. Whatever the psychology of philosophers and their audiences, the phenomenology of their careers is the clue to the historical survival of their classical mission: philosophers and those who ally themselves with philosophy are the only true subversives. As Husserl put it: "I would like to think that I, the supposed reactionary, am far more radical and far more revolutionary than those who in their words proclaim themselves so radical today."[22] Husserl does not

21. Edmund Husserl, *The Crisis of European Sciences and Transcendental Phenomenology*, p. 286.
22. *Ibid.*, p. 290.

blithely expect thousands to rally to the cause of genuine philosophy, but he does believe that, by carrying on his own work intensively and uncompromisingly, the philosopher makes it possible for civilization to reconstruct itself. If the crisis which he diagnoses is as profound as he makes it out to be—and I think it is—then the need for genuinely fundamental reflection is indeed absolute. In Husserl's terms, philosophy must be concerned with its own meaning if it is to remain true to its essential purpose. Thus, what might strike some as being a morbid self-concern is necessary to the career of the philosopher: he must again and again seek to justify his own activity. Husserl writes:

> The philosopher must always devote himself to mastering the true and full sense of philosophy, the totality of its horizons of infinity. No line of knowledge, no single truth may be absolutized and isolated. Only through this highest form of self-consciousness, which itself becomes one of the branches of the infinite task, can philosophy fulfill its function of putting itself, and thereby genuine humanity, on the road to realization. The awareness that this is the case itself belongs to the domain of philosophical knowledge at the level of highest self-reflection. Only through this constant reflexivity is a philosophy universal knowledge.[23]

The meaning of representation in phenomenology turns on the nature of reflexivity. In the kind of radical self-reflection which Husserl establishes as the ideal of philosophy, the phenomenologist accepts and affirms the directedness of concrete action toward its proper goal. In turn, man is comprehended always as bound teleologically to some end. The effort to understand the nature of such entelechies is itself a critical aspect of teleology. In reflecting on the meaning of Reason, the phenomenologist represents reason vivified, reason in practice. Here self-reflection implies a bringing to clarity of what is implicit in the experience in question. In phenomenological terms, the possibility of the philosopher's making his own activity explicit is sedimented in intentional consciousness. The thematization of some aspect of experience places that experience in a horizon of expectation. At every point, then, phenomenology honors the integrity of the aspect and the whole, the unit and the horizon in which it is viewed, the concrete and the universe in which it comes into clarity. Philosophy, in these terms, is practiced best

23. *Ibid.*, p. 291.

by remaining concerned at all times with the meaning of its own enterprise. At one and the same time, the philosopher represents, for Husserl, the possibility of philosophy, the life of reason, and the autonomy of self-reflection; but represented in philosophy is the philosopher's awareness of his own mission as a transcendental analogue of philosophical practice. The philosopher reflects on history only to find his reflection revealed in history; yet it is through that reflection that history is possible. To recognize in philosophy the intimacy between the inquirer and the inquirer's conception of what he is about is to appreciate the meaning of reflexivity.

Despite, or perhaps partly because of, the grandeur of the concept of representation and all the emphasis which has been placed on the idea of the philosopher as the servant of Reason, phenomenology may be accused of being a magnificent failure. In some philosophical quarters today, programmatic utterances and reliance on such terms as "Spirit" and "Reason" ("Hurrah" words, as they have been called) are in disfavor. It does not seem likely that still another call to self-responsibility will appeal to a community of thinkers whose intellectual lives are defined by a primordial nominalism: the belief that short views are preferable to transcendental vistas. On the side of the nonphilosophers, certainly, there has been no overwhelming turn to theory. Quite the reverse: if Western man was sick when Husserl wrote, he is sicker still today. The schools and colleges hardly promise a solution to our troubles, and those outside the universities are contemptuous of those within. At every turn, it seems that Husserl's warnings have had little effect. Where they are known, not much has changed; where they are unknown, not much has altered. It is understandable that, under these circumstances, one might lapse into what the Germans call "culture-pessimism." Yet Husserl persisted in his calling and refused to yield his conviction that the salvation of Man lies in the integrity of Reason. He asks:

Is it not the case that what we have presented here is something rather inappropriate to our time, an attempt to rescue the honor of rationalism, of "enlightenment," of an intellectualism which loses itself in theories alienated from the world, with its necessary evil consequences of a superficial lust for erudition and an intellectual snobbism? Does this not mean that we are being led again into the fateful error of believing that science makes man wise, that it is destined to create a genuine and contented humanity that is master of its fate? Who would still take such notions seriously today? [24]

It is Husserl's view that the modern tragedy of Western civilization comes from halfway measures, from a failure to turn to knowledge in its genuinely universal foundations, from a naïve acceptance of a limited and ultimately inadequate conception of objective science in place of rigorous science, from a refusal to recognize the meaningful status of the life-world in relation to knowledge, and from a despairing and benighted assessment of the nature of authentic subjectivity. The politics and sociology of culture are grounded on a fragmented conception of theory and a displacement of the vocation of philosophy. It may or may not be true that transcendental phenomenology alone has the power to reconstruct what unreason has demolished, but it is at least certain that Husserl has been able to present a philosophy which traces out the source of crisis in uncompromising terms. It is not his claim that sounding the alarm is equivalent to putting out the fire, but he has demonstrated what is wrong with a culture which no longer recognizes alarms. Husserl's perseverence in holding to Reason vindicates his own concern with history and brings into unity the full career of Man as a being whose roots define his destiny. Reason requires an acknowledgment of the past, just as it demands a lucid, reflective awareness of our present direction. To forget the past is to make it impossible to persist. In this sense, the future of phenomenology is allied with historical consciousness. The hope one may find in Husserl's insistence on Reason is that we are still rememberers, beings who not only become but seek to narrate that becoming. "In the beginning" is also the language of phenomenological genesis; it is the cry of origin.

24. *Ibid.*, p. 289–90.

Bibliography

THE LITERATURE ON HUSSERL and phenomenology is enormous. The list which follows is restricted to those titles mentioned in the text which are directly related to phenomenology and to a sampling of other books and articles which will provide the reader with varied interpretations and criticisms of Husserl's thought. Not all of Husserl's writings are cited, nor is there any serious attempt made to give an account of the periodical literature. The emphasis has been placed on works in English. A critical edition of Husserl is in the course of being published: *Gesammelte Werke* (edited under the direction of H. L. Van Breda), published in The Hague by Martinus Nijhoff. To date twelve volumes have appeared in this series, known as *Husserliana* (1950–present). A bibliography of Husserl's writings (up to June 30, 1959) by H. L. Van Breda appears in *Edmund Husserl, 1859–1959*, pp. 289–306 (cited below). For other bibliographies on Husserl see: Jan Patočka, *Revue internationale de philosophie*, II (1939), 374–97; Jean Raes, *ibid.*, XIV (1950), 469–75; J. D. Robert, *Tijdschrift voor Philosophie*, XX (1958), 534–44; Lothar Eley, *Zeitschrift für philosophische Forschung*, XIII (1959), 357–67; and Gerhard Maschke and Iso Kern, *Revue internationale de philosophie*, no. 71–72 (1965), pp. 153–202. Additional bibliographical aids will be found in: Herbert Spiegelberg, *The Phenomenological Movement* (cited below); E. Parl Welch, *The Philosophy of Edmund Husserl: The Origin and Development of His Phenomenology* (New York: Columbia University Press, 1941; reprint ed., New York: Octagon Books, 1965), which includes a listing of the contents of Husserl's

Jahrbuch für Philosophie und phänomenologische Forschung;
Raymond Klibansky, ed., *Philosophy in the Mid-Century,* Vol. II:
Metaphysics and Analysis (Florence: La Nuova Italia Editrice,
1961); and Gilbert Varet, *Manuel de bibliographie philosophique,*
Vol. II: *Les Sciences philosophiques* (Paris: Presses Universi-
taires de France, 1956). Also see Nigel J. Grant (with the as-
sistance of Harmke Kamminga), "A Selective Bibliography of
Works in Phenomenology and Related Topics (Excluding Major
Works) Published over the last Fifteen Years," *Journal of the
British Society for Phenomenology,* I (1970), 104–9. The following series and periodicals are noteworthy: Edmund Husserl,
ed., *Jahrbuch für Philosophie und phänomenologische For-
schung,* 11 vols., 1913–30; Marvin Farber, ed., *Philosophy and
Phenomenological Research,* 1940–present; Wolfe Mays, ed.,
Journal of the British Society for Phenomenology, 1970–present;
John Sallis, ed., *Research in Phenomenology,* 1971–present; and
Anna-Teresa Tymieniecka, ed., *Analecta Husserliana: The Year-
book of Phenomenological Research,* 1971–present. Numerous
books on Husserl's phenomenology are included in the following
collections: H. L. Van Breda, ed., *Phaenomenologica* (The
Hague: Martinus Nijhoff) and James M. Edie, ed., Northwestern
University Studies in Phenomenology and Existential Philosophy
(Evanston, Ill.: Northwestern University Press).

Adorno, Theodor W. *Zur Metakritik der Erkenntnis Theorie:
Studien über Husserl und die phänomenologischen Antino-
mien.* Stuttgart: Kohlhammer, 1956.

Bachelard, Suzanne. *A Study of Husserl's "Formal and Transcendental Logic."* Translated by Lester E. Embree. Evanston,
Ill.: Northwestern University Press, 1968.

Ballard, Edward G. *Philosophy at the Crossroads.* Baton Rouge,
La.: Louisiana State University Press, 1971.

Berger, Gaston. *The "Cogito" in Husserl's Philosophy.* Translated
by Kathleen McLaughlin with an Introduction by James M.
Edie. Evanston, Ill.: Northwestern University Press, 1972.
——. *Phénoménologie du temps et prospective.* Paris: Presses
Universitaires de France, 1964.

Boehm, Rudolf. "Basic Reflections on Husserl's Phenomenological Reduction." Translated by Quentin Lauer. *International
Philosophical Quarterly,* V, no. 2 (May, 1965), 183–202.

———. "Deux Points de vue: Husserl et Nietzsche" (written in collaboration with Isabelle Micha). *Archivo di filosofia,* no. 3 (1962), pp. 167–81.

———. "La Phénoménologie de l'histoire." *Revue internationale de philosophie,* LXVII, no. 71–72 (1965), 55–73.

Brand, Gerd. *Die Lebenswelt: Eine Philosophie des Konkreten Apriori.* Berlin: de Gruyter, 1971.

Bruzina, Ronald. *Logos and Eidos: The Concept in Phenomenology.* The Hague: Mouton, 1970.

Cairns, Dorion. "An Approach to Phenomenology." In *Philosophical Essays in Memory of Edmund Husserl,* edited by Marvin Farber, pp. 3–18. Cambridge, Mass.: Harvard University Press, 1940.

———. "Phenomenology." In *A History of Philosophical Systems,* edited by Vergelius Ferm, pp. 353–64. New York: Philosophical Library, 1950.

———. "The Philosophy of Edmund Husserl." Ph.D. thesis, Harvard University, 1933.

Carr, David, and Casey, Edward S., eds. *Explorations in Phenomenology.* The Hague: Nijhoff, 1973.

Chapman, Harmon M. *Sensations and Phenomenology.* Bloomington, Ind.: Indiana University Press, 1966.

Domarus, G. W. Eilhard A. von. "The Logical Structure of Mind." Ph.D. thesis, Yale University, 1930.

Dufrenne, Mikel. *The Notion of the A Priori.* Translated with an Introduction by Edward S. Casey. Evanston, Ill.: Northwestern University Press, 1966.

Edie, James M., ed. *An Invitation to Phenomenology: Studies in the Philosophy of Experience.* Chicago: Quadrangle, 1965.

———, ed. *New Essays in Phenomenology.* Chicago: Quadrangle, 1970.

———, ed. *Phenomenology in America: Studies in the Philosophy of Experience.* Chicago: Quadrangle, 1967.

Edmund Husserl, 1859–1959: Recueil commémoratif publié à l'occasion du centenaire de la naissance du philosophe. With an Avant-Propos by H. L. Van Breda and J. Taminiaux. The Hague: Nijhoff, 1959.

Elveton, R. O. ed., *The Phenomenology of Husserl: Selected Critical Readings.* Chicago: Quadrangle, 1970.

Farber, Marvin. *The Aims of Phenomenology: The Motives, Methods, and Impact of Husserl's Thought.* New York: Harper & Row, Torchbooks, 1966.

———. *The Foundation of Phenomenology: Edmund Husserl and the Quest for a Rigorous Science of Philosophy.* 3d ed. Albany, N.Y.: State University of New York Press, 1967.

———. *Naturalism and Subjectivism.* Springfield, Ill.: Thomas, 1959.

———. "Phenomenology." In *Twentieth Century Philosophy: Living Schools of Thought,* edited by Dagobert D. Runes, pp. 345–70. New York: Philosophical Library, 1943. Also published as *Living Schools of Philosophy.* Totawa, N. J.: Littlefield, Adams, 1962.

———. *Phenomenology and Existence: Toward a Philosophy within Nature.* New York: Harper & Row, Torchbooks, 1967.

———, ed. *Philosophical Essays in Memory of Edmund Husserl.* Cambridge, Mass.: Harvard University Press, 1940. Reprint, New York: Greenwood Press, 1968.

Findlay, J. N. "Phenomenology." In *Encyclopaedia Britannica,* 1964 ed., XVII, 699–702.

Fink, Eugen. "Les Concepts opératoires dans la phénoménologie de Husserl." In *Husserl.* Cahiers de Royaumont, Philosophie No. III, pp. 214–30. Paris: Editions de Minuit, 1959.

———. "The Phenomenological Philosophy of Edmund Husserl and Contemporary Criticism (with a Preface by Edmund Husserl)." In *The Phenomenology of Husserl: Selected Critical Readings,* edited, translated, with an Introduction by R. O. Elveton, pp. 73–147. Chicago: Quadrangle, 1970.

———. *Studien zur Phänomenologie: 1930–1939.* The Hague: Nijhoff, 1966.

———. "What Does the Phenomenology of Edmund Husserl Want to Accomplish?" Translated by Arthur Grugan. *Research in Phenomenology,* II (1972), 5–27.

Fondane, Benjamin. *La Conscience malheureuse.* Paris: Denoël et Steele, 1938.

Fulton, James Street. "The Cartesianism of Phenomenology." In *Essays in Phenomenology,* edited with an Introduction by Maurice Natanson, pp. 58–78. The Hague: Nijhoff, 1966.

Funke, Gerhard. "Geschichte als Phänomen." *Zeitschrift für philosophische Forschung,* XI, no. 2 (April–June, 1957), 188–234.

————. *Zur transzendentalen Phänomenologie*. Bonn: Bouvier, 1957.

Galay, Jean-Louis. "Essaie sur le problème de l'intelligibilité d'après la 'Critique de la raison logique' de Husserl." *Studia Philosophica*, XXIX (1970), 25–53.

Gibson, W. R. Boyce. "From Husserl to Heidegger: Extracts from a 1928 Freiburg Diary." Edited by Herbert Spiegelberg. *Journal of the British Society for Phenomenology*, II, no. 1 (January, 1971), 58–83.

Granel, Gérard. *Le Sens du temps et de la perception chez E. Husserl*. Paris: Gallimard, 1968.

Gurwitsch, Aron. *The Field of Consciousness*. Pittsburgh, Pa.: Duquesne University Press, 1964.

————. *Studies in Phenomenology and Psychology*. Evanston, Ill.: Northwestern University Press, 1966.

————. Review of "The Cartesianism of Phenomenology," by James Street Fulton. *Philosophy and Phenomenological Research*, II, no. 4 (June, 1942), 551–58.

Hartmann, Klaus. "Abstraction and Existence in Husserl's Phenomenological Reduction." *Journal of the British Society for Phenomenology*, II, no. 1 (January, 1971), 10–18.

Heidegger, Martin. *Being and Time*. Translated by John Macquarrie and Edward Robinson. New York: Harper, 1962.

————. "The Idea of Phenomenology." Translated by John N. Deely and Joseph A. Novak with the assistance of Eva D. Leo. *New Scholasticism*, XLIV, no. 3 (Summer, 1970), 325–44.

Hering, Jean. "Sub Specie aeterni: Réponse à une critique de la philosophie de Husserl." *Revue d'histoire et de philosophie religieuses*, VII, no. 4 (July–August, 1927), 351–64.

Hohl, Hubert. *Lebenswelt und Geschichte: Grundzüge der Spätphilosophie E. Husserls*. Munich: Alber, 1962.

Husserl, Edmund. *Briefe an Roman Ingarden: Mit Erläuterungen und Erinnerungen an Husserl*. Edited by Roman Ingarden. The Hague: Nijhoff, 1968.

————. *Cartesian Meditations: An Introduction to Phenomenology*. Translated by Dorion Cairns. The Hague: Nijhoff, 1960.

————. *The Crisis of European Sciences and Transcendental Phenomenology: An Introduction to Phenomenological Philosophy*. Translated with an Introduction by David Carr. Evanston, Ill.: Northwestern University Press, 1970.

———. *Erste Philosophie* (1923–24), Part II: *Theorie der phänomenologischen Reduktion.* Edited with an Introduction by Rudolf Boehm. The Hague: Nijhoff, 1959.

———. *Experience and Judgment.* Translated by James S. Churchill and Karl Ameriks, with a Foreword by Ludwig Landgrebe and an Afterword by Lothar Eley. Evanston, Ill.: Northwestern University Press, 1973.

———. *Formal and Transcendental Logic.* Translated by Dorion Cairns. The Hague: Nijhoff, 1969.

———. *The Idea of Phenomenology.* Translated by William P. Alston and George Nakhnikian with an Introduction by George Nakhnikian. The Hague: Martinus Nijhoff, 1964. Also included in *Readings in Twentieth Century Philosophy,* edited by William P. Alston and George Nakhnikian. New York: Free Press, 1963.

———. *Ideas: General Introduction to Pure Phenomenology.* Translated by W. R. Boyce Gibson. New York: Macmillan, 1931. German edition *Ideen zu einer reinen Phänomenologie und phänomenologischen Philosophie.* Vol. I. Halle: Niemeyer, 1913.

———. *Ideen zu einer reinen Phänomenologie und phänomenologischen Philosophie.* Vol. II: *Phänomenologische Untersuchungen zur Konstitution.* Vol. III: *Die Phänomenologie und die Fundamente der Wissenschaften.* Edited by Marly Biemel. The Hague: Nijhoff, 1952.

———. "Inaugural Lecture at Freiburg im Breisgau (1917)." Translated by Robert Welsh Jordan. In *Life-World and Consciousness: Essays for Aron Gurwitsch,* edited by Lester E. Embree, pp. 3–18. Evanston, Ill.: Northwestern University Press, 1972.

———. "Die Krisis der europäischen Wissenschaften und die transzendentale Phänomenologie: Eine Einleitung in die phänomenologische Philosophie." *Philosophia,* I, Fasc. 1–4 (1936), 77–176.

———. "A Letter to Arnold Metzger." Translated with an Introduction by Erazim V. Kohák. *Philosophical Forum,* XXI (1963–64), 48–68.

———. "A Letter to Dorion Cairns" (in German), in *Edmund Husserl, 1859–1959: Recueil commémoratif publié à l'occasion du centenaire de la naissance du philosophe,* pp. 283–85. The Hague: Nijhoff, 1959.

———. *Logical Investigations.* Translated with an Introduction

by J. N. Findlay. 2 vols. New York: Humanities Press, 1970.
———. *The Paris Lectures.* Translated with an Introduction by Peter Koestenbaum. The Hague: Nijhoff, 1964.
———. "Phenomenology." Translated by C. V. Salmon. In *Encyclopaedia Britannica,* 14th ed., 1927, XVII, 699–702. Also included in *Realism and the Background of Phenomenology,* edited by Roderick M. Chisholm. Glencoe: Free Press, 1960. New complete translation by Richard E. Palmer, *Journal of the British Society for Phenomenology,* II, no. 2 (May, 1971), 77–90.
———. "Phenomenology and Anthropology." Translated by Richard G. Schmitt. In *Realism and the Background of Phenomenology,* edited by Roderick M. Chisholm, pp. 129–42. Glencoe, Ill.: Free Press, 1960.
———. *Phenomenology and the Crisis of Philosophy: Philosophy as Rigorous Science and Philosophy and the Crisis of European Man.* Translated with an Introduction by Quentin Lauer. New York: Harper & Row, Torchbooks, 1965.
———. *The Phenomenology of Internal Time-Consciousness.* Translated by James S. Churchill and edited by Martin Heidegger with an Introduction by Calvin O. Schrag. Bloomington, Ind.: Indiana University Press, 1964.
———. *Philosophie als strenge Wissenschaft.* Edited by Wilhelm Szilasi. Frankfurt: Klostermann, 1965. English translation included in *Phenomenology and the Crisis of Philosophy.*
———. *Philosophie der Arithmetik: Mit ergänzenden Texten* (*1890–1901*). Edited with an Introduction by Lothar Eley. The Hague: Nijhoff, 1970.
Husserl. Cahiers de Royaumont, Philosophie No. III. With an Avant-Propos by M.-A. Bera. Paris: Editions de Minuit, 1959.
Husserl et la pensée moderne. With an Avant-Propos by H. L. Van Breda and J. Taminiaux. The Hague: Nijhoff, 1959.
Ingarden, Roman. "Edith Stein on Her Activity as an Assistant of Edmund Husserl: Extracts from the Letters of Edith Stein with a Commentary and Introductory Remarks." Translated, in part, by Janina Makota. *Philosophy and Phenomenological Research,* XXIII, no. 2 (December, 1962), 155–75.
Jeanson, Francis. *La Phénoménologie.* Paris: Téqui, 1951.
Kaufmann, Fritz, "Cassirer, Neo-Kantianism, and Phenomenology." In *The Philosophy of Ernst Cassirer.* Edited by Paul Arthur Schilpp, pp. 801–54. New York: Tudor, 1949.

———. "The Phenomenological Approach to History." *Philosophy and Phenomenological Research*, II, no. 2 (December, 1941), 159–72.

———. "Phenomenology of the Historical Present," *Proceedings of the 10th International Congress of Philosophy*, I (1949), 967–70.

Kelkel, Arion, and Schérer, René. *Husserl*. Paris: Presses Universitaires de France, 1971.

Kersten, Frederick I., and Zaner, Richard M., eds. *Phenomenology, Continuation and Criticism: Essays in Memory of Dorion Cairns*. The Hague: Nijhoff, 1973.

Kockelmans, Joseph J. *Edmund Husserl's Phenomenological Psychology: A Historico-Critical Study*. Translated by Bernd Jager and revised by the author. Pittsburgh, Pa.: Duquesne University Press, 1967.

———. *A First Introduction to Husserl's Phenomenology*. Pittsburgh, Pa.: Duquesne University Press, 1967.

———, ed. *Phenomenology: The Philosophy of Edmund Husserl and Its Interpretation*. Garden City, N.Y.: Doubleday, Anchor Books, 1967.

———, and Kisiel, Theodore J., eds. *Phenomenology and the Natural Sciences: Essays and Translations*. Evanston, Ill.: Northwestern University Press, 1970.

Landgrebe, Ludwig. "Husserl's Departure from Cartesianism." In *The Phenomenology of Husserl: Selected Critical Readings*, edited, translated, with an Introduction by R. O. Elveton, pp. 259–306. Chicago: Quadrangle, 1970.

———. "Phenomenology and Metaphysics." *Philosophy and Phenomenological Research*, X, no. 2 (December, 1949), 197–205.

———. "The World as a Phenomenological Problem." Translated by Dorion Cairns. *Philosophy and Phenomenological Research*, I, no. 1 (September, 1940), 38–58.

Laszlo, Ervin. *Beyond Scepticism and Realism: A Constructive Exploration of Husserlian and Whiteheadian Methods of Inquiry*. The Hague: Nijhoff, 1966.

Lauer, Quentin. *Phénoménologie de Husserl: Essai sur la genèse de l'intentionalité*. Paris: Presses Universitaires de France, 1955.

———. *The Triumph of Subjectivity: An Introduction to Transcendental Phenomenology* (with a Preface by Aron Gurwitsch). New York: Fordham University Press, 1958. Republished as *Phenomenology: Its Genesis and Prospect*. New York: Harper & Row, Torchbooks, 1965.

Lawrence, Nathaniel, and O'Connor, Daniel, eds. *Readings in Existential Phenomenology*. Englewood Cliffs, N. J.: Prentice-Hall, 1967.

Lee, Edward N., and Mandelbaum, Maurice, eds. *Phenomenology and Existentialism*. Baltimore: Johns Hopkins University Press, 1967.

Levin, David Michael. *Reason and Evidence in Husserl's Phenomenology*. Evanston, Ill.: Northwestern University Press, 1970.

Levinas, Emmanuel. *En Découvrant l'existence avec Husserl et Heidegger*. Paris: Vrin, 1949.

———. "Intentionalité et sensation." *Revue internationale de philosophie*, LXVII, no. 71–72 (1965), 34–54.

———. *The Theory of Intuition in Husserl's Phenomenology*. Translated by André Orianne. Evanston, Ill.: Northwestern University Press, 1973.

Luijpen, William A. *Existential Phenomenology*. Translated by Henry J. Koren with a Preface by Albert Dondeyne. Pittsburgh, Pa.: Duquesne University Press, 1960.

Lyotard, Jean-François. *La Phénoménologie*. Paris: Presses Universitaires de France, 1959.

Marx, Werner. *Reason and World: Between Tradition and Another Beginning*. The Hague: Nijhoff, 1971.

Mays, Wolfe, and Brown, S. C., eds. *Linguistic Analysis and Phenomenology*. London: Macmillan, 1972.

Merlan, Philip. "Time Consciousness in Husserl and Heidegger." *Philosophy and Phenomenological Research*, VIII, no. 1 (September, 1947), 23–53.

Merleau-Ponty, Maurice. *Phenomenology of Perception*. Translated by Colin Smith. New York: Humanities Press, 1962.

———. *The Primacy of Perception: And Other Essays on Phenomenological Psychology, the Philosophy of Art, History and Politics*. Edited with an Introduction by James M. Edie. Evanston, Ill.: Northwestern University Press, 1964.

———. *Signs*. Translated with an Introduction by Richard C. McCleary. Evanston Ill.: Northwestern University Press, 1964.

Mohanty, J. N. *Edmund Husserl's Theory of Meaning*. The Hague: Nijhoff, 1964.

------. *Phenomenology and Ontology*. The Hague: Nijhoff, 1970.

Muralt, André de. *L'Idée de la phénoménologie: L'Exemplarisme husserlien*. Paris: Presses Universitaires de France, 1958.

Natanson, Maurice. *The Journeying Self: A Study in Philosophy and Social Role*. Reading, Mass.: Addison-Wesley, 1970.

------. *Literature, Philosophy, and the Social Sciences: Essays in Existentialism and Phenomenology*. The Hague: Nijhoff, 1962.

------, ed. *Essays in Phenomenology*. The Hague: Nijhoff, 1966.

------, ed. *Phenomenology and Social Reality: Essays in Memory of Alfred Schutz*. The Hague: Nijhoff, 1970.

------, ed. *Phenomenology and the Social Sciences*. 2 vols. Evanston, Ill.: Northwestern University Press, 1973.

------, ed. *Philosophy of the Social Sciences: A Reader*. New York: Random House, 1963.

------, ed. *Psychiatry and Philosophy*. New York: Springer, 1969.

Ortega y Gasset, José. *Man and People*. Translated by Willard R. Trask. New York: Norton, 1957.

Osborn, A. D. *Edmund Husserl and His Logical Investigations*. 2d ed. Cambridge, Mass.: Edwards Brothers, 1949.

Paci, Enzo. *The Function of the Sciences and the Meaning of Man*. Translated with an Introduction by Paul Piccone and James E. Hansen. Evanston, Ill.: Northwestern University Press, 1972.

Pettit, Philip. *On the Idea of Phenomenology*. Dublin: Scepter, 1969.

Picard, Yvonne. "Le Temps chez Husserl et chez Heidegger." *Deucalion*, no. 1 (1946), pp. 95–124.

Pivčević, Edo. *Husserl and Phenomenology*. London: Hutchinson University Library, 1970.

Reinach, Adolph. "What is Phenomenology?" Translated with an Introduction by Derek Kelly. *Philosophical Forum*, n.s. I, no. 2 (Winter, 1968), 231–56.

Reyer, Wilhelm. *Einführung in die Phänomenologie*. Leipzig: Meiner, 1926.

Ricoeur, Paul. *Husserl: An Analysis of His Phenomenology*. Translated by Edward G. Ballard and Lester E. Embree. Evanston, Ill.: Northwestern University Press, 1967.

Salmon, C. V. *The Central Problem of David Hume's Philosophy: An Essay towards a Phenomenological Interpretation of the*

First Book of the "Treatise of Human Nature." Halle: Nie-meyer, 1929. Originally published in *Jahrbuch für Philosophie und phänomenologische Forschung*, Vol. X.

Sartre, Jean-Paul. *Being and Nothingness: An Essay on Phenomenological Ontology.* Translated with an Introduction by Hazel E. Barnes. New York: Philosophical Library, 1956.

————. "Faces, preceded by Official Portraits." Translated by Anne P. Jones. In *Essays in Phenomenology*, edited with an Introduction by Maurice Natanson, pp. 157–63. The Hague: Nijhoff, 1966.

————. "Intentionality: A Fundamental Idea of Husserl's Phenomenology." Translated by Joseph P. Fell. *Journal of the British Society for Phenomenology*, I, no. 2 (May, 1970), 4–5. The original appeared as "Une idée fondamentale de la phénoménologie de Husserl: L'Intentionalité," and is reprinted in Sartre's *Situations*, I, 31–35. Paris: Gallimard, 1947.

————. *The Transcendence of the Ego: An Existentialist Theory of Consciousness.* Translated and annotated with an Introduction by Forrest Williams and Robert Kirkpatrick. New York: Noonday, 1957.

Schérer, René. *La Phénoménologie des "Recherches Logique" de Husserl.* Paris: Presses Universitaires de France, 1967.

Schmitt, Richard. "Husserl's Transcendental-Phenomenological Reduction." *Philosophy and Phenomenological Research*, XX, no. 2 (December, 1959), 238–45.

————. "Phenomenology." In *Encyclopedia of Philosophy*, edited by Paul Edwards, VI, 135–51. New York: Macmillan and Free Press, 1967.

Schutz, Alfred. *Collected Papers*, Vol. I: *The Problem of Social Reality.* Edited with an Introduction by Maurice Natanson and a Preface by H. L. Van Breda. The Hague: Nijhoff, 1962. Vol. II: *Studies in Social Theory.* Edited with an Introduction by Arvid Brodersen. The Hague: Nijhoff, 1964. Vol. III: *Studies in Phenomenological Philosophy.* Edited by I. Schutz with an Introduction by Aron Gurwitsch. The Hague: Nijhoff, 1966.

————. *The Phenomenology of the Social World.* Translated by George Walsh and Frederick Lehnert with an Introduction by George Walsh. Evanston, Ill.: Northwestern University Press, 1967.

————. *Reflections on the Problem of Relevance.* Edited, annotated, with an Introduction by Richard M. Zaner. New Haven, Conn.: Yale University Press, 1970.

———, and Luckmann, Thomas. *Structures of the Life-World.* Translated by Richard M. Zaner and H. Tristram Engelhardt, Jr. Evanston, Ill.: Northwestern University Press, 1973.

Shestov, Lev. "In Memory of A Great Philosopher: Edmund Husserl." Translated by George L. Kline. *Philosophy and Phenomenological Research,* XXII, no. 4 (June, 1962), 449–71. Reprinted in *Russian Philosophy,* Vol. III. Edited by James M. Edie, James F. Scanlan, and Mary-Barbara Zeldin, with the collaboration of George L. Kline. Chicago: Quadrangle, 1965.

———. *Potestas Clavium.* Translated with an Introduction by Bernard Martin. Chicago: Regnery, 1968.

Shmueli, Efraim. "Critical Reflections on Husserl's Philosophy of History." *Journal of the British Society for Phenomenology,* II, no. 1 (January, 1971), 35–51.

Sinha, Debabrata. *Studies in Phenomenology.* The Hague: Nijhoff, 1969.

Smith, F. J., ed. *Phenomenology in Perspective.* The Hague: Nijhoff, 1970.

Sokolowski, Robert. *The Formation of Husserl's Concept of Constitution.* The Hague: Nijhoff, 1964.

Solomon, Robert C., ed. *Phenomenology and Existentialism.* New York: Harper & Row, 1972.

Spiegelberg, Herbert. *The Phenomenological Movement: A Historical Introduction.* 2 vols. 2d ed. The Hague: Nijhoff, 1965.

———. "Phenomenology." In *Encyclopaedia Britannica.* 1967 ed., XVII, 810–12.

———. "Phenomenology of Direct Evidence." *Philosophy and Phenomenological Research,* II, no. 4 (June, 1942), 427–56.

———. *Phenomenology in Psychology and Psychiatry: A Historical Introduction.* Evanston, Ill.: Northwestern University Press, 1972.

Stegmüller, Wolfgang. *Main Currents in Contemporary German, British, and American Philosophy.* Dordrecht: Reidel, 1969.

Stein, Edith. *On the Problem of Empathy.* Translated by Waltraut Stein with a Foreword by Erwin W. Straus. The Hague: Nijhoff, 1964.

Strasser, Stephan. *The Idea of Dialogal Phenomenology.* Translated by Henry J. Koren. Pittsburgh, Pa.: Duquesne University Press, 1969.

———. *Phenomenology and the Human Sciences: A Contribution to a New Scientific Ideal.* Translated by Henry J. Koren. Pittsburgh, Pa.: Duquesne University Press, 1963.

————. *The Soul in Metaphysical and Empirical Psychology.* Translated by Henry J. Koren. Pittsburgh, Pa.: Duquesne University Press, 1957.

Straus, Erwin W. *Phenomenological Psychology: Selected Papers.* Translated, in part, by Erling Eng. New York: Basic Books, 1966.

————, ed. *Phenomenology, Pure and Applied: The First Lexington Conference.* Pittsburgh, Pa.: Duquesne University Press, 1964.

Szilasi, Wilhelm. *Einführung in die Phänomenologie Edmund Husserls.* Tübingen: Niemeyer, 1959.

Thévenaz, Pierre. *What is Phenomenology?* Edited with an Introduction by James M. Edie, Preface by John Wild, and Translated by James M. Edie, Charles Courtney, and Paul Brockelman. Chicago: Quadrangle, 1962.

Toulemont, René. *L'Essence de la société selon Husserl.* Paris: Presses Universitaires de France, 1962.

Tran Duc Thao. *Phénoménologie et matérialisme dialectique.* Paris: Editions Minh-Tan, 1951.

Tymieniecka, Anna-Teresa. *Phenomenology and Science in Contemporary European Thought.* With a Foreword by I. M. Bochenski. New York: Noonday, 1962.

————, ed. *For Roman Ingarden: Nine Essays in Phenomenology.* The Hague: Nijhoff, 1959.

Van Breda, H. L., ed. *Problèmes actuels de la phénoménologie.* Paris: Desclée de Brouwer, 1952.

van Peursen, Cornelis A. *Phenomenology and Analytical Philosophy.* Translated by Rex Ambler and amended by Henry J. Koren. Pittsburgh, Pa.: Duquesne University Press, 1972.

Waelhens, Alphonse de. *Existence et signification.* Louvain: Nauwelaerts, 1958.

Wahl, Jean. *Husserl.* 2 vols. Cours de Sorbonne. Paris: Centre de Documentation Universitaire, 1958.

————. *L'Ouvrage posthume de Husserl: La Krisis: La Crise des sciences européenes et la phénoménologie transcendentale.* Cours de Sorbonne. Paris: Centre de Documentation Universitaire, 1958.

Wann, T. W., ed. *Behaviorism and Phenomenology: Contrasting Bases for Modern Psychology.* Chicago: University of Chicago Press, 1965.

Zaner, Richard M. *The Way of Phenomenology: Criticism as a Philosophical Discipline.* New York: Pegasus, 1970.

Index